Louis D. Brandeis and the Making of Regulated Competition, 1900–1932

This book provides an innovative interpretation of industrialization and state building in the United States. Most scholars cast the politics of industrialization in the Progressive Era as a narrow choice between breaking up large corporations and regulating them. Gerald Berk reveals a third way, regulated competition. In this framework, the government steered economic development away from concentrated power by channeling competition from predation to improvements in products and production processes. Louis Brandeis conceptualized regulated competition and introduced it into public debate. Political entrepreneurs in Congress enacted many of Brandeis's proposals into law. The Federal Trade Commission enlisted business and professional associations to make regulated competition workable. The commercial printing industry showed how it could succeed. And 30 percent of manufacturing industries used regulated competition to improve economic performance. In order to make sense of regulated competition, Berk provides a new theory of institutions he calls "creative syncretism," which stresses the capacity of creative actors to decompose and recombine institutional parts.

Gerald Berk is currently Associate Professor of Political Science at the University of Oregon. His first book, *Alternative Tracks: The Constitution of American Industrial Order, 1870–1916* (1994), was awarded the American Political Science Association's J. David Greenstone Award for Best Book in Politics and History. He is the recipient of fellowships from the American Council of Learned Societies, the Hagley Museum and Library, the American Philosophical Society, and the National Endowment for the Humanities. His work has been published in many venues, including *Studies in American Political Development*, *Theory and Society*, *Politics and Society*, the *Journal of Policy History*, and *Social Science History*.

Louis D. Brandeis and the Making of Regulated Competition, 1900–1932

GERALD BERK
University of Oregon

CAMBRIDGE
UNIVERSITY PRESS

CAMBRIDGE UNIVERSITY PRESS
Cambridge, New York, Melbourne, Madrid, Cape Town, Singapore, São Paulo, Delhi

Cambridge University Press
32 Avenue of the Americas, New York, NY 10013-2473, USA

www.cambridge.org
Information on this title: www.cambridge.org/9780521425964

First published 2009

Printed in the United States of America

A catalog record for this publication is available from the British Library.

Library of Congress Cataloging in Publication data
Berk, Gerald.
Louis D. Brandeis and the making of regulated competition, 1900–1932 / Gerald Berk.
p. cm.
Includes bibliographical references and index.
ISBN 978-0-521-42596-4 (hardback)
1. Trade regulation – United States – History – 20th century.
2. Antitrust law – United States – History – 20th century.
3. Brandeis, Louis Dembitz, 1856–1941. I. Title.
KF1609.B37 2009
343.73'0721–dc22 2008044130

ISBN 978-0-521-42596-4 hardback

For Karen

Contents

Figures and Tables

FIGURES

TABLES

Acknowledgments

I was fortunate to begin and end this project with wonderful collaborators. My interest in Brandeis started many years ago in discussions with Roger Karapin, Tony Levitas, Gretchen Ritter, and Chuck Sabel. They moved on. Happily, I got stuck and now have a chance to look back with gratitude for their inspiration. This book also ended with two collaborators: Marc Schneiberg and Dennis Galvan. Marc's passion for methodological rigor, rich data, and theoretical precision has had a profound influence on this book. Some of our collaborative work, previously published in *Politics and Society*, is reproduced in Chapter 6. Dennis's commitment to understanding human resilience under the most challenging of circumstances prodded me to think more deeply and broadly about my theoretical commitments. Together, we have attempted to rethink institutions as usable instruments, rather than confining iron cages, which are played creatively by their inhabitants. This book is deeply indebted to that work.

I was fortunate to work on this project at the Hagley Museum and Library. Its archives, conferences, and people have been indispensable to my work. Phil Scranton has been a wonderful friend, supporter, and mentor, whose work blazed a path for this book. Carol Lockman and Roger Horwitz made my many stays in Wilmington enjoyable and productive. Michael Nash's help in the archives was critical to the success of my research. Ken Lipartito and David Sicilia organized a terrific conference and edited volume, which gave me a chance to test Chapter 3 in a supportive and critical environment.

My colleagues at the University of Oregon have supported this book in countless ways – by listening to obscure stories about the history of cost accounting, by offering words of support when things weren't going well, and by helping to sharpen weak prose and confused ideas. In political science, I'm especially grateful to Deborah Baumgold, Dan Goldrich, Dick Kraus, Ron Mitchell, Lars Skalnes, Julie Novkov, Lennie Feldman, Joe Lowndes, and Craig Parsons. In the department of history, I thank Jim Mohr and Jeff Ostler for welcoming me into their fellowship and generously reading the manuscript. One couldn't ask for better colleagues and friends.

Anyone who knows the scholarship of Gary Herrigel, Chuck Sabel, and Jonathan Zeitlin will see their influence all over this book. I am grateful for their imagination, generosity, helpful suggestions, and friendship. They are models of creative and engaged scholarship, committed to a more just and emancipated world.

Stephen Skowronek and Karen Orren have been incredibly generous over the life of this project. It is a cliché to say that one criticizes the work that one admires the most. In this case it is true. I hope I have engaged their scholarship with the high regard in which I hold it and advanced the project that they have done so much to cultivate.

Many other people have read chapters or papers, listened to ideas, and offered help in conceptualizing tricky issues and conducting research. I am grateful to Steve Amberg, Chris Ansell, Richard Bensel, Amy Bridges, Coleen Dunlavy, Roy Edwards, Archon Fung, Mary Furner, Henrick Glimstedt, Terry Gourvish, Howell Harris, Ellen Herman, Richard John, Tom Johnson, Robert Johnston, Bill Keith, Lane Kenworthy, Bruce Kucklick, Naomi Lamoreaux, Walter Licht, Jim Livingston, Ned Lorenz, Chris McKenna, Chick Perrow, Dan Raff, Dave Robertson, Jeff Sklansky, Mark Stern, Philippa Strum, Fred Thompson, Jessica Wang, Kari Whittenberger-Keith, Frank Wilkinson, Jim Wooten, and three anonymous reviewers for Cambridge University Press.

I am also grateful to the participants in a number of small conferences and research seminars, sponsored by the following departments and programs: the Program in the History of Science at Oregon State University, the Institute for Governmental Studies at the University of California at Berkeley, the Department of History at the University of Pennsylvania, the Department of Political Science and the Atkinson Graduate School of Management at Willamette University, the Scandinavian Consortium on Organizations at Stanford University, the Center for Critical and Transnational Studies at the University of Oregon, the seminar on American capitalism in the Department of Sociology at the University of Arizona, the ESRC Centre for Small Business Research at Cambridge University, the Business History Unit of the Centre for Risk and Regulation at the London School of Economics, and the Stockholm School of Economics.

In addition to the Hagley Museum and Library, I thank the American Council of Learned Societies, the American Philosophical Society, and the National Endowment for the Humanities for their generous support. I am also grateful to archivists and librarians in the National Archives, the Library of Congress, the Federal Trade Commission Library, and the University of Oregon Library.

Peter, Lisa, Stefan, and Emma Berg made it possible to spend long periods in Washington, D.C., archives without missing my family too much. I'm forever grateful for their friendship, humor, and support.

I am grateful to the editors and staff at Cambridge University Press – to Lew Bateman for his patient guidance, and to Emily Spangler, Ernie Haim, Mark Fox, and James Dunn for the creativity and hard work it takes to bring a book to life. I also thank Beth Morel, David Estrin, and Mary Harper for their terrific work in editing and indexing this book.

I've dedicated this book to my life's spiritual partner, Karen Giese, who keeps me laughing regardless of the circumstances. More than anyone I know, she lives the aspirations spelled out in this book: self-reflection, craftsmanship, generosity, and deliberation in everyday life. My sons deserve special credit for their imagination and endurance. Adrian was present at the birth of this book; Jacob hardly knows life without it. Though animated by talents very different from my own, they both share the passion that went into this project.

Chapter 1

Creative Syncretism

Industrialization imperiled democracy and markets in the United States because it concentrated power in large corporations. Looking back at the Progressive Era, scholars generally see two options: break up corporations or regulate them. There was a third way, which contemporaries called regulated competition. In this framework, the state checked the tendency to concentrated power in the first instance by steering competition from predation into improvements in products and production processes. Louis Brandeis conceptualized regulated competition and introduced it into public debate during the presidential election of 1912.

Political entrepreneurs in Congress enacted many of Brandeis's proposals into law. They licensed the Federal Trade Commission (FTC) to check predatory rivalry before it turned into unassailable power and to cultivate business capacities to improve the quality of competition. The FTC enlisted business and professional associations to make regulated competition workable through better cost accounting and trade practice conferences. Trade associations in specialty manufacturing took up the FTC's challenge, and reinvented themselves from competition-suppressing cartels into developmental associations devoted to enhancing products, services, and productivity. The commercial printing industry showed how developmental associations could succeed. And nearly a third of the manufacturing industries in the United States adopted the tools of regulated competition and developmental association to improve economic performance. By a number of measures, regulated competition better reconciled traditional American aspirations to egalitarian democracy with modern ambitions to economic prosperity than either free markets or regulated corporations.

To be sure, regulated competition did not become hegemonic. It shared institutional and cultural space with other organizational forms, ideologies, and policy perspectives. Sometimes its practitioners battled opponents in competing institutional locations who saw the world quite differently; at other times, they practiced their craft without notice. In any case, regulated competition survived and the institutions of state and economy in the twentieth century remained diverse, multivocal, and essentially contested.

Regulated competition has been invisible to students of state building and industrialization in the United States. In the mainstream narrative, industrialization was about the rise of the big corporation; the politics of antitrust in the Progressive Era was about adjustment to it; and the FTC and trade associations during the 1920s were largely failed experiments in bureaucratic autonomy and liberal corporatism.

This story misses regulated competition because it divides tradition and modernity too sharply and evaluates the intrusion of the former into the latter as dysfunctional. The nineteenth-century era of courts and parties and competitive capitalism was fundamentally different from the twentieth-century era of administrative government and corporate capitalism. Each period had its defining cultural dispositions, constitutional principles, and institutional forms. When the old order intruded on the new one, principles and practices came into conflict. The result was paralysis, confusion, and administrative impotence.

This book argues otherwise: those who built regulated competition were successful precisely because they reached across historical, institutional, and cultural boundaries to find resources, which they creatively recombined in experiments in business regulation, public administration, accounting, and trade associations.

Brandeis decomposed the republican antimonopolist ideology of the movements that came before him and recombined its parts with principles drawn from the progressive movement's devotion to applied science and public administration. The result was a syncretic ideology I call republican experimentalism. Likewise, he recomposed the populist proposal to enforce competition with the progressive proposal to regulate monopoly to conceptualize regulated competition. Creative politicians in Congress continued Brandeis's work by recombining progressive Republican and populist Democratic proposals for a federal trade commission and then forging a majority coalition by interpreting their work to their colleagues through multiple frames. At the FTC, creative commissioners recomposed resources from civil society to create a network of business and professional associations devoted to upgrading competition through deliberation and cost accounting. Prodded by the commission, reflexive associationalists in the commercial printing industry reconfigured their association from a competition-suppressing cartel into a developmental association, devoted to reconfiguring competitive customs through new forms of cost accounting. The U.S. Chamber of Commerce assembled cost accountants, government officials, and trade association executives in a series of deliberative forums, where they culled generalizations from their experiences to create a usable model of developmental association.

It is difficult to make sense of these people's work or the institutions they created with the standard institutionalist assumptions, which inform the received narrative. This book develops a different theory of institutions I call creative syncretism, which rests on two propositions. Institutions are composed of an indefinite number of parts, which can be decomposed and recombined in unpredictable ways. Action within institutions is always potentially creative. Creative syncretism will help us understand how the builders of regulated competition created an experimentalist state, which was devoted to cultivating capacities for economic improvement in U.S. industry.

This chapter explains why the institutionalist narrative misses regulated competition, presents the theory of creative syncretism, and then shows how it informs the story told in this book. The first section outlines institutionalist principles and shows how they have been applied to industrialization, Progressive Era antitrust reform, and associationalism in the 1920s. The second section raises empirical objections to the institutionalist narrative, which reveal systematic theoretical problems. The third section explains the theory of creative syncretism. Finally, the fourth section summarizes the narrative developed in this book.

INSTITUTIONALISM AND THE CONVENTIONAL STORY

Historical institutionalists from various fields have missed or misunderstood regulated competition.[1] Despite progress in understanding comparative industrialization and state building, they have made theoretical commitments, which restrict empirical research, and make it difficult to account for the innovations described in this book.

[1] By "historical institutionalists," I mean new business and organizational historians, new institutional and economic sociologists, and historical institutionalists in political science. See the notes 2 through 14 for representative examples.

Institutionalists present industrialization as the rise of mass production and state building as the emergence of bureaucratic autonomy. Although they acknowledge deviations from these forms, their story begins with a master narrative that makes unwarranted assumptions about technology, institutional constraints on agency, and historical sequencing. The result is not only to miss regulated competition, but also to narrow our appreciation of diversity within institutions, mistakenly conceptualize institutional change as episodic rather than normal, and overlook the everyday creativity of institutional actors.

This section outlines the main principles of institutionalist theory and shows how they inform the mainstream narrative.

Institutionalist Principles

Institutionalist accounts of industrialization and state building make five critical assumptions: technology determines economic problems, historical sequence determines institutional form, institutions constrain action, institutions are historically layered, and institutions are path dependent.

Technology Determines Economic Problems. In institutionalist theory, the revolution in technology determined the characteristic economic problems associated with industrialization. For example, modern steelmaking was fundamentally different from iron forging, railroads from canals, and cigarette from cigar manufacture. Despite their differences, these innovations raised similar economic dilemmas and management problems. This is not to say that institutionalists are technological determinists. They recognize there were many efficient ways to manage modern technologies and show how context, culture, and institutions determined diverse solutions with varying degrees of success. Nonetheless, technology is exogenous, defines the vector of problems to solve, and constrains the range of effective solutions.[2]

Historical Sequence Determines Institutional Form. In mainstream institutionalism, all societies have multiple institutions, which have independent

[2] The classic statement of this perspective on technology in the new business history is Alfred D. Chandler, Jr., *The Visible Hand* (Cambridge, MA: Harvard University Press, 1977); and Alfred D. Chandler, Jr., *Scale and Scope* (Cambridge, MA: Harvard University Press, 1990). See also Herman Daems, "The Rise of the Modern Industrial Enterprise: A New Perspective," in Alfred D. Chandler, Jr. and Herman Daems, eds., *Managerial Hierarchies* (Cambridge, MA: Harvard University Press, 1980). Among organizational

histories. Economic institutions develop differently from institutions in the state, politics, or the family. One can learn a great deal about national variations in political and economic development by paying attention to variations in the sequence of democratization, industrialization, and state building.[3] For example, in Europe, where state building occurred under monarchies prior to industrialization, industrializing elites learned to consult with bureaucrats. In the United States, where state building occurred after industrialization and democratization, corporate elites saw efforts to build state capacity as intrusions on their autonomy.[4] Institutional sequencing shapes how actors define their identities and interests and the possible courses of reform in modern government and industry.

Institutions Constrain Action. Institutions constrain economic and political action through a variety of mechanisms: rules, taken-for-granted

historians who make this assumption, see Thomas K. McCraw, "Rethinking the Trust Question," in Thomas K. McCraw, ed., *Regulation in Perspective* (Boston: Harvard Business School Press, 1981), 1–55; and Louis Galambos, "Technology, Political Economy and Professionalization: Central Themes of the Organizational Synthesis," *Business History Review* 57 (Winter 1983): 471–93. This assumption is also shared by leading economic sociologists. See Neil Fligstein, *The Transformation of Corporate Control* (Cambridge, MA: Harvard University Press, 1900), 33–74; and Frank Dobbin and Timothy J. Dowd, "The Market That Anti-Trust Built," *American Sociological Review* 65 (2000): 631–57. Historical institutionalists in political science, studying business regulation, also assume technology determined the characteristic economic problems of industrialization. See, for example, Stephen Skowronek, *Building a New American State: The Expansion of National Administrative Capacities, 1877–1920* (Cambridge: Cambridge University Press, 1982), 121–25.

[3] Theda Skocpol, *Protecting Soldiers and Mothers: The Political Origins of Social Policy in the United States* (Cambridge, MA: Harvard University Press, 1992), 41–47; Edwin Amenta and Theda Skocpol, "Taking Exception: Explaining the Distinctiveness of American Public Policies in the Last Century," in Francis G. Castles, ed., *The Comparative History of Public Policy* (New York: Oxford University Press, 1989), 292–333; Skowronek, *Building a New American State;* Margaret Weir, Ann Shola Orloff, and Theda Skocpol, "Introduction: Understanding American Social Politics," in Margaret Weir, Ann Shola Orloff, and Theda Skocpol, eds., *The Politics of Social Policy in the United States* (Princeton, NJ: Princeton University Press, 1988), 3–36; Ira Katznelson, "Working-Class Formation: Constructing Cases and Comparisons," in I. Katznelson and A. Zolberg, eds., *Working Class Formation in Western Europe and the United States* (Princeton, NJ: Princeton University Press, 1986), 3–41; Martin Shefter, "Trade Unions and Political Machines: The Organization and Disorganization of the American Working Class in the Late Nineteenth Century," in Katznelson and Zolberg, eds., *Working Class Formation*, 197–275.

[4] David Vogel, "Why Businessmen Mistrust Their State," *British Journal of Political Science* 8 (January 1978): 45–78.

schemas, coercion, mimesis, and incentives. In analyzing the economy and economic policy, institutionalists usually draw upon rational choice theory to make sense of institutional forms. They find that institutional control mechanisms are especially important for minimizing transaction costs, resolving collective action problems, and ensuring public goods necessary for growth (e.g., labor training). If one learns about the organization of institutional mechanisms of control, one can predict, with some probability of success, the interests, identities, ideas, cultural dispositions, and actions of its agents and how well they work in maintaining order.[5]

Institutions Are Historically Layered. New institutions do not displace old ones. Instead, they exist side by side in incongruous and conflictual relations. Political scientists Karen Orren and Stephen Skowronek call this "intercurrence." In the United States, the administrative state did not displace the nineteenth-century order of courts and parties. Instead, older institutions became twentieth-century competitors to administration in a disorder, where ongoing conflicts over authority defined modern politics. Individual political institutions, such as the U.S. presidency, exhibit a similar dynamic. As political scientist Jeffrey Tulis shows, twentieth-century principles and practices did not displace old rules and routines in the U.S. presidency; they joined them in complex and incongruous "layers."[6]

Institutions Are Path Dependent. Seemingly small choices made at one moment in history can be cumulative and narrow the range of possibilities

[5] Kathleen Thelen and Sven Steinmo, "Historical Institutionalism in Comparative Politics," in Sven Steinmo, Kathleen Thelen, and Frank Longstreth, *Structuring Politics: Historical Institutionalism in Comparative Analysis* (Cambridge: Cambridge University Press, 1992). On institutions as solutions to collective action problems, see Peter Hall and David Soskice, "Introduction to Varieties of Capitalism," in Peter Hall and David Soskice, *Varieties of Capitalism* (New York: Oxford University Press, 2001), 9–12; Douglas North, *Institutions, Institutional Change and Economic Growth* (Cambridge: Cambridge University Press, 1990); John R. Bowman, "The Politics of the Market: Economic Competition and the Organization of Capitalists," *Political Power and Social Theory* 5 (1985): 35–88; Pepper D. Culpepper, "Employers, Public Policy, and the Politics of Decentralized Cooperation in Germany and France," in Hall and Soskice, eds., *Varieties of Capitalism,* 275–307; and Pepper D. Culpepper, *Creating Cooperation: How States Develop Human Capital in Europe* (Ithaca, NY: Cornell University Press, 2003). On institutions as solutions to transaction cost problems, see Oliver Williamson, *The Economic Institutions of Capitalism: Firms, Markets, Relational Contracting* (New York: Free Press, 1985).

[6] Karen Orren and Stephen Skowronek, "Beyond the Iconography of Order," in Lawrence C. Dodd and Calvin Jillson, eds., *The Dynamics of American Politics: Approaches and Interpretations* (Boulder, CO: Westview, 1994); Karen Orren and Stephen Skowronek, *The Search for American Political Development* (Cambridge: Cambridge University

in the future. Commitments to institutional practices can involve high initial costs and reap increasing returns from repetition, learning, or amortization of sunk costs. But path dependencies are not merely the result of increasing returns. Institutionalists have uncovered a variety of cognitive, rational, and coercive mechanisms that ensure reproduction because actors find it more attractive to follow routines than consider alternatives.[7]

The Institutionalist Story

The institutionalist account of industrialization and state building from the Civil War to the Great Depression is about the rise of and adjustment to mass production. It is told in three periods. In the first period, technological innovations created crises of overcapacity, which business tried to solve through cartels. When antitrust blocked this solution, organizational entrepreneurs abandoned association for consolidation in the largest merger wave in U.S. history. This conjuncture shaped future possibilities. The second period is about the politics of adjustment to the managerial corporation. When progressive state builders attempted to create a federal commission to regulate the corporation, old-order institutions (courts and parties) hamstrung their efforts. The third period returned to the economic issue that dominated the formative era: overcapacity. Although the new bureaucratic state collaborated with trade associations to solve overcapacity problems in the 1920s, path dependencies and institutional layering

Press, 2004), 108–18; Kathleen Thelen, *How Institutions Evolve: The Political Economy of Skills in Germany, Britain, the United States and Japan* (Cambridge: Cambridge University Press, 2004), 31–37; Wolfgang Streeck and Kathleen Thelen, eds., *Beyond Continuity: Institutional Change in Advanced Political Economies* (Oxford: Oxford University Press, 2005). On layering in the U.S. presidency, see Jeffrey Tulis, *The Rhetorical Presidency* (Princeton, NJ: Princeton University Press, 1987).

7 Paul Pierson, *Politics in Time: History, Institutions, Social Analysis* (Princeton, NJ: Princeton University Press, 2004); Paul Pierson, "Increasing Returns, Path Dependence, and the Study of Politics," *American Political Science Review* 94, no. 2 (June 2000): 251–67; Douglass C. North, *Institutions, Institutional Change and Economic Performance* (Cambridge: Cambridge University Press, 1990); Brian Arthur, *Increasing Returns and Path Dependence in the Economy* (Ann Arbor: University of Michigan Press, 1994); Fligstein, *Transformation of Corporate Control,* 5–10; Paul J. DiMaggio and Walter W. Powell, "The Iron Cage Revisited: Institutional Isomorphism and Collective Rationality in Organizational Fields," *American Sociological Review* 48 (1983), 147–60; Paul DiMaggio and Walter W. Powell, "Introduction," in Walter Powell and Paul DiMaggio, eds., *The New Institutionalism in Organizational Analysis* (Chicago: University of Chicago Press, 1991), 1–40.

impeded their efforts. Conflicts between the bureaucracy, parties, and the courts over competition policy left associations and government too weak to plan or discipline business. The result was a privately ordered economy, organized in markets and corporate hierarchies.

The nineteenth century witnessed a revolution in technology, which resulted in routine crises of overcapacity and cut-throat price competition. The steam engine, the open-hearth furnace in steel, and Bonsack rolling machine in tobacco greatly increased the speed of transportation and production. But these were expensive technologies that saddled firms with unprecedented debt. Where most costs had been "variable" in traditional industries (e.g., textiles, printing), most costs were "fixed" in modern industry (i.e., they did not vary with output). High fixed costs presented a novel economic problem: How could firms maintain production at a sufficiently high level to reap economies of scale, when their competitors, who had the same idea, were flooding the market with goods? This problem was compounded by depressions, which occurred every ten years between the 1870s and the second decade of the twentieth century. Business cut production traditionally in depressions. But modern manufacturers had the opposite incentive. In efforts to maintain scale economies, outcompete their rivals, and raise sufficient revenue to cover fixed costs and stave off bankruptcy, they maintained production levels and slashed prices. The result was cutthroat competition.[8]

The short-term solution to cutthroat competition was the creation of cartels, but it was notoriously unstable. In industry after industry, organizational entrepreneurs formed trade associations to manage overcapacity. However, as rational choice theorists predict and institutionalists argue, members had "high-powered incentives" to cheat on price and output agreements and profit at the expense of cooperators. As a result, cartels collapsed. To be sure, many cartels devised innovative methods to enforce agreements (the "trust certificate" is the most famous). However, by the 1880s they ran afoul of antitrust law. Unlike Germany or Japan,

[8] This paragraph and the following one are based on Chandler, *The Visible Hand;* Fligstein, *Transformation of Corporate Control*, 38–66; Dobbin and Dowd, "Market That Antitrust Built"; John R. Bowman, *Capitalist Collective Action: Competition, Cooperation and Conflict in the Coal Industry* (Cambridge: Cambridge University Press, 1989); Oliver E. Williamson, "The Modern Corporation: Origins, Evolution, Attributes," *Journal of Economic Literature* 19 (December 1981): 1537–68; J. Rogers Hollingsworth, "The Logic of Coordinating American Manufacturing Sectors," in John L. Campbell, J. Rogers Hollingsworth, and Leon L. Lindberg, eds., *Governance of the American Economy* (Cambridge: Cambridge University Press, 1991), 38–40.

where the state sanctioned and enforced cartels, U.S. courts refused to enforce trade agreements and state legislatures passed antitrust laws that empowered attorneys general to prosecute and dissolve them. Why?

Institutionalists explain the difference by historical sequencing. In the United States, nineteenth-century politics was organized around patronage parties and the judiciary. When the last vestiges of the property franchise ended in the 1830s, the first mass-based parties enlisted the petit bourgeoisie into politics. Without a central state bureaucracy that controlled policy and resources, patronage parties integrated the electorate through discrete benefits and appeal to the moral convictions of agrarian, small property, and artisanal norms. This class was overrepresented in legislatures.[9] Thus, when the "trusts" began to challenge traditional industry or set high prices for transportation and bulk commodities, the petit bourgeoisie registered its displeasure by instituting antitrust. In 1890, Congress passed the Sherman Antitrust Act, which outlawed all combinations in restraint of trade.

The absence of an autonomous bureaucracy in the United States also gave the judiciary far more influence and control over public policy than courts in Europe. Drawing on common-law precedents against restraints of trade before the advent of antitrust, the courts refused to enforce cartels. After antitrust, they read statutory law literally. For the first twenty years of Sherman Act jurisprudence, the courts declared all forms of business cartels illegal.[10]

Political institutions constrained and economic actors reacted. By the end of the 1890s, it was clear that association (or what business historians call "loose horizontal combination") was not an option. An alliance of industrialists, elite attorneys, and investment bankers seized the opportunity to solve the mounting crisis of overcapacity and cutthroat competition through mergers and acquisitions. They rearranged the principles of corporation law to facilitate consolidation. Between 1898 and 1904, the United States witnessed the largest merger wave in its history. Thousands

9 Martin Shefter, "Party, Bureaucracy, and Political Change in the United States," *Sage Electoral Studies Yearbook* 4 (1978): 211–65; Skocpol, *Protecting Soldiers and Mothers*, 44–45; Amenta and Skocpol, "Taking Exception," 314–15; Skowronek, *Building a New American State*, 19–35; Weir, Orloff, and Skocpol, "Introduction," 18–22.

10 Skowronek, *Building a New American State*, 19–35; Hans Thorelli, *The Federal Antitrust Policy* (Stockholm: Kungl, 1954), 155–60; McCraw, *Prophets of Regulation*, 65–68; Dobbin and Dowd, "The Market That Antitrust Built"; Hollingsworth, "The Logic of Coordinating American Manufacturing Sectors," 38–40.

of firms disappeared and some of the twentieth century's most prominent corporations – such as U.S. Steel and American Tobacco – were born.[11]

The great merger wave was a conjuncture, which created path dependencies. Capital-intensive industries continued to reap increasing returns from perfecting large-scale corporate hierarchies, whereas labor-intensive industries returned to open market competition. Trade associations became a lost alternative in the United States. Instead, antitrust created what students of "varieties of capitalism" call the archetype "liberal market economy." In contrast to Germany, where cartels were legal and most economic activity is "coordinated" by associations, the United States placed all economic activity in corporate hierarchies or open markets.[12]

The period following the great merger wave was marked by adjustment. In society, culture, and politics, Americans asked how they would adapt to the corporate reconstruction of U.S. capitalism. Some continued to resist, whereas others hoped to harness new forms to public ends. Nowhere was this struggle more evident than in the Progressive Era politics of antitrust, where old-order populists hoped to break up corporate monopolies and progressive state builders hoped to create an autonomous commission to regulate them. Although the progressives succeeded in 1914, institutional layering (or intercurrence) hampered the effectiveness of the FTC. Patronage parties refused to grant it sufficient authority or resources to exercise control. And the courts, jealous of competing authority, restricted the commission's powers. Thus, when the twin crises of overcapacity and redistribution reemerged in the 1920s and the Great Depression began, the bureaucracy was too weak to respond.[13]

[11] Hollingsworth, "The Logic of Coordinating American Manufacturing Sectors," 37–45; Naomi R. Lamoreaux, *The Great Merger Movement in American Business, 1895–1904* (Cambridge: Cambridge University Press, 1985); Dobbin and Dowd, "The Market That Antitrust Built"; McCraw, *Prophets of Regulation*, 68, 144–45; Jesse Markham, "Survey of the Evidence and Findings on Mergers," in *Business Concentration and Price Policy* (Princeton, NJ: Princeton University Press, 1955), 144; Ralph Nelson, *Merger Movements in American Industry, 1895–1956* (Princeton, NJ: Princeton University Press, 1959); William G. Roy, *Socializing Capital: The Rise of the Large Industrial Corporation* (Princeton, NJ: Princeton University Press, 1997).

[12] Hall and Soskice, "Introduction to Varieties of Capitalism," 27–33.

[13] On the weakness of the Federal Trade Commission, see Daniel P. Carpenter, *The Forging of Bureaucratic Autonomy* (Princeton, NJ: Princeton University Press, 2001), 7–11; Theodore Lowi, *End of Liberalism: The Second Republic of the United States* (New York: Norton, 1979), 97, 101, 111–12; Kenneth Finegold and Theda Skocpol, *State and Party in America's New Deal* (Madison: University of Wisconsin Press, 1995), 53–57; Thomas Lane Moore III, "The Establishment of a 'New Freedom' Policy: The Federal

Neither were trade associations able to overcome the burdens of institutional history. In 1919, as World War I came to a close, associations reemerged from the shadows of the U.S. economy. A partner in the successful war mobilization effort, they gained a new prestige nationally and became a key element in Republican economic policy during the 1920s. But path dependencies ruled. Unlike their corporatist counterparts in Europe, U.S. trade associations were too weak to solve the collective action problems associated with overcapacity and labor–management conflict. Like the bureaucracy, trade associations served only ancillary functions in the twentieth-century U.S. industrial order.[14] Instead, the United States became a privately ordered economy, organized in corporate hierarchies and competitive markets. Unlike Germany and Japan, the United States had few "coordinating institutions" between markets and hierarchies or elite bureaucracies capable of resolving economic dilemmas or improving performance. The failure of the National Recovery Administration to enlist trade associations to lift the U.S. economy out of depression in the 1930s is a paradigmatic example.

Empirical Problems with the Institutionalist Narrative

Research has uncovered many empirical problems with the institutionalist narrative. Four are salient: it mistakes the part for the whole, ignores competing systems, overestimates fixed costs, and mistakenly takes law as fixed and exogenous to economic development.

Trade Commission, 1912–1918" (PhD diss., University of Illinois, 1980); McCraw, *Prophets of Regulation*, 81, 125–28.

14 Robert H. Salisbury, "Why No Corporatism in the United States," in Philippe Schmitter and Gerhard Lembruch, eds., *Trends toward Corporatist Intermediation* (Beverly Hills, CA: Sage, 1972), 213–30; Colin Gordon, *New Deals: Business, Labor, and Politics in America, 1920–1935* (Cambridge: Cambridge University Press, 1994), 35–86, 128–65; Robert F. Himmelberg, *The Origins of the National Recovery Administration* (New York: Fordham University Press, 1976); Ellis Hawley, "Three Facets of Hooverian Associationalism: Lumber, Aviation, Movies," in Thomas K. McCraw, ed., *Regulation in Perspective* (Cambridge, MA: Harvard University Press, 1987); Finegold and Skocpol, *State and Party in America's New Deal*; Marc Allen Eisner, *From Warfare State to Welfare State: World War I, Compensatory State-Building, and the Limits of the Modern Order* (University Park: Pennsylvania State University Press, 2000), 106–21; Skowronek, *Building a New American State*, 267–71; Louis Galambos, *Competition and Cooperation: The Emergence of a National Trade Association* (Baltimore: Johns Hopkins University Press, 1966); Robert D. Cuff, *The War Industries Board: Business-Government Relations during World War I* (Baltimore: Johns Hopkins University Press, 1973).

First, the institutionalist story mistakes the part for the whole. Research on custom, specialty, and batch industries – from furniture and printing to machine tools – shows that there were many paths to industrialization in the United States. Moreover, these sectors rarely fit the institutionalists' picture of the alternative to corporate organization: a competitive market economy. They were organized in formal and informal networks, industrial districts, huge firms, relational contracts, and trade associations.[15] Firms in these sectors typically succeeded through product and process innovation and product quality and diversity. In addition, research on fire insurance and electricity shows how noncorporate legal forms, such as cooperatives, mutuals, and municipal ownership, persisted well into the twentieth century.[16] Add to these findings the fact that only 22 percent of U.S. industry participated in the great merger wave, and it appears that the institutionalist narrative mistakenly universalizes a partial account of U.S. economic development.[17]

Second, research on transportation and communications shows that there was no unambiguous relationship between technology and the definition of economic problems. All technologies can be deployed in multiple ways, each with unique challenges and advantages. My work on railroads

[15] See Philip P. Scranton, *Endless Novelty: Specialty Production and American Industrialization, 1865–1925* (Princeton, NJ: Princeton University Press, 1997); Phillip P. Scranton, "Diversity in Diversity: Flexible Production and American Industrialization, 1880–1930," *Business History Review* 65 (Spring 1991): 27–90; John K. Brown, *The Baldwin Locomotive Works, 1831–1915* (Baltimore: Johns Hopkins University Press, 1995); Howell J. Harris, "Getting It Together: The Metal Manufacturers' Association of Philadelphia," in Sanford M. Jacoby, ed., *Masters to Managers: Historical and Comparative Perspectives on American Employers* (New York: Columbia University Press, 1991); Gary Herrigel, *Industrial Constructions: The Sources of German Industrial Power* (Cambridge: Cambridge University Press, 1996); Charles F. Sabel and Jonathan Zeitlin, eds., *World of Possibilities: Flexibility and Mass Production in Western Industrialization* (Cambridge: Cambridge University Press, 1996), 241–380; Gerald Berk, *Alternative Tracks: The Constitution of American Industrial Order, 1865–1917* (Baltimore: Johns Hopkins University Press, 1994); Gerald Berk, "Communities of Competitors: Open Price Associations and the American State, 1911–1929," *Social Science History* 3 (1996): 375–400.

[16] Marc Schneiberg, "Political and Institutional Conditions for Governance by Association: Private Order and Price Controls in American Fire Insurance," *Politics and Society* 27 (1999): 67–103; Marc Schneiberg, "Organizational Heterogeneity and the Production of New Forms: Politics, Social Movements and Mutual Companies in American Fire Insurance, 1900–1930," in Michael Lounsbury and Marc Vantresca, eds., *Research in the Sociology of Organizations* (Greenwich, CT: JAI Press, 2002).

[17] Naomi Lamoreaux, *The Great Merger Movement in American Business, 1895–1904* (Cambridge: Cambridge University Press, 1985), 88n1; Fligstein, *Transformation of Corporate Control,* 318–19.

and historian Kenneth Lipartito's on telephones show that regional carriers rivaled their larger national competitors by inventing different methods to lower costs, serve customers, and organize administration. The victors in these battles of competing systems were determined in politics, not Darwinian market competition. Thus, the struggles over institutional form were not merely about how to solve economic problems determined exogenously by technology. These struggles determined the definition of economic problems in the first instance.[18]

Third, the attribution of high fixed costs to modern industry is overdrawn and cost structures are an unreliable predictor of consolidation. My study of the railroads shows that cost structures were determined more by struggles over corporation and receivership law than they were by technology. Indeed, when half the mileage of the industry went bankrupt and fell into receivership in the late nineteenth century, debt (fixed costs) was written down by one-third in order to keep national systems intact.[19] Transportation planner Gregory Thompson's study of railroad costs demonstrates that fixed costs never accounted for more than 35 percent of total costs. During most of the period of rapid industrialization, they were well under 20 percent. He concludes that the "relationship between fixed and variable railroad costs ... is precisely the opposite of the conventional wisdom."[20] Studies of industrial consolidations in the great merger wave also show that the relationship between cost structures and mergers is sketchy at best. Lamoreaux demonstrates that many industries learned to cope with overcapacity problems without price fixing or mergers. And Roy shows that most industries that underwent consolidation in the great merger wave did not have high fixed costs.[21] So the assumption that technology determined cost structures, and cost structures determined cutthroat competition, the creation of cartels, and consolidation does not stand up to scrutiny.

Fourth, the idea that economic legislation was dominated by nonprogrammatic political parties, which brokered patronage among economic

[18] Berk, *Alternative Tracks;* Sabel and Zeitlin, *World of Possibilities;* Kenneth Lipartito, "The Strategy of System Building: Telephony in the American South," in William Aspray, ed., *Technological Competitiveness: Contemporary and Historical Perspectives on the Electrical, Electronics and Computer Industries* (Piscataway, NJ: IEEE Press, 1993).

[19] Berk, *Alternative Tracks,* 47–72.

[20] Gregory L. Thompson, "Misused Product Costing in the American Railroad Industry: Southern Pacific Passenger Service between the Wars," *Business History Review* 63 (Autumn 1989): 510–54, quotation on 524.

[21] Lamoreaux, *The Great Merger Wave;* Roy, *Socializing Capital,* 21–41.

interests, does not always fit the facts. Studies of financial policy, railroad regulation, and antitrust show how legislative politics raised fundamental questions about political identity, narrative meaning, citizenship, and the cultural authority of the corporation and the market.[22] Moreover, the debate over antitrust remained unresolved, and competition became what political theorist William Connelly calls an "essentially contested concept" throughout the twentieth century.[23] As a result, it is impossible to hold antitrust exogenous to economic strategy. Although it is true that late-nineteenth-century courts outlawed price fixing, they left the legal status of associations wide open. Organizational entrepreneurs exploited legal ambiguities to experiment with new designs and lobbied the political branches to reshape antitrust to reflect what they learned.[24]

In summary, U.S. economic development was diverse, fixed costs did not determine the characteristic economic problems of industrialization, politics raised fundamental questions of cultural authority, and antitrust was unsettled. These anomalies raise difficult questions for institutionalist assumptions. Technology looks economically indeterminate. Institutions do not necessarily constrain action. Path dependencies do not close off alternatives or ensure institutional homogeneity. Although these insights demonstrate where institutionalists go wrong, it remains to outline an alternative framework that can make better sense of these anomalies and the evidence presented in this book.[25]

[22] Victoria Hattam, *Labor Visions and State Power: The Origins of Business Unionism in the United States* (Princeton, NJ: Princeton University Press, 1993); Gretchen Ritter, *Goldbugs and Greenbacks: The Antimonopoly Tradition and the Politics of Finance in America* (Cambridge: Cambridge University Press, 1997); John Ashworth, *Agrarians and Aristocrats: Party Political Ideology in the United States, 1837–1846* (Cambridge: Cambridge University Press, 1987); Berk, *Alternative Tracks*.

[23] William Connelly, *The Terms of Political Discourse* (Lexington, MA: D. C. Heath, 1974), chapter 1.

[24] On the continuing debate over the meaning of competition, see Ellis W. Hawley, *The New Deal and the Problem of Monopoly: A Study in Economic Ambivalence* (Princeton, NJ: Princeton University Press, 1966); Rudolph J. R. Peritz, *Competition Policy in America* (Oxford: Oxford University Press, 1996); Michael H. Best, *The New Competition: Institutions of Industrial Restructuring* (Cambridge, MA: Harvard University Press, 1990), 88–92; Marc Allen Eisner, *Antitrust and the Triumph of Economics: Institutions, Expertise and Policy Change* (Chapel Hill: University of North Carolina Press, 1991).

[25] I join a second generation of institutionalists in their efforts to overcome the excessive determinism of the first generation and its inability to theorize diversity and change. I believe it is necessary to replace the structuralist foundations of institutional theory with a constructivist or pragmatist approach to realize these goals. For excellent recent efforts to theorize diversity and change from a structuralist perspective, see Wolfgang Streeck and Kathleen Thelen, eds., *Beyond Continuity* (Oxford: Oxford University Press, 2005),

CREATIVE SYNCRETISM

This book draws on constructivist and pragmatist traditions in social theory to develop a different theory of institutions, which rests on four propositions. First, all institutions are syncretic. They are composed of an indeterminate number of features, which are decomposable and recombinable in unpredictable ways. Second, action within institutions is always potentially creative. Actors draw on a wide variety of cultural and institutional resources to create novel combinations. Third, deliberation occurs through narrative. Creative actors open new possibilities by recomposing the stories of their problems. Fourth, creative actors elaborate and diffuse otherwise isolated institutional experiments through creative conceptualization. Political scientist Dennis Galvan and I call this approach to institutions *creative syncretism* and I draw upon it to inform the history of regulated competition.[26]

This section ends with a fifth proposition, which is more particular to the story of regulated competition. Costs are social constructions. Measurement did not merely reflect economic reality, it shaped actors' perceptions of possibilities in economic organization and public policy.

Institutions Are Syncretic. Galvan and I conceptualize institutions as bundles of rules, cognitive principles, or instruments that can be decomposed and recombined in unpredictable ways. We call this characteristic of institutions *syncretism*.[27]

It is a mistake to think of institutions as composed of a finite set of essential and complementary features, which can be apprehended by their

1–39; Kathleen Thelen, *How Institutions Evolve* (Cambridge: Cambridge University Press, 2004); Karen Orren and Stephen Skowronek, *The Search for American Political Development* (Cambridge: Cambridge University Press, 2004); and Powell and Dimaggio, "Introduction."

[26] Gerald Berk and Dennis Galvan, "How People Experience and Change Institutions: A Field Guide to Creative Syncretism," *Theory and Society* (forthcoming). For a sympathetic perspective on political science methodology more generally, see Mark Bevir and Asaf Kedar, "Concept Formation in Political Science: An Anti-Naturalist Critique of Qualitative Methodology," *Perspectives on Politics* 6 (2008): 503–17.

[27] The idea of syncretism derives from religious and cultural studies. See Charles Stewart and Rosalind Shaw, *Syncretism/Anti-Syncretism: The Politics of Religious Synthesis* (London: Routledge, 1994). On syncretic or "recombinant" institutions, see Roberto Unger, *Social Theory: Its Situation and Its Task* (Cambridge: Cambridge University Press, 1987), 33–37; Charles Sabel and Jonathan Zeitlin, "Stories, Strategies, Structures," in Charles F. Sabel and Jonathan Zeitlin, *World of Possibilities: Flexibility and Mass Production in Western Industrialization* (Cambridge: Cambridge University Press, 1997); Jonathan Zeitlin and Gary Herrigel, eds., *Americanization and Its Limits*

agents or social scientists. Instead, this book conceptualizes institutions as combinations of indefinite numbers of features, the salience of which always depends on context, interpretation, and the use actors make of them. There are no essential defining features of a liberal judiciary, a corporate economy, or a parliamentary democracy. As sociologist Colin Crouch puts it, all institutions have "redundant" features that lie dormant at any given time.[28] Moreover, the strength of the ties between institutional components (e.g., rules, role descriptions, functional divisions of labor, or aspects of an institution's symbolic apparatus) are highly variable. Organization theorist Karl Weick and sociologists Walter Powell and Paul DiMaggio call this "coupling" and argue that the picture of the rational organization, in which components are integrated by clear rules into a hierarchy, does not fit reality.[29] All institutions have complex combinations of clear and vague rules and roles. Hence, their components are both "loosely" and "tightly" coupled. The more loosely they are coupled, the more they necessitate interpretation and recomposition in the normal course of institutional action.

Syncretism, redundancy, and loose coupling mean that the particular mix of active and dormant features depends on the purposes to which institutional actors put them. In this sense, institutions are better thought of as a bundle of resources (or repertoires of practices) that can be accessed

(New York: Oxford University Press, 2000); Rudra Sil, *Managing "Modernity": Work, Community, and Authority in Late-Industrializing Japan and Russia* (Ann Arbor: University of Michigan Press, 2002); Colin Crouch, *Capitalist Diversity and Change: Recombinant Governance and Institutional Entrepreneurs* (Oxford: Oxford University Press, 2005); Dennis Galvan, *The State Must Be Our Master of Fire: How Peasants Craft Sustainable Development in Senegal* (Berkeley: University of California Press, 2005); David Stark and Laszlo Bruszt, *Postsocialist Pathways: Transforming Politics and Property in East Central Europe* (Cambridge: Cambridge University Press, 1998); William H. Sewell, "A Theory of Structure: Duality, Agency and Transformation," *American Journal of Sociology* (July 1992): 1–29; Elisabeth S. Clemens, "Afterward: Logics of History? Agency, Multiplicity, and Incoherence in the Explanation of Change," in Julia Adams, Elisabeth S. Clemens, and Ann Shola Orloff, eds., *Remaking Modernity: Politics, History, and Sociology* (Durham, NC: Duke University Press, 2005), 499–507. On "technical syncretism," see Lewis Mumford, *Technics and Civilization* (New York: Harcourt, Brace, 1934), 107–9.

[28] Crouch, *Capitalist Diversity and Change*, 64–65, 88–91; Colin Crouch and Henry Farrell, "Breaking the Path of Institutional Development: Alternatives to the New Determinism," *Rationality and Society* 16, no. 1 (February 2004): 5–43.

[29] Karl E. Weick, *Making Sense of the Organization* (Malden, MA: Blackwell, 2001), 33–56; Paul DiMaggio and Walter W. Powell, "Introduction," in Walter W. Powell and Paul DiMaggio, eds., *The New Institutionalism in Organizational Analysis* (Chicago: University of Chicago Press, 1991), 1–40.

for problem solving through decomposition and recombination, than they are as order-making machines.

This is not to say that institutions are infinitely plastic or that any combination of features will do. Institutional actors settle on provisional combinations in response to collectively defined problems. Dewey calls them "habits," Bourdieu "habitus."[30] But habits are not routines, the "mere slothful repetition of what has been done before," as the founder of pragmatism, C. S. Pierce, put it.[31] Two features of habit make compulsive repetition unlikely. First, habits are always partial: human experiences overflow the ability of habits to make sense of the world. Thus, experience inevitably perturbs what at first glance look like stable combinations of institutional features.[32] Second, Dewey argues that routine is difficult to sustain, because it "artificially" separates habit and thought. Habit without thought is artificially undiscerning; the more it faces new circumstances and unfamiliar experiences, the more it produces unintended consequences, confusion of expectation and outcome. But, thought, when it only occurs in response to such difficulties, and becomes detached from ordinary habits of action, Dewey adds, "lacks a means of execution. In lacking application, it also lacks tests, criteria. Hence it is condemned to a separate realm. If we try to act upon it our actions are clumsy, forced." To be sure, Dewey recognizes that sometimes the powerful benefit from imposing routine upon the weak. But in this instance, the powerful themselves are not immune from the fragility of routine. They must constantly adjust to reproduce it. Thus, routine is exceptional, not as most institutionalists argue, the normal consequence of functional necessity, taken-for-granted schemas, path dependencies, political legitimacy, or authoritative coercion. More commonly, when experience overflows

[30] John Dewey, *Human Nature and Conduct* (Amherst, NY: Prometheus Books, 2002 [1922]); Pierre Bourdieu, *Outline of a Theory of Practice* (Cambridge: Cambridge University Press, 1977).

[31] Hans Joas and E. Klippen, "Creativity and Society," in H. Joas and J. Margolis, eds., *A Companion to Pragmatism* (Oxford: Blackwell, 2006), 325. On the similarity between Dewey's distinction between "habit" and "routine" and Bourdieu's distinction between "disposition" and "rule," see Richard Shusterman, "Introduction: Bourdieu as Philosopher," in Richard Shusterman, ed., *Bourdieu: A Critical Reader* (Malden, MA: Blackwell, 1999), 1–13; and Richard Shusterman, "Bourdieu and Anglo-American Philosophy," in Shusterman, ed., *Bourdieu*, 14–28; Gary Herrigel, "Institutionalists at the Limits of Institutionalism: A Constructivist Critique of Two Volumes by Wolfgang Streeck and Kozo Yamamura," *Socio-Economic Review* 3 (2005): 559–67.

[32] See Dewey's discussion of impulse and habit in *Human Nature and Conduct*; and Hans Joas, *The Creativity of Action* (Chicago: University of Chicago Press, 1996), 126–44.

habit or routine breaks down, institutional actors draw on their capacity for creative action to "deliberate."[33]

This book shows how syncretism pervaded traditional and modern culture and institutions in the Progressive Era and made it impossible for actors to follow routine. For example, we shall see how the principles of republicanism and self-regulating markets were loosely coupled in nineteenth-century ideology, and how efforts to bind them in unreflective routine resulted in perverse consequences. We shall also see how scientific management and public administration were composed of loosely coupled instruments, which had to be hived off and recombined with traditional business and government practices to form workable experiments in regulation and trade association.

Action Is Creative.[34] If institutions are complex bundles of loosely coupled features, then action is never determined by rules, norms, or taken-for-granted schemas. Actors are no institutional dopes. Instead, as Dewey writes, faced with unfamiliar experiences and the perturbation of habit, they can deliberate. Deliberation involves the application of reflective imagination to sort out competing paths of action suggested by new experiences, circumstances, and prior habits. Institutional actors respond by drawing on a repertoire of partially salient ways of responding to similarly shaped circumstances from the past. But prior habits, or combinations of institutional resources, may apply only up to a point in new circumstances, and are unlikely to represent complete or coherent expectations for action "because old habits as far as they are checked, are also broken into objects which define the obstruction of ongoing activity."[35]

When actors deliberate, they work in effect as anthropologist Claude Levi-Straus's "bricoleur,"[36] rummaging through available and partially relevant institutional resources, as well as salient experiences, to cobble together a new solution, or, in Dewey's terms, a "path of action." When

[33] Dewey, *Human Nature and Conduct*, 72–77.

[34] On creativity in institutions, see also the recent literature on entrepreneurship. Adam Scheingate, "Political Entrepreneurship, Institutional Change and American Political Development," *Studies in American Political Development* 17 (2003): 185–203; Crouch, *Capitalist Diversity and Change*; Hokyu Hwang and Walter W. Powell, "Institutions and Entrepreneurship," *Handbook of Entrepreneurship Research* (Norwell, MA: Kluwer, 2005): 179–210.

[35] Dewey, *Human Nature and Conduct*, 182.

[36] Claude Levi-Strauss, *The Savage Mind* (Chicago: University of Chicago Press, 1966).

they deliberate, actors consider a set of novel possibilities, each taking its "turn in projecting itself upon the screen of the imagination. It unrolls a picture of its future history, of the career it would have if it were given head." This is not a utilitarian weighing of options, but a recombinatory process of putting together creative new possibilities, "an experiment in making various combinations" of habits and experiences. Deliberation, moreover, is an inherently social process, which involves taking the attitude of others or enlisting them in experiments. In institutions, Galvan and I call this deliberative process of decomposing and recombining habits "creative syncretism."[37]

Creative syncretism occurs in three settings: within institutions, across institutional boundaries, and over time. If actors within institutions deliberate and experiment through recombination, living in a world of plural institutions multiplies the necessity for syncretism. As Orren and Skowronek, Alford and Friedland, Crouch and Keune, and others show, all societies are populated by multiple, hybrid, and incongruous institutions.[38] Therefore, actors inevitably experience uncertainty about how to reconcile conflicts between institutions. But institutional pluralism also enlarges the basket of resources available for problem solving. In a world of syncretic institutions, ideas and instruments can be hived off of one institution and exported to another. Syncretism occurs between, as well as within, institutions.

Syncretism also occurs across the boundaries of time. Faced with conflict among habits or unfamiliar terrain, actors can also access resources by reaching back in time to resurrect ideas or instruments once thought lost or abandoned.[39] Archeological resources can then be combined with

[37] Dewey, *Human Nature and Conduct*, 156–98. On experimentation, see also Gary Herrigel, "Rules and Roles: Ambiguity, Experimentation and New Forms of Stakeholderism in Germany," *Industrielle Beziehungen* 15, no. 2 (2008): 111–32.

[38] Robert R. Alford and Roger Friedland, "Bringing Society Back In: Symbols, Practices, and Institutional Contradictions," in DiMaggio and Powell, *The New Institutionalism in Organizational Analysis*, 232–63; Orren and Skowronek, *The Search for American Political Development;* Colin Crouch and Maarten Teune, "Changing Dominant Practice: Making Use of Institutional Diversity in Hungary and the United Kingdom," in Wolfgang Streeck and Kathleen Thelen, eds., *Beyond Continuity* (Oxford: Oxford University Press, 2005), 83–103; Robert Boyer, "Hybridization and Models of Production: Geography, History and Theory," in Robert Boyer, Elsie Charron, Ulrich Jurgens, and Steven Tolliday, eds., *Between Imitation and Innovation* (Oxford: Oxford University Press, 1998), 23–56.

[39] See Marc Schneiberg, "What's on the Path? Path Dependence, Organizational Diversity and the Problem of Institutional Change in the U.S. Economy, 1900–1950," *Socioeconomic Review* 5, no. 1 (January 2007): 47–80.

institutional features more commonly thought appropriate to a contemporary or emerging institutional order. Syncretism is temporal, as well as spatial.

Creative syncretism pervades the history of regulated competition. We shall see how Louis Brandeis built the theory of regulated competition by reaching across the divisions of time to reconfigure nineteenth-century principles of republican antimonopolism and combine them with features of twentieth-century administration. Brandeis decomposed scientific management and nineteenth-century common law, and recombined their parts in a syncretic blueprint for a federal trade commission. We shall also see how creative syncretists in Congress forged a majority coalition for a federal trade commission by writing a law with multiple meanings. In doing so, they licensed multiple projects, regulated competition among them. Drawing on the principles of regulated competition, creative administrators at the Federal Trade Commission recomposed resources from their institutional environment to forge innovative programs in cost accounting and setting industry standards for competition. By assembling peak business, professional, and trade associations on new ground, they cultivated capacities to upgrade competition in U.S. manufacturing. Finally, we shall see how creative syncretists in specialty manufacturing combined ancient craft solidarities with features of modern scientific management to reinvent trade associations from competition-suppressing cartels into developmental associations devoted to collaborative learning.

Deliberation Involves Cultural Narrative. Deliberation is an inescapably cultural, as well as practical, activity. When institutional actors project future possibilities, they accord them meaning in light of ongoing cultural debates over authority, power, and social relations. Even the most instrumental questions, such as how to measure manufacturing costs, inevitably raise broader questions of social and political meaning.[40]

But cultural interpretation does not enter deliberation or creative action in the abstract. That is, actors do not apply abstract principles to particular situations. Instead, as sociologist Margaret Somers shows, institutional actors tell one another concrete stories about how they got into a fix, what it means in light of cultural dispositions,

[40] William H. Sewell, "Toward a Post-Materialist Rhetoric for Labor History," in Lenard R. Berlanstein, ed., *Rethinking Labor History: Essays on Discourse and Class Analysis* (Urbana and Chicago: University of Illinois Press, 1993), 15–38.

and possible futures to reconnect cultural aspirations to institutional practice.[41]

To be sure, cultural narratives, like institutions, are contested and syncretic. They are devised from a repertoire of principles and symbols, which can be decomposed and recombined in unpredictable ways. Therefore, cultural narratives do not cause actions; they are the devices by which we communicate their meaning and alter our social sense of the possible.

The history of regulated competition is full of examples of deliberation as cultural story telling, some more obvious than others. We shall see, for example, how Brandeis attempted to forge a common project among petit bourgeois populists and cosmopolitan progressives by reworking their narratives about the rise of the trusts into a new story about the concentration of economic power and its alternatives. We shall also see how the practitioners of regulated competition at the FTC and in trade associations retold the story of the most challenging economic problem of their age: cutthroat price competition. Instead of the prevailing causal story, which attributed destructive competition to the immutable forces of technology and human greed, they showed how competition issued from accounting conventions that overvalued volume. By doing so, they opened the door to experimentation. Alter those conventions, they conjectured, and manufacturers would find more healthy ways to compete.

Creative Actors Conceptualize Institutional Projects. Once they create new possibilities through deliberation and narrative, how do creative actors turn otherwise isolated responses to pressing problems into institutional projects? How do they elaborate, diffuse, and institutionalize experiments? How do they enlist collaborators, imitators, and allies

[41] Margaret R. Somers, "Narrativity, Narrative Identity, and Social Action: Rethinking English Class Formation," *Social Science History* 16 (Winter 1992): 591–630; Donald Polkinghorne, *Narrative Knowing and the Human Sciences* (Albany: State University of New York Press, 1988). On the role of narrative in policy reasoning, see Deborah Stone, *Policy Paradox: The Art of Political Decision Making* (New York: Norton, 2002); Thomas J. Kaplan, "Reading Policy Narratives: Beginnings, Middles, and Ends," in Frank Fischer and John Forrester, eds., *The Argumentative Turn in Policy Analysis and Planning* (Durham, NC: Duke University Press, 1993), 167–85; and John Forrester, "Learning from Practice Stories: The Priority of Practical Judgment," in Fischer and Forrester, *The Argumentative Turn*, 186–212; Dvora Yanow, "Built Space as Story: The Policy Stories That Buildings Tell," *Policies Studies Journal* 23, no. 3 (1995): 407–22. On scientific economics as narrative, see Dierdre McCloskey, *The Rhetoric of Economics* (Madison: University of Wisconsin Press, 1998).

to their projects? Creative actors conceptualize.[42] By this I mean, they create categories, models, ideal types, typologies, or stylized accounts of social processes in which others find culturally resonant solutions to pressing problems. Concepts gain traction because actors see people like themselves doing things that better realize their ends. This does not mean that would-be collaborators or imitators evaluate concepts with settled identities, cultural dispositions, or goals. As in deliberation, new concepts become compelling because they provide the intellectual resources for reconfiguring goals or identities in the midst of institution building. People conceptualize in order to engage others in the process of finding their way about, discovering common goals, and settling on provisional identities and Deweyan habits.

Conceptual formulations can be highly contextual and concrete or they can be universal and abstract. The former includes typologies or ideal types drawn from experience; stylized accounts of economic or political processes that reveal unexpected opportunities for agency; or detailed institutional visions and organizational designs. The latter typically involve complex models deduced from first principles, or highly abstract concepts from which specific conclusions are drawn. There are many variations in between.

In this book, the architects of regulated competition tend to conceptualize their projects inductively and contextually, whereas their opponents tend to deduce universal abstractions. We shall see how Louis Brandeis conceptualized competition as a concrete historical process with ambiguous consequences for the distribution of power and economic performance. By doing so, he showed business, trade associations, and government how to channel competition from predation into improvement in products and production processes. We shall see how creative administrators at the FTC institutionalized trade practice conferences by developing concepts to explain how competitive customs were formed, performed, and reformed. Likewise, the U.S. Chamber of Commerce assembled trade commissioners, cost accountants, and trade association

[42] For a similar idea, see David Strang and John W. Meyer, "Institutional Conditions for Diffusion," *Theory and Society* 22, no. 4 (August 1993): 492. I do not use their term, "theorization," because it refers mainly to the work of prestigious professionals and policy makers who build "complex and highly integrated models." On theorization, see also Hokyu Hwang and Walter W. Powell, "Institutions and Entrepreneurship," in Sharon A. Alvarez, Olav Sorenson, and Rajshree Agrawal, eds., *The Handbook of Entrepreneurship Research* (New York: Springer, 2005), 179–210.

executives in a national forum to cull generalizations from their experience with trade association cost accounting. The result was a model of developmental association defined by four features: a common language, deliberation, benchmarking, and the coupling of price stabilization and improvement. By contrast, the economists and judges who challenged trade practice conferences and developmental associations deduced highly abstract models and universal categories to evaluate concrete cases.

Costs Are Socially Constructed.[43] Like the institutionalist account of industrialization and business regulation, my story begins with the cost structure of modern industry. Whereas institutionalists conceptualize costs as exogenous constraints on economic action and public policy, this book sees them as endogenous social constructions. Measurement did not mirror economic reality; instead, it shaped actors' understanding of work, technology, competition, and the division of labor in modern industry. As accounting scholar Peter Miller writes, "accounting is not a neutral device that merely documents 'the facts' of economic activity." It is better understood as a "set of practices that affects the world we live in, the social reality we inhabit ... and the way we administer the lives of others and ourselves."[44] In this book, costs are conceptualized as an artifact of contests over accounting conventions, the outcome of which legitimated

[43] On the social construction of economies more generally, see Michel Callon, ed., *The Laws of the Markets* (Oxford: Blackwell, 1998). On the social construction of science, see Bruno Latour and Steve Woolgar, *Laboratory Life: The Construction of Scientific Facts* (Princeton, NJ: Princeton University Press, 1986); Steven Shapin and Simon Schaffer, *Leviathan and the Air-Pump: Hobbes, Boyle and the Experimental Life* (Princeton, NJ: Princeton University Press, 1985); and Steve Fuller, *Philosophy of Science and Its Discontents* (Boulder, CO: Westview, 1989).

[44] Peter Miller, "Accounting as Social and Institutional Practice: An Introduction," in Anthony G. Hopwood and Peter Miller, eds., *Accounting as Social and Institutional Practice* (Cambridge: Cambridge University Press, 1994). There has been lots of excellent scholarship on the social studies of accounting in recent years. In addition to the articles in Hopwood and Miller, see Theodore M. Porter, *Trust in Numbers: The Pursuit of Objectivity in Science and Public Life* (Princeton, NJ: Princeton University Press, 1995); Mary Poovey, *A History of the Modern Fact* (Chicago: University of Chicago Press, 1998); and Michael Power, *Accounting and Science: Natural Inquiry and Commercial Reason* (Cambridge: Cambridge University Press, 1996). Postpositivist policy studies have also taken up the social construction of measurement in the public sector. See, for example, Stone, *Policy Paradox*, 163–87, 305–23; and Dvora Yanow, *Constructing "Race" and "Ethnicity" in America: Category Making in Public Policy and Administration* (Armonk, NY: M. E. Sharp, 2003).

some techniques over others and made corresponding economic problems and institutional strategies appear more or less natural.

From a constructivist perspective, it is less important to resolve, once and for all, whether railroads, steel, oil, or tobacco had high "fixed" costs than it is to understand how actors made sense of costs and acted on those understandings. Despite the foregoing evidence that railroads did not have a high ratio of fixed to variable costs, business historians have demonstrated that many railroad managers assumed fixed costs were an immutable constraint. Accounting conventions thus shaped economic action.

As sociologist David Stark puts it, accounting has two meanings, one scientific, the other political: bookkeeping and narration.

> Accountants prepare story lines according to established formulae, and in the accountings of a good story we know what counts. In everyday life, we are all bookkeepers and storytellers. We keep accounts and we give accounts, and most importantly, we can all be called to account for our actions.[45]

This book analyzes the way practitioners and opponents of regulated competition created and deployed accounting conventions to license agency and assign accountability. We shall see how some actors naturalized the language of "fixed" costs to circumscribe agency, accountability, and public policy, while others challenged the fixed cost assumption to enable experimentation and creative conceptualization. Among the latter were the architects and practitioners of regulated competition. Reflexive policy makers, cost accountants, trade association executives, and bureaucrats asked whether the defining economic problem of their age – cutthroat price competition – was caused by the immutable features of modern technology or simply by accounting conventions that overvalued volume. Posing the question enabled experimentation. By reconfiguring accounting conventions so that most costs were variable (and so subject to human agency), they showed manufacturers how to invent less predatory ways to compete. Brandeis proposed Congress empower a federal trade commission to set cost accounting standards. Creative commissioners at the FTC devised an ambitious project to cultivate cost accounting capacities in peak business, professional, and trade associations. And those associations succeeded in reconfiguring many of their members' destructive habits.

[45] David Stark, "Recombinant Property in East European Capitalism," *American Journal of Sociology* 101, no. 94 (January 1996): 993–1027.

The opponents of regulated competition conceived of costs differently. Like institutionalists looking back, economists, judges, and officials in the Department of Justice naturalized the costs of modern industry. They used the conceptual distinction between fixed and variable costs to build deductive theories, which they deployed to evaluate experiments in regulated competition when they came before the courts and Congress. The outcome of these clashes over the social construction of costs, not an intercurrent struggle between fading and emergent institutions, determined the fate of regulated competition in the twentieth century.

A CREATIVE SYNCRETIST NARRATIVE

This book recounts the story of regulated competition in three parts: Brandeis and the theory of regulated competition, regulated competition in practice, and regulated competition contested. It applies the theory of creative syncretism both to the narrative and to the institutions of regulated competition. I show not only how actors invented new institutional forms by recombining resources from unlikely places, but also how they designed those institutions to make use of their participants' capacity for creativity, deliberation, and recombination. The result was innovative and unfamiliar forms of regulation, public administration, professional organization, and trade associations.

Our story begins with the great merger wave at the turn of the nineteenth century. For cosmopolitan progressives (economists, attorneys, public intellectuals, and some political leaders), this event signaled the modernization of U.S. industry. They created theories to explain how corporate concentration was inevitable and efficient. Progressives were hardly apologists for corporate power. Acknowledging its dangers, they proposed to build countervailing power in a federal agency, staffed by experts and empowered to regulate monopoly. Another group of reformers opposed the progressives. Drawing on nineteenth-century republican principles, petit bourgeois populists (farmers, craftspeople, and small manufacturers) contended that corporate power was cause and consequence of corruption. They hoped to break up concentrated power and prevent the predatory tactics, which led to it in the first place, by strengthening antitrust law and enforcement. This contest is conventional wisdom for institutionalists who study the politics of industrialization in the United States.

Louis Brandeis entered this struggle in the presidential election of 1912 with a third perspective. A Boston reformer and small business attorney,

Brandeis had long been sympathetic to the populists. But he was also a creative syncretist, who saw an opportunity to forge a common project between progressives and populists. And he found in Democratic candidate Woodrow Wilson a sympathetic sponsor who shared his desire to forge a coalition of populist Democrats and progressive Republicans. In 1912, Brandeis and Wilson deliberated in the Deweyan sense.

As Brandeis saw it, the problem was to renarrate the causes of American distress in a way that both populists and progressives could find a place for themselves. In his view, populist Democrats were correct: corporate power endangered the republic, and it was unlikely that a commission could redress that power. Progressives were also correct: markets were no longer self-regulating and a commission was necessary to ensure that they realized civic ends. But Brandeis thought both factions falsely reified particular institutional forms and in doing so, they reached unwarranted conclusions about the causes of big business, restricted policy imagination, and diminished the possibilities for experimentation.

Populist Democrats failed to see the ambiguities of competition, because they placed blind faith in self-regulating markets. Brandeis and others knew through observation, however, that competition could be predatory or productive. Hence, a blanket rule against restraints of trade would undermine the many productive restraints business had learned to place on rivalry. Enforced competition, in other words, would have perverse outcomes.

Similarly, Brandeis held that the progressives mistakenly reified the large-scale corporation as inevitable and efficient. In the absence of a policy that distinguished predatory from productive competition, however, no one really knew whether economic concentration was caused by efficiency or the desire for power. The progressive economists, Brandeis charged, were incorrect to naturalize bigness as scientific law. He learned that another group of professionals, engineers and cost accountants, questioned the economists' explanation of bigness. They have remained completely out of view of institutionalist scholars of this period.

The cost accountants had demonstrated how the obsession with mass production and bigness was driven more by cost conventions that overvalued volume than by the immutably high fixed costs of modern technology (as the economists theorized). In experiments with manufacturing and railroads, they showed that when firms adopted new cost metrics, they found many ways to increase efficiency and profits without augmenting the scale of production. Drawing on these successes, Brandeis criticized the advocates of regulated monopoly for capitulating to unnecessary power and cutting short the search for the technical means to reconcile American aspirations to equality and economic prosperity.

Instead of reifying markets or corporations, Brandeis proposed an ongoing experiment. Create an agency with the capacity to distinguish predatory from productive competition and then use it to channel rivalry from the former to the latter. Brandeis called this option "regulated competition" and proposed two warrants for the Federal Trade Commission. The first combined deliberation and coercion. Empower the commission to work with business to identify predatory methods of competition and check them before they turned into unassailable power. The second warrant was what I call cultivational: empower the commission to perturb destructive business habits though education, information, and disciplined comparison between the best and worst of business practices (benchmarking). Brandeis proposed the FTC hire cost accountants, not economists, to oversee its cultivational mission.

Thus, even though institutional conditions seemed conducive for the crystallization of routine (path dependency) after the great merger wave, regulated competition challenged progressives and populists to set aside blind faith in markets or administration for an experiment. Empower a trade commission to channel competition from predation into improvements in products and production processes and see what happens. Brandeis bet that the outcome would better reconcile the populist goal of equality with the progressive goal of scientific mastery than either enforced competition or regulated monopoly.

Although Brandeis cracked open the terms of debate in 1912, he did not succeed in convincing populists and progressives to merge their identities into a single political bloc. Wilson exploited divisions within the Republican Party to win the election with a plurality, and the problem of assembling a reform coalition remained.

Under Wilson's watchful eye, Congress took up the cause of reform. By 1914, creative syncretists in Congress had forged a majority coalition in support of a federal trade commission by writing a law with multiple meanings. The heart of the Federal Trade Commission Act empowered the FTC to regulate "unfair methods of competition." Legislative entrepreneurs told their populist colleagues in the Democratic Party this was a prophylactic power. The FTC would use it to check predatory activity before it turned into unassailable power. They told their progressive Republican colleagues that it meant that once firms grew big for reasons of efficiency, the FTC would ensure they used that power responsibly. In the end, both factions took credit for the statute. And the law with multiple meanings licensed multiple projects, among them regulated competition. Part II recounts the implementation of regulated competition.

In 1914, creative administrators at the FTC picked up Brandeis's project and carried it forward. Their work has been invisible to institutionalists, because institutionalists believe the FTC was born a structurally weak agency. It had a vague mission, few resources, little autonomy from business or Congress, and an unwieldy mandate to regulate the whole economy. Seen from the perspective of creative syncretism, however, the story recounted in this book shows how administrators found resources for innovation, where institutionalists see only constraints. By collaborating with peak business, professional, and trade associations, the FTC built a nimble agency with the capacity to steer a diverse economy from destructive competition to product diversity, innovation, and productivity.

In 1915, the FTC's second chair, Edward Hurley, invited Brandeis to address the commission. To their surprise, Hurley and Brandeis found they shared an enthusiasm for cost accounting. (Hurley was a Chicago manufacturer who had learned about cost accounting when he served as president of the Illinois Manufacturer's Association.) A great deal of destructive competition in manufacturing, Hurley and Brandeis agreed, was caused by the unreflective obsession with volume. This was Deweyan routine. But the cost accountants provided a deliberative alternative, which showed there was nothing inevitable about accounting conventions that valued volume over all other ends.

Hurley and Brandeis agreed that the commission ought to take up the accountants' project and teach business new methods to measure costs and then pool information about what worked and what did not. By doing so, the FTC could help channel competition from cutthroat pricing into improvements in products and production processes.

Hurley considered approaching Congress for a license to set uniform national cost accounting standards and the resources to carry it out, but the political conditions appeared inhospitable. This did not block creativity. Hurley searched instead for resources in civil society, where he found the cost accountants, the U.S. Chamber of Commerce, and a number of trade associations in manufacturing industries, which were in the midst of developing their own accounting systems. Under Hurley's guidance, the FTC turned to these groups to cultivate business capacities for regulated competition.

Hurley's successors at the FTC elaborated his experiments in cultivational administration through trade practice conferences, which assembled industries to distinguish predatory from productive competition. The commission's third chair, Nelson Gaskill, creatively conceptualized trade practice conferences as deliberative interventions into the process of trade custom formation. By doing so, he provided a legal foundation for trade practice rules, which made it possible to institutionalize FTC conferences. In 1926, the commission created a Trade Practice Conference Division, which anticipated the federal government's efforts to upgrade competition during the Great Depression through the National Recovery Administration. By the end of the decade the division had approved hundreds of trade practice rules, among them fifty that endorsed trade association cost accounting systems.

Institutionalists overlook cultivational administration because they have searched for bureaucratic hierarchy and autonomy. But creative administrators at the FTC valued different ends and organizational features. Cultivational administrators sought to build deliberative, scientific, and evaluative capacity in peak business, professional, and trade associations through public/private collaboration, not state autonomy. Moreover, FTC cost accounting and trade practice conferences worked most effectively when they violated cardinal principles of bureaucracy: hierarchical communication, a sharp division between plan and execution, and a clear division of labor between departments. These characteristics might have been workable had the FTC faced well-known, homogeneous, and static problems. But having defined its mission otherwise, the FTC valued different organizational features. The Trade Practice Conference Division combined functions (deliberation, research, and legal interpretation); top FTC administrators descended the hierarchy to run trade practice conferences; and the Trade Practice Conference Division engaged in routine horizontal communication with the legal department. In order to distinguish this form from Weberian hierarchy, I adopt the concept of heterarchy from organization theory. Heterachies combine functions, blur the sharp distinction between plan and execution, and flatten organizational hierarchies in order to respond creatively to uncertainty, diversity, and constant change.

The FTC's efforts bore fruit in innovations in civil society. Between 1918 and 1929, 246 associations in 96 manufacturing industries participated in the development and diffusion of cost accounting. In doing so, they invented a new form of association, which I call developmental. Developmental associations abandoned efforts to suppress competition, taking up instead improvement through collaborative learning. They had three defining features: uniform cost accounting, benchmarking, and interfirm deliberation. The goal of better cost accounting was to shift rivalry from cutthroat competition over volume into improvements in products and production processes. The goal of benchmarking was to provide firms with detailed data on average costs in their industry, so that they could compare their own performance with that of others and learn where they most needed to improve. And the goal of deliberation was to build the capacity of firms to use benchmarking data to perturb habits and to enhance industry cost systems and trade association benchmarking services. The U.S. Chamber of Commerce, the National Association of Cost Accountants, and the American Trade Association Executives worked closely with the FTC and trade associations to conceptualize and diffuse developmental associations.

Did regulated competition through developmental associations work? In order to answer this question, I present a detailed case study of the commercial printing industry. Commercial printers devised the first and the most elaborate developmental association. Moreover, this industry had all the characteristics that institutionalists, who have been influenced by game theory, believe make effective price coordination within trade associations impossible: easy entry, large numbers of firms, and diverse products. Therefore, the printing industry is a good case to test my interpretaton of developmental associations as collaborative learning systems against the institutionalist interpretation of information-pooling associations as a new form of price fixing cartel.

The printers' story begins in 1910. After repeated failures to enforce cartels, the printers did not – as institutionalists would have predicted – consolidate or revert to competitive markets. Instead, drawing on old craft solidarities and modern cost accounting techniques, they reinvented Ben Franklin Clubs and Typothetae associations. Like the creative administrators at the FTC, reflexive associationalists conjectured that the causes of cutthroat competition in printing lay not in technology or intractable collective action problems, but in accounting conventions that prized volume over all other ends. (They named them the "volume bug.") Alter accounting techniques, they hypothesized, and printers might find other paths to prosperity. The United Typothetae of America (UTA) devised just such a system. But the UTA's Standard Cost System sat on the shelf until the FTC took up cost accounting in 1915 and prodded the association to launch an ambitious organizing plan. By 1927, more than one-third of the fifteen thousand printers in the United States had adopted the UTA's cost system and the association had devised an elaborate benchmarking system by which printers could compare their costs with one another. The result was to shift production and technology from volume to specialty production, increase labor skills, increase the number of small and medium-sized firms in the industry, and treble productivity in the industry. In short, the developmental association was successful in commercial printing and helped shape an alternative model of industrial organization.

With the help of the U.S. Chamber of Commerce, the National Association of Cost Accountants, the American Trade Association Executives, and the FTC, developmental associations spread from printing to other specialty sectors (e.g., metalworking and lithography), batch industries, (e.g., tanning and awnings), and finally into continuous-processing sectors (e.g., pharmaceuticals and paper).

By 1929, more than 13 percent of all manufacturing trade associations had adopted the features of developmental associations in whole or in part. And by a number of measures, they succeeded in upgrading competition and improving economic performance.

In sum, efforts to regulate competition through FTC-sponsored cost accounting, trade practice conferences, and developmental associations were remarkably successful. But success did not ensure institutional or cultural hegemony. The unresolved struggle over antitrust reemerged in the 1920s in a battle over the accountability of trade practice conferences and developmental associations. Part III recounts that struggle.

On one side were the partisans of regulated competition: cost accountants, trade associations, trade commissioners, and Brandeis (now an associate justice on the U.S. Supreme Court). Following Brandeis, they conceptualized competition as an ambiguous process, which could result in economic improvement or concentrated power. Under a regime of regulated competition, it was the state's responsibility to steer rivalry from the latter to the former. Hence, they advocated principles of process, power, and performance to evaluate trade practice conferences and trade association accounting activities. Competitive customs, they argued, were formed in a social process of tender, acceptance, and generalization. Therefore, it made sense to judge trade practice conferences and trade association accounting activities according to three criteria. First, did they intervene in that process by which trade customs were formed and reformed effectively to channel competition from predation to improvement? Second, did they check the concentration of power and keep open possibilities for new forms of rivalry? Third, did those interventions in the process of forming trade customs improve economic performance?

On the other side of the debate were the Department of Justice, the courts, and the economics profession. They used economic science to draw a bright line between public and private interests and then compared the facts with their categories. Hence they advocated principles of classification to evaluate trade practice conferences and trade association behavior. Trade association activities, they postulated, were inherently competitive or monopolistic; government regulation served either the public or private interests. Thus, the relevant question for trade practice conferences was whether they realized the public interest in perfecting competition or merely rearranged private advantages in the market. Likewise, classifiers asked whether trade association efforts to pool information served the public interest in realizing the economist's ideal of perfect competition by improving individual decision-making capacity or fostered monopoly by coordinating collective action. With these distinctions in mind, the Department of Justice, the courts, and the economists weighed the facts and policed the boundaries between public and private and competition and monopoly.

The classifiers won the contest over the principles of accountability, but only after they had revised their theories to accommodate many features of regulated competition. Thus, many – not all – trade practice rules and developmental associations survived the fight over accountability. The result was a twentieth-century regulatory and industrial order rife with diversity; syncrestism; and an ongoing conflict over antitrust, competition, and economic form.

Notice how different this narrative is from the institutionalist story. Where institutionalists see the politics of antitrust in the Progressive Era as a debate over how to assimilate the modern corporation, I see it as a contested site for multiple economic and regulatory projects. Where institutionalists see antitrust as a constraint on economic form, I see it as a contested resource for experimentation and creative syncretism. Where institutionalists see layering as the source of confusion, incapacity, and capture at the FTC, I see multiple possibilities and resources for nonbureaucratic organization and public/private collaboration in the FTC's legislative mandate and organizational environment. Where institutionalists see path dependencies, which precluded associations from solving overcapacity problems, I see creative associationalists who navigated a path around collective action problems with cost accounting, benchmarking, and collaborative learning. Where institutionalists see a U.S. industrial order, which settled into liberal market institutions, I see diversity in industry and government and ongoing possibilities for creative syncretism.

PART I

BRANDEIS AND THE THEORY OF REGULATED COMPETITION

Chapter 2

Republican Experimentalism and Regulated Competition

The election of 1912 divided antitrust reformers and Louis Brandeis proposed to unite them. Populist Democrats hoped to decentralize economic power by enforcing competition. Progressive Republicans accepted the concentration of economic power, but wanted to regulate it with an independent commission. Louis Brandeis offered a third way. Neither self-regulating markets nor regulated monopoly, regulated competition would harness a regulatory commission and civil society to channel rivalry from predation into improvements in products and production processes. By recomposing the relationship between public administration and competition, Brandeis's proposal promised to reconcile the populist desire for decentralized power with the progressive desire for administrative mastery and economic progress.

The contest over antitrust reform raised fundamental questions of narrative identity and cultural authority. It would not be won or lost by technical considerations alone. The election of 1912 turned on who spoke most directly to U.S. anxieties over the relationship among economic prosperity, democracy, and power. But cultural conflict seemed mired in irreconcilable differences in 1912: populists lashed out at progressives for capitulating to despotic power; progressives charged populists with unwarranted faith in individualism and self-regulating markets. Reconciliation promised immense political vitality and Brandeis took up the challenge. He disassembled ancient republican fears of monopoly power and recombined their parts with modern faith in science in a cultural schema I call republican experimentalism.

This chapter situates, explains, and defends republican experimentalism and regulated competition. The first part situates Brandeis's approach within a debate between populists and progressives – a debate that was structured by the U.S. Supreme Court. Brandeis combined the concerns of the republican antimonopoly movements that went before him with technical sensibilities of engineers in republican experimentalism. The second part explains regulated competition through three examples: machine leasing in the shoe industry, resale price maintenance, and trade associations.

THE PREDICAMENT OF ANTITRUST REFORM

In 1911, antitrust enthusiasts won a Pyrrhic victory when the Supreme Court ruled against the oil and tobacco trusts. They looked on with dismay as Justice White gutted two decades of antitrust jurisprudence with the stroke of a pen. Not *every* combination or contract in restraint of trade was unlawful, he wrote, only those that *unreasonably* restrained trade. The rulings against Standard Oil and American Tobacco signaled the Court's intent to evaluate public regulation of private contracts according to strict standards of classification. Did antitrust practice serve a genuine public interest in preventing monopoly or merely redistribute private advantages in the market? Like protective labor legislation, railroad rate regulation, and taxation, antitrust would be held accountable to a strict constitutional distinction between public and private. Otherwise, *every* contract would be subject to state supervision and no market activity would be safe from public control. The Court's distinction between reasonable and unreasonable contracts in restraint of trade was the first step in that direction.[1]

[1] On the "literalist" era of antitrust jurisprudence, when the courts declared every contract in restraint unlawful, instead of only "unreasonable" ones, see Rudolph J. R. Peritz, *Competition Policy in America: History, Rhetoric, Law*, rev. ed. (New York: Oxford University Press, 1996), 26–50; William Letwin, *Law and Economic Policy in America: The Evolution of the Sherman Antitrust Act* (New York: Random House, 1965), 103–6; Hans Thorelli, *Federal Antitrust Policy: Origination of an American Tradition* (Baltimore: Johns Hopkins University Press, 1955), 534–37. On the *Standard Oil* decision and the rule of reason, see Peritz, *Competition Policy*, 50–58; Marc Winerman, "The Origins of the FTC: Concentration, Cooperation, Control and Competition," *Antitrust Law Journal* 71 (2003): 12–13. On parallels between *Standard Oil* and other areas of Lochner Court jurisprudence, see Howard Gillman, *The Constitution Besieged: The Rise and Demise of Lochner Era Police Powers Jurisprudence* (Durham, NC: Duke University Press, 1993), 125–31; and Peritz, *Competition Policy*, 45–48. On the foundations of the Court's logic in laissez-faire constitutionalism more generally, see Herbert Hovencamp, *Enterprise and American Law, 1836–1937* (Cambridge, MA: Harvard University Press, 1991), chapter 14; Morton J. Horwitz, *The Transformation of American Law*, 1890–1960 (New York: Oxford University Press, 1992), 9–64;

The *Standard Oil* decision incensed populist Democrats because it reversed the strict prohibition of restraints of trade. "The Trusts Have Won," declared three-time Democratic presidential candidate, William Jennings Bryan. The Court usurped the legislative function and trampled popular sovereignty. The Sherman Act was clear: Congress outlawed *every* contract and combination in restraint of trade, not merely those that were unreasonable. The Court was obliged to enforce competition. Bryan called on the friends of antitrust to challenge judicial arrogance, win control over the political branches, and set the law on a sound foundation again. The stakes for populists were high. Not merely the separation of power, but the republic itself was threatened by judicial capitulation to despotic power.[2]

Although progressives were sympathetic to the populist plea for active government, they welcomed the *Standard Oil* decision. Most progressives thought contracts and combinations in restraint of trade were inevitable in modern industry, as hierarchical organization steadily replaced market exchange. An antitrust doctrine that condemned them all was of little use. The Court's distinction between reasonable and unreasonable restraints deserved praise. But progressives also thought the Court had overreached. Classification was increasingly a technical matter, ill served by legal niceties such as the rule of reason. Judges were not well equipped to distinguish competition from monopoly – a necessary prerequisite to knowing whether the public interest would be served by breaking up giant enterprise or accepting it and subjecting it to government regulation. Fortunately, two decades of progress in scientific economics had established a field with sufficient rigor, institutional autonomy, and status to meet the challenge.[3]

Charles W. McCurdy, "Justice Field and the Jurisprudence of Government-Business Relations: Some Parameters of Laissez-Faire Constitutionalism, 1863–1897," *Journal of American History* 61 (March 1975): 970–1005.

2 Scott C. James, *Presidents, Parties, and the State: A Party System Perspective on Regulatory Choice, 1884–1936* (Cambridge: Cambridge University Press, 2000), 150–53; Winerman, "Origins of the FTC," 13–15.

3 On the difficulties in establishing professional autonomy in economics, see Mary O. Furner, *Advocacy and Objectivity: The Crisis in the Professionalization of American Social Science, 1865–1905* (Lexington: University Press of Kentucky, 1975); Dorothy Ross, *Origins of American Social Science* (Cambridge: Cambridge University Press, 1991), 98–116; Daniel T. Rodgers, *Atlantic Crossings: Social Policy in a Progressive Age* (Cambridge, MA: Harvard University Press, 1998), 77–111; Dorothy Ross, "Socialism and American Liberalism: Academic Social Thought in the 1880s," *Perspectives in American History* 11 (1977–1978); Robert L. Church, "Economists as Experts: The Rise of an Academic Profession in the United States, 1870–1920," in Lawrence Stone, ed., *The University in Society*, vol. 2 (Princeton, NJ: Princeton University Press, 1974).

Among the founders of the American Economics Association in 1886 were two influential economists who took up the Court's challenge to classify economic activity more rigorously. A founder of the marginalist revolution in economics in North America, John Bates Clark, applied his theories to rework the classical distinction between competition and monopoly. Henry Carter Adams, an accomplished statistician, government servant, and theoretician, applied the tools of marginalism to the Court's demand for a rigorous distinction between public and private economic activities. Clark and Adams were influential innovators and active participants in regulatory debates; their ideas were representative of an emerging perspective within their profession.[4]

Consider Clark's theory of monopoly. All too often, he wrote, laymen and lawyers confuse monopoly and centralization. The former was a technical condition, in which the price mechanism failed to allocate resources to their highest value. The latter was a condition associated with production. In order to understand monopoly, it was necessary to reconceptualize competition. Clark's famous innovation was the law of "diminishing marginal utility." The more consumers accumulated a single commodity, he wrote, the less utility they derived from it. As a result, they continued to acquire additional units until the value of the last (or "marginal") unit was equal to the marginal utility derived from it. Thus, in a perfectly competitive economy, traders exchanged goods until resources were allocated to their highest value. By contrast, when an individual, firm, or cartel had sufficient power to set prices or output, resources deviated from their "natural channel." This was "monopoly" and it was improper, Clark wrote, because it distorted the allocation of resources.[5] Centralization,

[4] On the marginalist revolution in American economics, see James Livingston, "The Social Analysis of Economic History and Theory: Conjectures on Late-Nineteenth Century American Development," *The American Historical Review* 92 (1987): 69–95; James Livingston, *Pragmatism and the Political Economy of Cultural Revolution, 1850–1940* (Chapel Hill: University of North Carolina Press, 1994), 53–59; John Bates Clark, *The Distribution of Wealth* (New York: Macmillan, 1899), 36–51; Ernesto Screpanti and Stefano Zamagni, *An Outline of the History of Economic Thought* (Oxford: Oxford University Press, 1993), 147–49, 169; Craufurd D. W. Goodwin, "Marginalism Moves to the New World," in R. D. C. Black, A. W. Coats, and C. D. W. Goodwin, eds., *The Marginal Revolution in Economics* (Durham, NC: Duke University Press, 1973), 285–304; Joseph Dorfman, *The Economic Mind in American Civilization, 1865–1918*, vol. 3 (New York: Viking, 1959), 188–204; T. W. Hutchison, *A Review of Economic Doctrines, 1870–1929* (Oxford: Oxford University Press, 1953), 251–62. On the roots of marginalism in nineteenth-century physics, see Philip Mirowski, "Physics and the 'Marginalist Revolution,'" *Cambridge Journal of Economics* 8 (December 1984): 361–79.

[5] John Bates Clark, *The Problem of Monopoly* (New York: Columbia University Press, 1904), 13–20; *Chicago Conference on Trusts* (Chicago: The Civic Federation

by contrast, was a condition associated with production. When a small number of large firms could produce goods more cheaply than their smaller counterparts, industries became centralized. Centralization was inevitable and efficient. In some cases, it resulted in monopoly and then government regulation was warranted. But more often than not, huge firms stopped short of exercising their full weight in the market for fear of encouraging competitors. Although progressive economists debated Clark's empirical conclusion, they accepted his categories.

Like Clark, Adams also took up the Court's challenge to classify. If there was any "virtue" in the new "science" of economics, he wrote, it should be able to "determine, with some degree of accuracy" the conditions under which market competition or government regulation will best serve the "rational ends of society."[6] Drawing on the work of British marginalist Stanley Jevons, Adams classified industries by defining features of production. In most industries, there was a relatively low threshold of production, after each additional unit of labor and materials resulted in diminishing marginal units of output. However, in many modern industries, with high fixed-cost technologies, additional units of input yielded increasing marginal units of output. In the former, firms remained relatively small and competition "depressed" the cost of service. Therefore, there was no need for state action. The latter, by contrast, tended toward centralization. In many cases, "such businesses are by their nature monopolies ... [and] no law can make them compete." Hence, only public regulation of prices – that is, regulated monopoly – would overcome festering grievances and "restore social harmony."[7]

Progressives welcomed the marginalist revolution in economics, even as they continued to debate the facts. It justified state autonomy, supplied a ready source of government experts, and provided objective standards to discipline the judiciary. In 1905, Theodore Roosevelt initiated a campaign for an independent commission to apply marginalist distinctions and regulate monopoly power where appropriate. Through close consultation with Clark and the National Civic Federation, Roosevelt's commissioner of corporations, Herbert Knox Smith, outlined a blueprint for a federal trade commission.[8] In 1906, the president enlisted Representative William

of Chicago, 1900), 35, 404–9; John Bates Clark, *The Control of Trusts* (New York: Macmillan, 1901), 12.

6 Henry Carter Adams, "Relation of the State to Industrial Action," *Publications of the American Economic Association* 1 (1887): 54.

7 Adams, "Relation of State to Industrial Action," 64.

8 Martin J. Sklar, *The Corporate Reconstruction of American Capitalism* (Cambridge: Cambridge University Press, 1988), 203–85.

Hepburn (R-IA) to initiate a bill in Congress. The Hepburn Bill made good on the promise of the new economics. It empowered the Federal Trade Commission to license interstate corporations, supervise corporate finance so consumers were not saddled with serving undue financial obligations, and monitor trade practices for violations of the law. Though the Hepburn Bill failed, it reframed the debate.[9] By the time the Supreme Court released its opinion against Standard Oil in 1911, the idea of an independent commission, staffed by economists, was familiar. Thus, when Taft Republicans responded to the *Standard Oil* decision with complacency, this was the final straw in the conflict between conservative and progressive Republicans. It was no surprise that progressives bolted the party and enlisted Roosevelt to seek a third term as president.

With the Republicans divided, Democrats saw their first opportunity to win the presidency since 1897 and take control over national government. But party leaders knew their ambitions were impossible without a majority in favor of antitrust reform. Therefore, they searched for a candidate who might appeal to progressive Republicans as well as the party's agrarian populist base. In Woodrow Wilson, they found a Southerner, an intellectual, and a reformist governor who had successfully initiated antitrust reform in New Jersey.[10] Wilson searched for a language with which to frame the predicament of antitrust: he distinguished between good and bad trusts, talked about a government agency devoted to enhancing rather than replacing the market, and appealed to a "middle ground" between capitalism and socialism.[11] But it was not until he enlisted Brandeis's counsel in the summer of 1912 that he identified a third way to antitrust reform: regulated competition.

Like Wilson, Brandeis was a master syncretist who recomposed populist and progressive politics. However, where Wilson recombined coalitions, Brandeis recombined cultural resources and policy designs. He spoke to the progressive preoccupation with science and the populist anxiety about power through republican experimentalism. He combined the populist desire to check economic power before it became unassailable with the progressive desire for technical mastery in regulated competition. In doing so, Brandeis shifted the debate away from the judicial preoccupation with classification and the public/private distinction. Instead, he showed how

[9] On the Hepburn Bill, see Sklar, *Corporate Reconstruction*, 228–53; George Mowry, *The Era of Roosevelt, 1900–1912* (New York: Harper, 1958), 202–6.

[10] James, *Presidents, Parties, and the State*, 153–62.

[11] Sklar, *Corporate Reconstruction*, 394–419.

economic arrangements were better evaluated according to how well they intervened in an ongoing process of trade custom formation and the consequences of that intervention for economic performance.

REPUBLICAN EXPERIMENTALISM

Brandeis recast the possibilities of antitrust policy by retelling the history of industrialization. Like the populists, he stressed the effects of corruption and power on the rise of big business. All conspicuous trusts, he said, achieved their positions through the ruthless exercise of power and there was every reason to think they would continue do so in order to maintain it in the future. Like the progressives, Brandeis stressed the dynamic nature of applied science in modern industry. Industrialization was replete with examples of innovation that reduced human toil, increased creativity, and made it possible to imagine a future of endless novelty. The reformer's task, Brandeis thought, was to weave these strands together into a coherent image of the future. In this narrative, republican ends (equality, citizenship, and democracy) would be realized through scientific means (experimentation, measurement, and evaluation). But scientific ends (efficiency, invention, and technical mastery) would be also be realized by republican means (deliberation, individual development, and honorable rivalry). This was the republican experimentalist solution to the conflict between the populist and progressive position.

Republican Resources

Brandeis had a deep affinity for small business and the sentiments of nineteenth-century republican antimonopolism. A partner in the law firm Brandeis, Dunbar, and Nutter, he served a petit bourgeois clientele: the many small firms in the boot and shoe, paper, and mercantile industries that populated the New England landscape. He represented the shoe manufacturers against the giant monopoly United Shoe Machinery, merchants and manufacturers in their repeated conflicts with the railroads, and savings banks against giant insurance companies.[12]

[12] Brandeis, Dunbar, and Nutter had no business in the industry that dominated the Massachusetts economy, textiles, whose average factory employed more than three hundred wage earners. This was about four times the number employed in the average shoe factory. Nor did Brandeis and his partners serve Boston's leading investment bankers, who financed large-scale railroad development in the West. Allon Gal, *Brandeis of Boston* (Cambridge, MA: Harvard University Press, 1980), 15–21, 43–46, 50.

But it is a mistake to reduce Brandeis's republican sensibilities to the material interests of his clients.[13] He served as legal counsel to United Shoe Machinery and the innovative mass retailer Edward Filene. He admired the inventors of brand-name, trademarked consumer goods and defended their practice of fixing the retail prices. And his most creative work as an attorney involved fashioning collaborative relations between small and large firms. Brandeis also devoted endless hours to progressive causes generally opposed by small business: scientific management, protective labor law, collective bargaining, and conservation.

Although Brandeis was not an academic thinker – he never wrote a treatise on antitrust or constitutional law – he rarely lost an opportunity to articulate the broader implications of practical problems. And when he did, he sounded much like the republican antimonopoly movements that went before him: the self-styled "producers" of the Greenback-Labor Party, the Knights of Labor, and the Farmer's Alliance.[14] Like them, Brandeis's first questions about the economy were moral and political, not technical. Did economic arrangements develop independent citizens capable of participating in a vigorous democracy? Or did they lock in power, aggrandize the rich, and dispirit the poor? Did they engender

[13] See, for example, Thomas K. McCraw, *Prophets of Regulation* (Cambridge, MA: Harvard University Press, 1984), 86–87, 133–34, 141; Janice Mark Jacobson, "Mr. Justice Brandeis on Regulation and Competition: An Analysis of His Economic Opinions" (PhD diss., Columbia University, 1973), 126–27, 255; Albro Martin, *Enterprise Denied: Origins of the Decline of American Railroads, 1897–1917* (New York: Columbia University Press, 1971), 160–62, 206–18, 252–54.

[14] A generation of research on late-nineteenth-century social movements shows that, despite enormous variation in social origins, they shared an ideology of republican antimonopolism. See Victoria Hattam, *Labor Visions and State Power: The Origins of Business Unionism in the United States* (Princeton, NJ: Princeton University Press, 1993); Lawrence Goodwyn, *Democratic Promise: The Populist Moment in America* (New York: Oxford University Press, 1976); Leon Fink, *Workingmen's Democracy: The Knights of Labor and American Politics* (Urbana: University of Illinois Press, 1983); Eric Foner, *Free Soil, Free Labor, Free Men: The Ideology of the Republican Party before the Civil War* (London: Oxford University Press, 1970); Richard Oestreicher, "Terrence Powderly, the Knights of Labor and Artisinal Republicanism," in Melvyn Dubofsky and Warren Van Tine, eds., *Labor Leaders in America* (Urbana: University of Illinois Press, 1987), 30–60; Nick Salvatore, *Eugene V. Debs: Citizen and Socialist* (Urbana: University of Illinois Press, 1982); Gerald Berk, *Alternative Tracks: The Constitution of American Industrial Order, 1865–1916* (Baltimore: Johns Hopkins University Press, 1993), 75–115; Gretchen Ritter, *Goldbugs and Greenbacks: The Antimonopoly Tradition and the Politics of Finance in America* (New York: Cambridge University Press, 1997); Robert D. Johnston, *The Radical Middle Class: Populist Democracy and the Question of Capitalism in Progressive Era Portland* (Princeton, NJ: Princeton University Press, 2003).

respect for the law or encourage opportunism and deceit? Did they add legitimacy to the constitutional order or ignite social unrest and demands for revolutionary socialism?

Brandeis also refused to separate political from economic motivation. The will to power, he thought, not economic improvement, was the motive behind the trusts. For a generation now, Americans had watched Standard Oil, American Tobacco, United Shoe Machinery, the big three meatpackers, and the railroads perfect the predatory tactics of the "prize ring." They drove independent producers to the wall with secret railroad rebates, predatory pricing, intimidation, industrial espionage, and tying contracts.[15] Although the trusts often financed their tactics from savings, many found support from investment bankers, who mobilized "other people's money" in service of corporate power.[16]

There was nothing inevitable about this outcome, because no "conspicuous trust," formed in the great merger wave, was motivated by the "desire for increased efficiency." U.S. Steel was typical. Formed to suppress "annoying competition," and realize a huge commission for the House of Morgan, it set the standard for corporate development in the twentieth century.[17]

Brandeis worried about the effects of economic power on democracy. He had seen how J. P. Morgan, Consolidated Edison, and United Shoe Machinery influenced the Massachusetts legislature. He thought the progressives' faith in countervailing state power naïve. Despotism "with safeguards," he said, was still despotism.[18]

[15] Philippa Strum, *Louis D. Brandeis: Justice for the People* (Cambridge, MA: Harvard University Press, 1984), 146–55.

[16] Louis D. Brandeis, "Our Financial Oligarchy," chapter 1 in Richard M. Abrams, ed., *Other People's Money and How the Bankers Use It* (New York: Harper Torchbooks, 1967), 1–19.

[17] U.S. Congress, Senate, Committee on Interstate Commerce, *Hearings on Control of Corporations, Persons, and Firms Engaged in Interstate Commerce*, 62d Cong., 2d sess., 1911, vol. 1, pt. 16, 1171 (hereafter cited as *Clapp Committee*); Brandeis, "Trusts and Efficiency," *Collier's Weekly*, September 14, 1912, reprinted in *Business – a Profession* (Boston: Small, Maynard, 1925), 205–24. For recent corroborations of Brandeis's interpretation of the great merger wave, see Naomi Lamoreaux, *The Great Merger Wave in American Business, 1895–1904* (New York: Cambridge University Press, 1985); William Roy, *Socializing Capital* (Princeton, NJ: Princeton University Press, 1997); Neil Fligstein, *The Transformation of Corporate Control* (Cambridge, MA: Harvard University Press, 1990), 75–115.

[18] Louis D. Brandeis, "Competition," *American Legal News* 44 (January 1913), reprinted in O. K. Fraenkel, *The Curse of Bigness* (New York: Viking, 1934), 112–13. On Brandeis's involvement with the regulation of Boston natural gas and Morgan's effort

Economic power also undermined democracy indirectly by destroying the conditions for individual development. In a world arranged by hierarchy and power, Americans would become narrow in vision, opportunistic, and timid in public life. Democracy would fall to decadent citizens. Progressive economists were wrong: the antitrust impasse was not a technical problem with moral implications. It was a moral and political problem for which reformers ought to imagine technical possibilities. Brandeis told Congress "the trust problem can never be settled ... by looking at it through the spectacles of bonds and stocks." It was a civic enterprise. A person must study from the perspective of the "people," understand its effects on "liberty" and the "development of American democracy." And when that happens, one will realize that the trusts have "stabbed industrial liberty in the back," fostered widespread disrespect for the law, and imperiled "our institutions."[19]

By "industrial liberty," Brandeis meant "positive liberty" – the opportunity to develop intelligence, empathy, and "civic courage." Unlike laissez-faire constitutionalists, he did not mean the liberty of autonomous individuals to freely enter into contracts and accumulate property. "Those who won our independence," Brandeis wrote, aspired to create an active people, courageous, hopeful, imaginative, and outspoken.[20] "Always and everywhere, the intellectual, moral and spiritual development of ... the individual is both a necessary means and the end sought."[21]

> Democracy in any sphere is a serious undertaking. It substitutes self-restraint for external constraint. ... It demands continuous sacrifice by the individual and more exigent obedience to moral law than any other form of government. Success in any democratic undertaking must proceed from the individual. It is possible only where the process of perfecting the individual is pursued.[22]

"Human faculties" develop only when responsibility and discussion are extended from politics to everyday life. For the mind and the moral sense, Brandeis wrote, are "like the hand. [They] grow with using" and

to consolidate railroads in New England, see Alpheus T. Mason, *Brandeis: A Free Man's Life* (New York: Viking, 1946), 126–40, 177–213.

19 *Clapp Committee*, 1166.

20 *Whitney v. California*, 247 U.S. 357, 372–80 (1927), cited in Pnina Lahav, "Holmes and Brandeis: Libertarian and Republican Justifications for Free Speech," *Journal of Law and Politics* 4, no. 3 (Winter 1988): 458–59; *Filene Co-operative Association Echo* (May 1905), excerpted in Alfred Lief, ed., *The Brandeis Guide to the Modern World* (Boston: Little, Brown, 1941), 97.

21 Letter to Robert W. Bruere, February 25, 1922, excerpted in Lief, *The Brandeis Guide*, 51.

22 Letter to Robert W. Bruere, 70–71.

atrophy in neglect.[23] Freedom of speech was necessary to democracy not because it maximized the liberal free trade in ideas, as Justice Holmes and John Stuart Mill argued. Instead, it cultivated civic personality. "Public discussion" was not a privilege; it was a "political duty." This, Brandeis wrote, ought to be the "fundamental principle" of American life.[24]

The trusts not only corrupted politics and undermined the conditions for individual development, they also encouraged cynicism and disrespect for the law. Although Standard Oil and American Tobacco found refuge in liberal incorporation laws, trade unions came under constant attack as conspiracies before the law. Many Americans perceived a double standard. They learned "our sacred Constitution" protected "vested wrongs" more than "vested rights," Brandeis said. It was little wonder that the social unrest of the late nineteenth century continued into the twentieth. Respect for the law was unlikely to return, until Americans "restored" industry to "health" and equality.[25]

A state attuned to the development of individual moral personality, spirit, and intelligence was a tall order. In contrast to laissez-faire constitutionalists and progressives, who imaged state action in compensation for the failures of individual action, Brandeis envisioned a government devoted to cultivating the conditions for citizenship. In a democracy, "it devolves upon the state . . . to fit the rulers for their task." In the nineteenth century, this meant steady withdrawal from the market. But industrialization proved unregulated markets provided as many opportunities for self-aggrandizement as virtue. Active government was necessary not only to nurture the conditions for civic development, but also to "stimulate the desire" to take advantage of them. Unless the state cultivated "education and character" in its citizens, Brandeis worried, "our great experiment in democracy must fail."[26]

Brandeis's appeal to "civic courage,"[27] individual development, and economic decentralization seemed anachronistic to many progressives, who thought his jeremiad against the modern corporation gave twentieth-century voice to a waning petit bourgeoisie. Brandeis's critics, then and now, are correct to charge him with a yeoman sensibility,

[23] *Filene Co-operative Association Echo*, 97.
[24] Lahav, "Holmes and Brandeis," 458–66.
[25] Statement before the Senate Committee on Interstate Commerce (December 14, 1911), excerpted in Lief, *Brandeis Guide*, 181–82.
[26] Fourth of July Oration (Faneuil Hall, Boston, 1915), excerpted in Lief, *The Brandeis Guide*, 3–4.
[27] Strum, *Louis D. Brandeis*, 237; Lahav, "Holmes and Brandeis," 460–64.

which valued the political and the moral over purely economic values.[28] However, to conclude this was the whole of Brandeis's beliefs is to read the record selectively and force him into an indefensibly rigid distinction between tradition and modernity. In a more fluid world, where the opportunities for syncretic combination of old and new practices were more the norm than the exception, Brandeis's turn to science is no less important than his republicanism.

Scientific Resources

Brandeis was a modernist. Like John Bates Clark, Henry Carter Adams, and Theodore Roosevelt, he believed science and modern industry could do much to alleviate poverty and human toil, and provide the leisure necessary for social progress. A founder of the "sociological jurisprudence" movement, he showed how scientific evidence could be used to justify state action before an increasingly skeptical Supreme Court.[29] In 1913, he enlisted his sister-in-law, Josephine Goldmark, and Felix Frankfurter to write a lengthy brief in support of protective labor law for women, which presented reams of evidence on the health effects of poor working conditions and long hours.[30] The same year, he made Frederick Taylor and Harrington Emerson famous when he told the Interstate Commerce Commission that the railroads did not need a rate increase because they could save a million dollars a day with scientific management. And in 1914, he told members of the FTC they could no greater service to U.S. industry than to sponsor a national program in cost accounting.[31]

[28] See, for example, Walter Lippmann, *Drift and Mastery* (first published 1914), Spectrum edition (Englewood Cliffs, NJ: Prentice Hall, 1961), 42–43; Charles Forcey, *Crossroads of Liberalism: Croly, Weyl, Lippmann and the Progressive Era, 1900–1925* (New York: Oxford University Press, 1961), 207–8; Louis Hartz, *The Liberal Tradition in America* (New York: Harcourt Brace, 1955), 232; George E. Garvey and Gerald J. Garvey, *Economic Law and Economic Growth: Antitrust, Regulation and the American Growth System* (New York: Praeger, 1990), 65–66; Robert Bork, *The Antitrust Paradox: A Policy at War with Itself* (New York: Basic Books, 1978), 41–47; McCraw, *Prophets of Regulation*, 80–142.

[29] Morton J. Horwitz, *The Transformation of American Law, 1870–1960: The Crisis of Legal Orthodoxy* (New York: Oxford University Press, 1992), 188–89; William W. Fisher III, Morton J. Horwitz, and Thomas A. Reed, eds., *American Legal Realism* (New York: Oxford University Press, 1993), 232–41.

[30] Louis D. Brandeis and Felix Frankfurter, assisted by Josephine Goldmark, *The Case for the Shorter Working Day; Brief for the State of Oregon, Defendant in Error* (New York: National Consumer's League, 1914).

[31] See Chapter 3.

Nevertheless, Brandeis used science differently from most progressives. Where they thought science could resolve political conflict, Brandeis subordinated it to moral and political ends. Where the progressive economists believed science could reveal natural constraints on policy choice and institutional design, Brandeis found tools in applied science that could be put to diverse ends. Where progressives hoped scientific laws could resolve constitutional debate, Brandeis thought truth an elusive goal. He mistrusted the dualities that served as foundations to progressive thought: objectivity and self-interests, politics and administration, public and private, and perfect competition and natural monopoly. Instead, like philosopher John Dewey, Brandeis found in scientific method a process that accorded well with his ideas of democratic deliberation and social learning.[32] Where Roosevelt turned to economic science to resolve the conflict between competition and contract in antitrust, Brandeis turned to the practical sciences of cost accounting and engineering, where he found techniques that promised to overcome limitations in the debate and reconcile republican equality with economic prosperity.

When Brandeis honed his critique of the trusts, rethought antitrust policy, and participated in railroad regulation, he was more apt to consult the *Engineering News* than the *Quarterly Journal of Economics*. When he lectured on corporation law in the 1890s, it was to engineers at the Massachusetts Institute of Technology, not to students of law, economics, or business administration. By the election of 1912, Brandeis counted some of the nation's leading engineers (such as Frederick Taylor, Henry Gantt, Harrington Emerson, and F. Lincoln Hutchins) among his most trusted advisers.[33]

To be sure, Brandeis was aware that engineers, like economists, wrote about the technological causes of bigness; but he also thought the engineers were more aware of the limits of bigness. With all due respect to his critics then and now, Brandeis understood the principle of economies of scale. Working with technicians from the New England paper industry, he learned about the high costs of "idle capacity" in industries with "continuous processing" technologies. In 1903, he began a three-decade involvement with public utility regulation, where he learned about natural

[32] On Dewey's thinking about the relationship between science and democracy, see Robert B. Westbrook, *John Dewey and American Democracy* (Ithaca, NY: Cornell University Press, 1991), 140–47.

[33] McCraw, *Prophets of Regulation*, 95. For more on Brandeis's relationship with the engineers, see Chapter 3.

monopoly in local markets.[34] Like many engineers, however, Brandeis thought economies of scale were mostly physical, not economic. All too often his contemporaries naturalized the trusts by overestimating the advantages of size and underestimating the costs to economic progress in diminished competition, organizational sclerosis, and unimaginative management. Like the pragmatist thinkers of his age, Dewey and James, Brandeis thought human beings creatures of habit and limited vision, who nevertheless had the capacity for creative problem solving. Efforts to control the environment about them, like the search for scientific truth, were elusive. In the law, this meant that the more abstract the foundational distinctions – public and private, contract and competition, the rule of reason – the less likely they could be applied determinately to facts. To be relevant and effective, practical jurisprudence necessitated a "living law" attuned to ongoing changes in meaning and context. The elusive search for truth was no less a problem in business management. In a world of changing conditions, managers developed rules of thumb, customs, or habits to make decisions. Consequently, economic activity had a tendency to settle into a routine that slowed economic progress and human development.[35] "The margin between what men naturally

[34] See *Clapp Committee*, 1158–59, 1206, 1209–10. Additional evidence of Brandeis's understanding of scale economies in continuous process technologies in steel can be found in testimony before the *House Committee on Investigation of United States Steel Corporation*, 62d Cong, 2d sess., no. 40, 2837–39, where he argues that because critical parts of the smelting and hot-rolling processes necessitated 24-hour operation, the workday should be shortened to 8, not 10, hours. On Brandeis's understanding of scale economies in public utilities see Louis D. Brandeis, "How Boston Solved the Gas Problem," *American Review of Reviews* (1907), reprinted in Brandeis, *Business – a Profession*, 109. For a more extensive discussion, see Gerald Berk, "Neither Markets nor Administration: Brandeis and the Antitrust Reforms of 1914," *Studies in American Political Development* 8 (Spring 1994): 33–37.

[35] On pragmatist doubts about scientific truth and its alternative, nonfoundational, epistemology, see Daniel J. Wilson, "Fertile Ground: Pragmatism, Science, and Logical Positivism," in Robert Hollinger and David Depew, eds., *Pragmatism: From Progressivism to Postmodernism* (Westport, CT: Praeger, 1995), 122–41; Clarence Irving Lewis, "Logical Positivism and Pragmatism," in John D. Goheen and John L. Mothershead Jr., eds., *The Collected Papers of Clarence Irving Lewis* (Palo Alto, CA: Stanford University Press, 1970), 92–112. On the relationship between progressivism and pragmatism more generally, see James T. Kloppenberg, *Uncertain Victory: Social Democracy and Progressivism in European and American Thought, 1870–1920* (New York: Oxford University Press, 1986); Richard Rorty, *Philosophy and Social Hope* (London: Penguin, 1999); Hollinger and Depew, *Pragmatism: From Progressivism to Postmodernism;* James Livingston, *Pragmatism and the Political Economy of Cultural Revolution, 1850–1940* (Chapel Hill: University of North Carolina Press, 1994). On Brandeis as a pragmatist, see Daniel A. Farber, "Reinventing Brandeis: Legal

do and that which they can do is ... great," Brandeis wrote. Therefore, they must be prodded "on to action, enterprise and initiative." No more effective stimulus had been devised in economic life than competition. It perturbed routine and showed unreflective managers a better way.[36] "Monopoly has a deadening effect; ... economic progress only flows from struggle."[37]

If monopoly undermined the stimulus to experimentation, excess size and rigid hierarchies impaired business's capacity to do something new. Brandeis recognized that "organization can do much to make the [large] concern more efficient," but he thought organization had its limits. "There is a point where the centrifugal force necessarily exceeds the centripetal." And bureaucracy "can never supply the combined judgment, initiative, enterprise and authority" of experienced management. "Nature sets limits to his possible achievement,"[38] and at some point "demoralization sets in," because the human capacity for prediction and control under conditions of uncertainty was finite.[39] "Real efficiency in any business in which conditions are ever changing," Brandeis wrote, "must ultimately depend, in large measure, upon the correctness of the judgment exercised, almost from day to day, on the important problems as they arise." This capacity became more and more remote with increasing scale and organizational hierarchy.[40]

The engineers, Brandeis wrote, repeatedly complained that huge firms, which prized volume over all other goals, were unlikely to experiment or innovate. Quoting testimony from the *Engineering News*, Brandeis wrote that "modern trade combinations tend ... toward constancy of process and products, and by their very nature are opposed to new processes and new products originated by independent inventors." They "discourage independent inventive thought" and restrain competition in the development and sale of patents and patent rights.[41] The engineers, Brandeis noted, complained that the United States had fallen further

Pragmatism for the Twenty-first Century," *University of Illinois Law Review* (Winter 1995): 163–90.

36 *American Legal News* (January 1913), excerpted in Lief, *The Brandeis Guide*, 55.

37 Address before Southern New England Textile Club, Providence (December 28, 1912), and Address before the New England Dry Goods Ass'n, Boston (February 11, 1908), quoted in Lief, *The Brandeis Guide*, 179.

38 Louis D. Brandeis, "Trusts and Efficiency," *Collier's Weekly*, September 14, 1912, reprinted in Brandeis, *Business – a Profession*, 223–24.

39 *Clapp Committee*, 1147–48.

40 *Harper's Weekly*, January 30, 1914, quoted in Lief, *The Brandeis Guide*, 27.

41 Brandeis, *Other People's Money*, 102–3.

and further behind in applied metallurgy after the organization of U.S. Steel in 1901. Engineers in the United States were no less ingenious than their German counterparts. The problem was caused by the relationship between market power and mass production. "With the market closely controlled and profits certain by following standard methods, those who control our trusts do not want the bother of developing anything new." Besides, "a huge organization is too clumsy to take up the development of an original idea." The same was increasingly true, the engineers complained, in machinery production, where "the real advances in the art are being made by European inventors and manufacturers."[42]

Brandeis's critique of the trusts has often been taken as a sign of his republicanism: he prized "moral and political" values, regardless of their economic consequences.[43] It is true that his first question was ethical: What sort of economy enlarged opportunities for individual development and democracy in everyday life? But Brandeis did not neglect technical questions. Drawing on the practical sciences of accounting and engineering, rather than economics, he found the tools to imagine novel forms of efficiency and alternative possibilities for realizing republican ends. He told Woodrow Wilson, Congress, the public, and regulators that economic progress flowed mostly from perturbing habit, from doing something new. In engineering, he found a framework for deliberation, experimentation, and evaluation that not only promised invention, but also accorded with his republican worldview and democratic sensibilities. It is true that many engineers thought science could resolve political conflict. Taylor is best known for his promise to find the "one best way" to manage modern enterprise. But in Brandeis's view, scientific management was a decomposable bundle of principles and techniques. Some of its features – efficiency analysis, problem solving, and measurement – could be combined with republican ends – civic courage and individual development – in novel ways.

NB

REGULATED COMPETITION

Brandeis welcomed the *Standard Oil* decision. Unlike the progressives, who thought it legitimated corporate capitalism and regulated monopoly,

[42] Brandeis, *Other People's Money*, 102–3.

[43] Hartz, *The Liberal Tradition in America*, 232; Garvey and Garvery, *Economic Law and Economic Growth*, 65–66; Bork, *The Antitrust Paradox*, 41–47; McCraw, *Prophets of Regulation*.

Brandeis thought it challenged Americans to admit that the economy was diverse, contracts were always social, and the effects of competition were ambiguous. He tried to teach that competition was a social process, with bad and good outcomes, and to show how it was the role of government and civil society to steer it from the former to the latter. With this knowledge, Americans might choose regulated competition over enforced competition or regulated monopoly.

The Social Nature of Contract

Although Brandeis was sympathetic to Bryan's republicanism, he thought a literal reading of the Sherman Act and the policy of enforced competition incoherent, capricious, and self-defeating. Restraints on trade had become so common, that the problem was to distinguish destructive from productive ones and channel economic organization from the former to the latter.

Practical men knew it was impossible to apply a rule outlawing all combinations and contracts in restraint of trade, Brandeis wrote, because all contracts forged social relations between individuals. "In a sense *every* contract restrains trade; for after one has entered into a contract, he is not as free in trading as he was before he bound himself. But the right to bind one's self is essential to trade development." Experience and observation taught Brandeis that contracts were rarely the arm's-length utilitarian calculations contemplated by economists. Instead, diffuse, reciprocal relations among business, labor, and consumers made markets. The trouble was once parties bound themselves to trade relations, they were imperiled by exploitation. Unforeseen circumstances or disparities in power could easily demoralize the social relations that were necessary for markets.[44]

From Brandeis's perspective, the progressive economists were mistaken in their search for foundational laws. Though more rigorous than the

[44] Brandeis, "The Competition That Kills," in Brandeis, *Business – a Profession*, 251, emphasis added. For similar discussions of contract as a social tie, see Mark Granovetter, "Economic Action and Social Structure: The Problem of Embeddedness," *American Journal of Sociology* 91 (November 1985): 481–510; Ronald Dore, "Goodwill and the Spirit of Market Capitalism," *British Journal of Sociology* 34 (1983): 459–82; Edward Lorenz, "Neither Friends nor Strangers: Informal Networks of Subcontracting in French Industry," in Diego Gambetta, ed., *Trust: Making and Breaking Cooperative Relations* (Oxford: Basil Blackwell, 1988); Charles F. Sabel, "Flexible Specialization and the Re-emergence of Regional Economies," in Paul Hirst and Jonathan Zeitlin, eds., *Reversing Industrial Decline? Industrial Structure and Policy in Britain and Her Competitors* (Oxford: Berg, 1989), 26–31.

judicial distinction between competition and restraint, their categories of perfect competition and natural monopoly were hopelessly abstract and reified standards. Applied to antitrust, they often resulted in perverse consequences by undermining the combination of rivalry and restraint necessary for economic progress. Particular decisions, Brandeis wrote, cannot be "determined by abstract reasoning. Facts only can be safely relied upon to teach us whether a trade practice is consistent with the general welfare."[45] The same actions may have different meaning and effect in different contexts. Even "words of advice, seemingly innocent and perhaps benevolent [may be destructive] when uttered under circumstances that make advice equivalent to command." Or contractual restraints productive in one context can be destructive in another. "For the essence of [illicit] restraint is power" and power relations can only be determined in historical context.[46]

For Brandeis, competition, like contract, was a social process, which could have good or bad consequences. The initial problem was to figure out whether the restraints businesses imposed upon one another were productive or destructive for competition. Did they channel rivalry in productive directions or suppress it altogether? Did they cultivate new markets and invention or, as Dewey worried, lock in compulsive routine?

These questions could not be posed deductively or answered without careful attention to industrial history, so Brandeis taught by example. On the campaign trail for Wilson, in *Harper's Weekly,* or testifying before Congress, he told stories about creative combinations of rivalry and restraint, predatory competition, and overpowering restraints. Consider three industrial tales Brandeis told repeatedly: the history of tying contracts in the shoe machinery industry, resale price maintenance, and price regulation by trade associations. The first involved an effective balance of rivalry and restraint gone badly; the second, an example of effective regulated competition misunderstood; the third, a potential alternative to corporate hierarchy, which merited experimentation and monitoring.

Tying Contracts

The New England shoe industry provided the firm Brandeis, Dunbar, and Nutter with its most lucrative clients. Like other industrializing

[45] Brandeis, "The Competition That Kills," in *Business – a Profession,* 251.
[46] Dissent in American Column Co. v. U.S., 257 U.S. 377 at 414, 1921.

sectors, shoe manufacture witnessed mechanization, factory concentration, and rapid productivity growth in the late nineteenth century. Prior to the Civil War, this was largely a rural workshop trade, in which craft workers specialized in one of roughly ten steps in the production process. In 1856, the McKay Company transformed the industry when it introduced the first commercially viable sewing machine for leather. Other innovations followed. By the turn of the century, manufacturers had mechanized eyeleting, pegging, bottoming, heeling, soling, and burnishing. Between 1862 and 1900, the average number of annual shoe machinery patents increased from 27 to 117. As a result, productivity soared. In 1862, a shoe worker produced an average of 299 pairs per year. Forty years later that number had grown to 1,314.[47]

The shoe industry was a networked industry. It was neither corporate nor purely competitive. Machinery tended to aid, not replace, handwork; factories remained relatively small; firms were geographically clustered in industrial districts.[48] Shoe manufacturing shared the network characteristics associated with other batch and specialty industries, such as furniture, jewelry, machine tools, and ceramics. In order to cultivate and protect assets in skilled labor, product reputations, and the goodwill of subcontractors, Massachusetts shoe manufacturers clustered in four counties, or "industrial districts," where they developed a variety of formal and informal restraints upon predatory competition.[49]

[47] U.S. Department of Commerce and Labor, Bureau of Census, *Manufactures, 1905* (Washington, DC: Government Printing Office, 1907), 499; Carl Kaysen, *United States v. United Shoe Machinery Corporation: An Economic Analysis of an Anti-Trust Case* (Cambridge, MA: Harvard University Press, 1956), 28; Ross Thomson, *The Path to Mechanized Shoe Production in the United States* (Chapel Hill: University of North Carolina Press, 1989), 180, 183–84.

[48] Kaysen, *U.S. v. United Shoe Machinery*, 3–5.

[49] On industrial districts see Phillip P. Scranton, *Endless Novelty: Specialty Production and American Industrialization, 1865–1925* (Princeton, NJ: Princeton University Press, 1997); Phillip P. Scranton, "Diversity in Diversity: Flexible Production and American Industrialization, 1880–1930," *Business History Review* 65 (Spring 1991): 27–90; John K. Brown, *The Baldwin Locomotive Works, 1831–1915* (Baltimore: Johns Hopkins University Press, 1995); Howell J. Harris, "Getting It Together: The Metal Manufacturers' Association of Philadelphia," in Sanford M. Jacoby, ed., *Masters to Managers: Historical and Comparative Perspectives on American Employers* (New York: Columbia University Press, 1991); Regina Blaszczyck, *Imagining Consumers: Design and Innovation from Wedgwood to Corning* (Baltimore: Johns Hopkins University Press, 2000); Philip Scranton, "Supple Cities: Flexible Manufacturing and Industrial Districts in the United States, 1870–1930" (unpublished paper, Rutgers University, Camden, NJ, n.d.), 12–16, 19–20; Mark Stern, *The Pottery Industry of*

However, the Massachusetts shoe industry was successful in the late nineteenth century mostly because the vertical relationship between machinery makers and manufacturers regulated competition. There were two reasons for this. First, most inventors came from shoe factories, and the machinists, who translated their ideas into practice, remained in close contact with artisans on the shop floor. As a result, machinery makers clustered in manufacturing districts, where they shared a great deal of technical information. Second, the legal relationship between machinery makers and manufacturers was organized around patent law and long-term leasing arrangements that fostered innovation, not spot-contract sales. In order to protect patent rights and reduce the risks of adopting new technology, machine makers charged an initial leasing fee of $300–$500 and then a royalty of 3–5¢ on each pair of shoes made. Often as long as seventeen years, leases obligated vendors to provide a variety of services: access to new parts and machinery, loans, and regular service by traveling technicians or "roadies." The roadie system was critical to innovation, as service technicians became a conduit for performance information.[50] In sum, rapid technical innovation in the shoe industry came not from the growth of huge firms through the vertical integration of machinery makers and manufacturers or free competition between independent entrepreneurs, but from regulated competition.

As counsel to both the manufacturers and the United Shoe Machinery Corporation, Brandeis wrote many of the key contracts that regulated competition in this industry. His service to New England shoe manufacturers began in the 1880s, when he helped negotiate labor contracts, secure finance, and perfect the leasing system. At the dawn of the great merger wave in 1897, he took on a new client with heavy holdings in the McKay Machinery Company. Two years later, when McKay merged with four other companies to form United Shoe Machinery Corporation, Brandeis joined the board of trustees and signed on as legal counsel. A merger of firms with complementary lines, United was the first enterprise to offer a full line of equipment from cutting to finishing. By 1905, it had secured a virtual monopoly over two operations and as much as 65 percent of the market in others.[51]

Trenton: A Skilled Trade in Transition, 1850–1929 (New Brunswick, NJ: Rutgers University Press, 1994).

[50] Thomson, *Path to Mechanized Shoe Production*, 68–70, 121, 185–86.

[51] Kaysen, *U.S. v. United Shoe Machinery*, 6–16.

In 1900, a conflict between United and the manufacturers ensued when management reformed the leasing systems inherited from its component companies. They proposed a tying contract, in which all customers would be obligated to take a full line of United equipment appropriate to their production system. Those who adopted a competitor's product would forfeit their lease. The manufacturers protested, and after a protracted negotiation with the New England Association of Boot and Shoe Manufacturers, United agreed to limit its tying requirement to departmental clusters and offer individual leases at a premium.[52]

Notwithstanding Brandeis's ties to the manufacturers, he defended United against an alliance of shoe manufacturers and independent machinery firms, who brought their case to the Massachusetts legislature. In 1906, the Joint Committee on the Judiciary held hearings on a bill to regulate leasing. Brandeis testified for United Shoe Machinery. Despite its vast market power, he thought the corporation effectively regulated competition. In the first place, Brandeis explained, United's leasing system did not discriminate by size. Unlike Standard Oil or American Tobacco, who favored large customers, United lowered entry barriers into the shoe industry and placed all manufacturers on a level playing field in technology. Also, by making the latest technology available to every manufacturer, United standardized a critical resource in competition. As a result, shoe manufacturers were more likely to compete over productivity and product quality, diversity, and novelty than access to capital. Third, by reducing the cost of new technology, United encouraged rapid diffusion. Finally, by consolidating the roadie system, the corporation improved service and communication between manufacturers and inventors. In short, Brandeis thought United increased the pace of innovation, preserved small and medium-sized manufacturers, and improved the diversity and quality of products by regulating competition in the shoe industry.[53]

Although Brandeis defended United, he pressed the company to reform its leasing arrangements without success. When the manufacturers' bill died in committee in 1907, the manufacturers asked Brandeis to renegotiate their leases with United. In response, he attended a meeting with

[52] Thomson, *Path to Mechanized Shoe Production*, 228–31.

[53] See Brandeis testimony before the Joint Judiciary Committee of the Massachusetts Legislature on the Bill (H. 472) to Regulate the Sale and the Leasing of Shoe Machinery (April 18, 1906) in *Brandeis and Brandeis: The Reversible Mind* (publisher unknown), 12–20; and *Clapp Committee*, 1160; Mason, *Brandeis*, 216–17.

company president, Sidney Winslow, and a group of manufacturers, at which he urged the tying clauses be eliminated. Winslow's response was swift and harsh: he instructed the marketing department to extend tying clauses from machinery clusters to the full line and to add a rider, by which United reserved the right to terminate a lease on thirty days' notice, without cause. Captured by an intransigent monopoly, Brandeis later explained, the manufacturer had no choice but to comply. Brandeis resigned his position on the corporation's board and stepped down as counsel.[54]

For the next three years, Brandeis removed himself from the controversy until he witnessed United's successful effort to prevent Thomas Plant from entering the market. Brandeis had learned of Plant's plan to introduce a competing line in 1908, when the shoe manufacturer asked him to serve as his counsel. Hoping to remain neutral, Brandeis refused. But just as Plant was about to commence production, a $1.5 million credit obligation came due, and he found himself frozen out of the New York and Boston money markets. Plant had little choice but to sell to the most attractive suitor, United Shoe Machinery.

In 1911, Brandeis reentered the fray. Once again, he suspected the work of the "money trust." Heavily invested in United Shoe Machinery, the First National Bank of Boston used its influence to block Plant's loan. Speaking for the Western Shoe Alliance (New Englanders no longer dared challenge United), Brandeis took the manufacturers' case to the press, Congress, and Wilson. Testifying before the Senate Committee on Interstate Commerce, he recounted his experience with United Shoe Machinery. Until 1907, Brandeis said, he believed the restraining aspects of the leasing system upgraded competition in the shoe industry. But monopoly proved to do the same "deadly work" in this industry as it had in others. Once the "shoe machinery trust" gained control over an "indispensable article of commerce," it used it to "kill competition." Tying contracts ought to be prohibited, Brandeis believed. Like the experience of steel and oil, this case proved that effective competition necessitated regulation; otherwise, it led inevitably to monopoly.[55]

Brandeis's experience with the shoe industry taught him about regulated competition. Economic progress flowed not from free competition or organizational hierarchy. By structuring the conditions under which machines were adopted in the shoe industry, leasing arrangements upgraded

[54] Mason, *Brandeis*, 217–22.

[55] Mason, *Brandeis*, 220–26; *Clapp Committee*, 1160–62.

competition. But regulated competition, when carried out by business alone, risked public and private exploitation. Therefore, government standard setting, monitoring, and prosecution were also necessary. To be effective, Brandeis concluded, regulated competition necessitated joint action by enterprise and the state, not – as laissez-faire constitutionalists demanded – by drawing a sharp line between them.

Resale Price Maintenance

The second industrial tale by which Brandeis explained regulated competition involved his defense of resale price maintenance, or the practice by which manufacturers set the retail prices of their products.

A month before the *Standard Oil* decision, the Supreme Court pronounced resale price maintenance illegal. A drug manufacturer, Dr. Miles Medical Company, charged a retailer, John D. Parks and Sons, with violating its contract with the manufacturer by cutting prices set therein. Writing for the majority, Justice Hughes held for the retailer. The contract was void, because it "eliminated all competition" in retail sales. Like all forms of price fixing, resale price maintenance was always an unreasonable restraint of trade. Economists applauded the decision for protecting the price mechanism from distortion.[56]

Brandeis protested, because he thought resale price maintenance was an advance in "trade morals." By cultivating confidence among manufacturers, retailers, and consumers, it made a market for innovation. Moreover, it checked predatory competition by mass retailers, who selectively cut prices on brand-name products to entice customers into their stores, where they paid full price for other products. Resale price maintenance, Brandeis said, regulated competition. It should be encouraged, not condemned.

Brandeis first became aware of the controversy over resale price maintenance in 1911. Waiting to testify before the House Committee on Patents, he heard a litany of complaints against the Court's ruling in *Dr. Miles*, levied by the leading manufacturers of brand-name and trademarked goods: Ingersoll, Kellogg, Eastman Kodak, Waterman, and Gillette.[57] But why did the pioneers in mass-produced consumer goods want to fix resale prices? After all, one might expect that mass-producers and mass retailers would both wish to expand the size of the market.

[56] Peritz, *Competition Policy*, 53–59; McCraw, *Prophets of Regulation*, 101–2.

[57] U.S. Congress, House of Representatives, Committee on Patents, *Hearings on Oldfield Revision and Codification of the Patent Statutes*, 62nd Cong., May 12, 1912, 3–25.

But manufacturers realized that, although profitable, there were risks to homogeneous products. Tastes and technologies inevitably changed; rivals introduced products that competed as much on novelty and diversity as on price. In order to hedge the risks of being locked in, manufacturers diversified into "line" and "franchise extensions," that is, new models, sizes, or flavors of an existing product or related products with the same brand name or trademark as the original.[58]

Brandeis observed how price cutting by mass retailers undermined this strategy. Ingersoll's testimony taught him how chain and department stores selectively cut prices on brand-name goods to entice consumers into their stores, where they then paid full price on other products. Such "loss leaders" only worked when trade names and prices were well known (Ingersoll's "dollar pocket watch" is the best example). "More appropriately...termed a 'mis-leader,'" Brandeis said, this practice created the "false impression" that competing products of unknown value were equally well priced. Loss leaders also conveyed the message that brand-name products were usually overpriced. Consumers lost confidence that standard prices represented good value and the small retailer, unable to compete, dropped the article altogether. "Thus a single prominent price-cutter can ruin a market for both the producer and the regular retailer."[59] Trade was demoralized and competition was curtailed, not advanced, by resale price cutting.[60]

Resale price maintenance, by contrast, "has tended to develop not to suppress competition," wrote Brandeis, "because it has made it possible in the distribution of goods to go to an expense to open up another sphere of merchandizing which would have been absolutely impossible without a fixed price. The whole world can be drawn into that field. And when you have developed a product market for a trusted product, you are inciting invention; more important, you are inciting the commercial development of the competing article. Every success is constantly inciting a large number of other men to go into that business. You are making a market

[58] Susan Strasser, *Satisfaction Guaranteed: The Making of the American Mass Market* (New York: Pantheon, 1989), 124–46, 269–77. On the "hedging" strategies of mass-producers more generally, see Charles F. Sabel and Jonathan Zeitlin, "Stories, Strategies and Structures: Rethinking Historical Alternatives to Mass Production," in Charles F. Sabel and Jonathan Zeitlin, eds., *World of Possibilities* (Cambridge: Cambridge University Press), 5–20.

[59] Brandeis, "Competition That Kills," 252–55.

[60] On opposition to resale price maintenance by mass retailers, see Strasser, *Satisfaction Guaranteed*, 282.

for invention, and you are doing it by means of the reputation of the particular article that cannot be made and cannot be conserved without some limit upon the price at which the article goes to the community."[61]

Progressives and historians have incorrectly criticized Brandeis for advocating resale price maintenance. Perceiving him as a lawyer to the petit bourgeoisie, they argue he wanted to protect "mom and pop" stores from their more efficient rivals: department and chain stores, and mail order houses.[62] But observation taught Brandeis that manufacturers, not retailers, led the movement to overturn the Court's decision in *Dr. Miles*. It is true that Brandeis thought resale price maintenance benefited independent retailers, and he applauded Ingersoll, Kellogg, and Hamilton Watch for abandoning quantity discounts in order to preserve them.[63] Nevertheless, he thought the mass retailers performed valuable services. "We should be poorer if we lost any one of them." Small stores and consumers are "better off for [their] honest competition.... It is," however, "a question of the *kind* of competition. We stop unfair competition and it is because this competition [price cutting on trademarked goods] is unfair and has injurious effect that it ought to be stopped, and for that reason alone."[64]

[61] Testimony before the House Committee on Patents, *Oldfield Revision and Codification of the Patent Statutes, No. 18*, 62d Cong. (Washington, DC: Government Printing Office, 1916), 4, emphasis added. Hereafter cited as *Oldfield Patent Committee*. For a similar defense of resale price maintenance by Kellogg see Strasser, *Satisfaction Guaranteed*, 280–81.

[62] McCraw, *Prophets of Regulation*, 101–8; Richard S. Tedlow, *New and Improved: The Story of Mass Marketing in America* (New York: Basic Books, 1990), 214; John H. Bunzel, *The American Small Businessman* (New York: Arno Press, 1979), 179–80; Richard C. Schragger, "The Anti-Chain Store Movement, Localist Ideology, and the Remnants of the Progressive Constitution, 1920–1940," *Iowa Law Review* 90, no. 3 (March 2005): 1011–94.

[63] U.S. Congress, House of Representatives, Committee on Interstate and Foreign Commerce, *Hearings on Regulation of Prices*, 64th Cong., 1st sess. (Washington, DC: Government Printing Office, 1916), 225. Hereafter cited as *Regulation of Prices*.

[64] *Regulation of Prices*, 227–28, emphasis added. To be sure, Brandeis also thought the preservation of independent retailers was an added benefit of resale price maintenance. Much has been made of Brandeis's support for these goals at the cost to efficiency in a 1930 case against a Florida law that taxed chain stores. In supporting the state's right to levy such a tax, Brandeis said the preservation of independent proprietors was a legitimate and laudable goal. Nonetheless, as Brandeis pointed out, the Florida legislature preferred not merely small proprietors but "cooperative retail associations" to integrated chains. It is telling that the chain stores themselves argued there was no need for a tax to equalize competition, because the cooperatives had attained external economies of scale equal to their internal economies and actually had lower costs at the level of the enterprise. See Liggett v. Lee, 288 U.S. 577–80.

Even so, Brandeis remained cautious about resale price maintenance, because, like United's leasing system, it could fall prey to power. As long as the field of competition remained open, standard prices were likely to have a positive effect. Kellogg did not hazard a corn flake monopoly when it fixed retail prices, because it had 106 competitors. However, American Tobacco created a monopoly when it fixed retail prices of some products to cross-subsidize predatory pricing on others. Brandeis looked forward to a federal trade commission with the ability to monitor industry for such differences.

Trade Associations

Brandeis thought trade associations could also regulate competition. He recognized they had a spotty record: the trusts began as competition-suppressing cartels. But personal experience, observation of Europe, and the trade association work of American innovator Arthur Jerome Eddy taught Brandeis how associations could improve competition through standard setting, price regulation, information pooling, and education.

Early in his career, Brandeis worked closely with trade associations to reform labor relations, monopoly power, and banking in Massachusetts and New York. The New England Shoe and Leather Association and the Brockton Shoe Manufacturers' Association tackled seasonal unemployment and United's unfair leasing practices with Brandeis's help. Between 1905 and 1910, Brandeis worked with the Massachusetts Savings Bank Insurance League to provide inexpensive life insurance to working people. By mobilizing hundreds of small mutual banks, the league also succeeded in shifting control over mortgage funds from the "big three" oligopoly (Mutual, Equitable, and New York Life) to locally controlled institutions. In 1910, Brandeis worked with the New York Cloak, Suit, and Shirt Manufacturers' Association to pioneer the nation's first modern collective bargaining agreement. Thus, experience taught Brandeis that associations could set competitive standards, develop new markets, and improve labor relations.[65]

Brandeis also looked abroad to Europe, where associations appeared to have far more legitimacy. He took a keen interest in worker, retail, and agricultural cooperatives, subscribing to the *International Cooperative*

[65] Strum, *Louis D. Brandeis*, 186–90; Mason, *Brandeis*, 153–77, 289–315; Steve Fraser, *Labor Will Rule: Sidney Hillman and the Rise of American Labor* (Ithaca, NY: Cornell University Press, 1993), 62–83.

Bulletin. Brandeis was particularly taken with Denmark, where farmers accomplished through producer cooperatives much of what the American Farmers' Alliance had tried but failed to do in the 1890s. He encouraged his wife, Alice, and his sister-in-law, Josephine Goldmark, to publish a volume on the subject. *Democracy in Denmark* showed how dairy cooperatives and folk schools sponsored technical innovation and export marketing in family farms through training in husbandry, entrepreneurship, mechanical engineering, and Danish folk culture. As economic historian Charles Kindleberger shows, these institutions were responsible for Denmark's successful response to a global wheat glut in the 1870s by using its grain domestically to produce butter and cheese for export.[66]

Brandeis found another example of successful association in the German Steel Cartel, whose accomplishments he repeatedly compared to the failure of U.S. Steel. U.S. Steel was formed in 1901 from a merger of Federal Steel and Carnegie Steel. Federal had been through a merger several years earlier. Over the next five years, U. S. steel acquired firms in transportation, mining, and fabricated steel. By 1905, it controlled 67 percent of all production in the United States.

The German Steel Works Association was formed in 1904 from twenty-nine companies, which controlled 74.5 percent of domestic production. Like U.S. Steel's component firms, many members were vertically integrated and produced both primary and fabricated products. The association was authorized to regulate prices and allocate capacity.[67]

In 1911, Brandeis compared the German Steel Association to U.S. Steel while testifying before the Senate Committee on Interstate Commerce. Since 1904, he charged, German steel exports increased by 480 percent, whereas U.S. exports grew by only 33 percent. In 1901, the United States held approximately 22 percent of the world's market; by 1910, its share

[66] Philippa Strum, *Brandeis: Beyond Progressivism* (Lawrence: University of Kansas Press, 1993), 40–42; Strum, *Louis D. Brandeis,* 187; Josephine Goldmark and A. H. Hollman, *Democracy in Denmark,* trans. Alice G. Brandeis (Washington, DC: New Home Library Foundation, 1936). On the place of cooperatives in the Danish political economy more generally, see Charles F. Sabel and Peer Hull Christensen, "The Small Holder Economy in Denmark: The Exception as Variation," in Charles F. Sabel and Jonathan Zeitlin, eds., *World of Possibilities* (Cambridge: Cambridge University Press, 1997), 344–78. On Danish adaptation to the wheat glut of the 1870s in comparative perspective, see Charles Kindleberger, *Economic Response: Comparative Studies in Trade, Finance and Growth* (Cambridge, MA: Harvard University Press, 1978).

[67] Gary Herrigel, *Industrial Constructions: The Sources of German Industrial Power* (Cambridge: Cambridge University Press, 1996), 87–90; Chandler, *Scale and Scope,* 491–6; Steven Webb, "Tariffs, Cartels, Technology, and Growth in the German Steel Industry, 1879–1914," *Journal of Economic History* 40, no. 2 (June 1980): 309–30.

had fallen to 13 percent. The German manufacturers outperformed their U.S. counterparts on every measure: technological innovation, metallurgy, and product diversity. What happened? Brandeis asked.[68]

According to Brandeis, U.S. Steel's poor performance was caused by banker control, overcentralization, and monopoly power. In return for negotiating the steel merger, the House of Morgan had taken generous amounts of voting stock. Overrepresented on the board, the bankers used their influence to plow savings into dividends instead of investment. The more U.S. Steel centralized control over labor, investment, and production, the more it prized volume and stability over innovation. Engineers in the United States, Brandeis noted, complained that the industry had become less and less receptive to technical improvement since the merger of 1901.

Although it set prices and output quotas for primary steel, the German combine remained "independent" in "methods ... of manufacture," raw material procurement, and "labor policy." Its twenty-nine members learned to compete over nonvolume improvements to productivity and over product quality and diversity. Because the German Steel Association set quotas only on primary products destined to market, member firms were free to use as much steel as they wanted to "work up into ... more highly manufactured goods." Thus, Brandeis concluded, where Americans solved the overcapacity crisis in steel by suppressing competition, the Germans solved it by channeling rivalry from mass to specialty production.[69]

Economic historian Steven Webb's study of German steel corroborates much in Brandeis's account. According to Webb, the cartel increased productivity and competitiveness by encouraging member firms to integrate backward into mining and forward into finished products. Moreover, like Brandeis, he notes that the cartel was unable to forge agreements over finished products so it limited its quotas to primary products. As a result, member firms dodged quotas on primary products by moving up market into finished goods.[70]

[68] *Clapp Committee*, 1168–71, 1181–82, 1249, 1253, 1262; Brandeis, "Trusts and the Export Trade," *Collier's Weekly*, September 21, 1912, reprinted in Brandeis, *Business – a Profession*, 225–42.

[69] *Clapp Committee*, 1182, 1249. See also Brandeis testimony in U.S. Congress, Senate, Committee on Interstate Commerce, *Hearings on Control of Corporations, Persons, and Firms Engaged in Interstate Commerce* (Washington, DC: Government Printing Office, 1912), 3–6.

[70] Webb, "Tarriffs, Cartels, Technology."

Brandeis did not need to look abroad for a model of regulated competition by association, because he found an indigenous one in business attorney Arthur Eddy's experiments with open price associations. These were associations that attempted to regulate competition by pooling price, production, and cost information. Chapter 5 will describe Eddy's experiments with open price associations in great detail and show how they grew into developmental associations. For now, it is important understand Eddy's influence over Brandeis and the similarities in their thinking. Brandeis corresponded with Eddy, read his work, acknowledged his influence, and recommended him to others. By explaining how trade associations could achieve "cooperative competition," Eddy helped Brandeis distinguish cartels and trusts from developmental associations.[71]

Like Brandeis, Eddy thought the *Standard Oil* decision reopened the debate over trade associations. In response, he wrote a series of articles on associations, cooperative competition, and antitrust reform. In 1912, he collected them in a book called *The New Competition.*

Like Brandeis, Eddy thought competition was morally and economically ambiguous. Left alone, it could be the "life" or the "death" of trade. At times, competition was "the most powerful incentive toward perfection, ethical, aesthetic, and material." At others, it became "vicious," "brutal," and "vindictive." The difference turned on custom. Nineteenth-century Americans associated competition with three conventions: autarky, opportunism, and secrecy. Under the "old competition," Eddy wrote, business counted "secrecy" and "deceit" among legitimate means to best a rival. Though functional for a time, the old competition became "brutal" after the Civil War and fell into crisis.[72] In industry after industry, visionaries organized trade associations to regulate cutthroat competition. But they failed because customs – secrecy, mistrust, and opportunism – prevailed.

Eddy explained how he attempted to overcome the weight of custom through experimentation and in doing so he invented a new form of competition. He asked firms in steel construction and cotton printing to submit pricing data in the midst of a bidding competition. When the bidding ended, he compiled the data, distributed it to participants, and

71 On Brandeis's correspondence with Eddy, see A. J. Eddy to LDB, March 17, 1913; LDB to A. J. Eddy, March 26, 1913 in *Papers of Louis Dembitz Brandeis* (University of Louisville, Microfilm), Series I, Reel 30, Box 53–1.

72 Arthur Jerome Eddy, *The New Competition* (New York: D. Appleton, 1912), 22, 60–62, 100.

organized a forum to discuss the outcome. Participants inevitably raised broader questions about productivity and the state of the industry. Eddy found that the more competitors learned to play with "their cards on the table," the more they stood back from the precipice of cutthroat pricing and concentrated instead on service, product quality, and productivity. The "new competition," Eddy concluded, was "cooperative." By pooling and discussing information, business learned to channel rivalry from opportunism to genuine improvement in products and production processes.[73]

For all Eddy's success, he thought custom weighed heavily on all early-twentieth-century Americans. The public, he wrote, "made a fetish" out of the old competition and assumed its right to low prices, even if they were driven below costs. Economists mistakenly turned their observations of ruthless competition among autarkic firms into scientific law. Business assumed its rights to autarky and secrecy inalienable under the Constitution. And the Supreme Court mistook freedom of contract for natural law. But the old competition, Eddy wrote, had the "force of custom, nothing more." It could be changed.[74]

Like Brandeis, Eddy seized the opportunity afforded by the presidential campaign of 1912 to reconfigure U.S. ideas about competition. He proposed the state license experiments in cooperative competition by trade associations. Experience would show experts and citizens alike how information pooling and deliberation upgraded competition. In time, cooperative competition would become custom.[75]

Brandeis applauded Eddy's innovations and ideas. "Combinations in unreasonable restraint of trade are a grave evil," he told William Smyth of the American Dental Trade Association. But, as Eddy's work demonstrated, many combinations are "possible which do not stifle competition and ... greatly advance the common weal." "Competition," Brandeis added, "should be regulated. That is, we should have combinations which nourish," not "kill" competition. Experience has shown that "salutary competition" always necessitates "careful study of the facts" concerning costs, prices, supply and demand, and "wholesome methods" of rivalry. Information pooling demands "cooperation." As Eddy's experiments in association showed, cooperative competition channels business activity from "trade abuse" to "initiative," invention,

[73] Eddy, *New Competition*, 100–45.
[74] Eddy, *New Competition*, 68–79, 193–94.
[75] Eddy, *New Competition*, 2, 193–94, 200–201.

and "enterprise." Thus, open price associations should be distinguished from competition-suppressing associations, whose only purpose is "monopoly" power.[76]

Brandeis rejected self-regulating markets and corporate hierarchies. Industrializing business had developed a wide range of forms to check predatory competition and encourage invention in products, manufacturing process, and service. Complex contracts in shoe machinery, resale price maintenance, and trade associations provided three successful examples of regulated competition. But privately regulated competition risked exploitation and market power. Thus, it necessitated state monitoring and cooperation. Chapter 4 will explore the policy implications of regulated competition in more detail.

CONCLUSION

The Supreme Court reshaped the Progressive Era debate over antitrust when it insisted that complainants classify restraints of trade and provide convincing evidence. Populists, argued Justice White, demanded state action without a clear foundation to distinguish legitimate exercises of the police power. Progressives took up the Court's challenge. In antitrust and regulation, economists devised scientific foundations to classify economic activities and rigorous research methods to test their categories against the facts. Drawing on the marginalist revolution, they deduced criteria to distinguish perfect competition from natural monopoly and both from artificial restraints on trade. They proposed state action accordingly.

Although sympathetic to the progressive project, Brandeis rejected the method of classification in antitrust. As laissez-faire constitutionalists and progressive economists quarreled over categories and facts, Brandeis tried to shift the debate. Like the pragmatists of his time and the legal realists after him, he thought efforts to match facts to deductive categories elusive. The bright lines between competition and monopoly or public and private proved chimerical. Judges and economists who held rigidly to these distinctions condemned productive arrangements, such as resale price maintenance, and absolved destructive ones, such as tying contracts.

[76] LDB to William Ellsworth Smythe, June 28, 1915, in Melvyn Urofsky and David Levy, eds., *Letters of Louis D. Brandeis*, vol. 3 (Albany: State University of New York Press, 1973), 559–60. See also *Boston Evening Transcript*, November 21, 1910, quoted in Mason, *Brandeis*, 327, where Brandeis says, "We have had combinations to increase prices.... What we need [now] are combination[s] to reduce the costs of production."

Instead of classification, Brandeis asked judges, politicians, and economists to consider the facts in antitrust cases according to three criteria: the process of business development in the industry in question, the distribution of economic power in the industry, and the effects of business arrangements on economic performance. All economic activity, he said, was a social process. Business coordinated actions through customs and competition always had social content. Antitrust practitioners should ask three questions: Did social restraints on trade enhance or undermine competition? Did they lock in power or ensure it could be challenged? Were competitive practices predatory or productive? Vertical restraints in shoe machinery channeled competition from deep financial pockets to improvements in manufacturing and products, whereas tying contracts killed rivalry altogether and locked in unassailable power. Resale price maintenance ensured a ready market for product innovation, whereas loss leaders undermined consumer confidence and concentrated power in mass retailers. In both cases, performance was measurable in productivity, the entry of new firms, and new products. The method of evaluating process, power, and performance, in short, was a realistic alternative to classification.

Although Brandeis's third way was technically sophisticated, the election of 1912 turned more on cultural aspirations and anxieties than it did on technical considerations. The *Standard Oil* decision was a powerful signifier for reformers. For populist Democrats, it meant the corruption of all that was hopeful in the American spirit. With a stroke of the pen, Justice White entrenched privilege and silenced civic discourse. For progressives, the *Standard Oil* decision forced Americans to grow up and face the realities of power. It unmasked the myth of the self-regulating market and gave professionals a chance to steer the nation from drift to mastery. Irreconcilable as these differences seemed, Brandeis and Wilson envisioned immense vitality in their marriage.

Republican experimentalism promised to reconcile populist and progressive ends. Brandeis saw in engineering a model of deliberative problem solving, which accorded well with older republican aspirations to individual development and modern aspirations to technical progress. Moreover, he recomposed competition from its nineteenth-century meaning, as a means to reproduce equality, virtue, and republican government, into a project with syncretic meaning. When effectively regulated, competition would perturb custom, spark experimentation, and stimulate discussion. These were ends in themselves, but also means to individual development and economic progress. Human beings were fallible. But, if they were prodded to question habit, they would invent surprising means to economic and social betterment. Republican experimentalism, in short, promised to reconcile individual development and technical progress by extending deliberation from politics to everyday economic life.

Republican experimentalism failed to forge a common project among reformers. Woodrow Wilson won the presidential election of 1912 with a plurality and the antitrust debate raged on. By 1914, populists and progressives converged on a federal trade commission, even as they continued to fight over what it should do. Once again, Brandeis proposed a third way. Drawing from his work with engineers at the Interstate Commerce Commission, he proposed a commission devoted to upgrading, rather than replacing or enforcing, competition. In order to make sense of that proposal, we turn first to Brandeis's participation in railroad regulation and then use it to retell the origins of the FTC.

Chapter 3

Learning from Railroad Regulation

Brandeis formulated a blueprint for a federal trade commission from his experience with railroad regulation. He learned about the limits of progressivism and applied economics when he became involved in a series of Interstate Commerce Commission (ICC) rate cases between 1910 and 1914. Although he was a partisan participant, and his side won, Brandeis came to see railroad regulation as a failure. Instead of realizing the progressive promise to autonomy, legitimacy, and objectivity, applied economic science led to stalemate and paralysis. Brandeis proposed an alternative, which I call cultivational administration. Although the ICC did not take up his proposal, it became the basis for his Federal Trade Commission design and, as we shall see in Chapter 4, a third way to organize a commission. This chapter explains what Brandeis learned from railroad regulation and outlines his alternative.

Brandeis's relationship with the engineers flourished in railroad regulation, where they taught him new ways to think about efficiency and regulation. He consulted them on matters of railroad efficiency, enlisted their service as expert witnesses, and drew on their expertise to craft an alternative design for railroad regulation. And as he did, he deepened the chasm between the way engineering and economics approached the construction of knowledge. He learned four lessons from the engineers, which would reshape his understanding of economic efficiency and regulation. First, railroad cost accounting practices short-circuited improvement, because they prized volume over all other ends. Second, the economists who designed railroad rate regulation mistakenly reified railroad accounting practices as scientific law. As a result, railroad managers, economists, and regulators fell prey to customs that arrested policy imagination and inhibited economic improvement. Third, ICC economists made false promises to resolve distributive conflict through statistical objectivity. Instead of ending the battle between ratepayers and railroads, the ICC's efforts to base rates on the physical value of railroad property resulted in stalemate and paralysis. Fourth, Brandeis learned that the progressive design for rate regulation provided railroads with perverse incentives to increase capitalization instead of improving service. Brandeis concluded that the progressive promise to objectivity, autonomy, and legitimacy was unattainable.

Brandeis proposed an alternative, which was based on a dramatically different theory of social relations and economic knowledge. Cultivational regulation promised to nurture civic development, economic growth, and scientific learning through sliding-scale rate making and performance benchmarking. Drawing on his experience in natural gas regulation in Massachusetts, Brandeis suggested the ICC replace its efforts to cap railroad profits with a profit sharing system called "sliding scales." In this technique, increases in railroad dividends would be pegged to proportionate decreases in rates. Therefore, railroads always had an incentive to improve. Sliding scales promised to foster civic mindedness in railroad managers and cooperation between them and the state.

Drawing on the work of engineer F. Lincoln Hutchins, Brandeis also proposed the ICC create a benchmarking system, which would allow railroads to compare their costs to one another. The commission would mandate a uniform system of cost accounts and ask the carriers to submit data to a central efficiency bureau that would calculate industry benchmarks and disseminate them back to the railroads. This proposal was based on a dramatically different theory of the way economic knowledge was useful to regulation from the one advocated by the economists, who thought objective knowledge was necessary to resolve the intractable conflict between regulators and railroads. However, Brandeis and the engineers thought knowledge that fostered disciplined comparison between the railroads could forge a common interest between railroads and regulators in economic improvement and provide everyone with information, unavailable from the market or within the firm, about how to improve.

This chapter develops this theme in three sections. The first section recounts the law and economics of early railroad regulation. I explain the judicial logic for rate-of-return regulation, show how it paralleled the Court's thinking in antitrust, and explain how progressive economists responded with a suitable regulatory design. The second section recounts Brandeis's involvement in the railroad rate cases. I focus on the lessons he learned from this experience: how railroad accounting practices impeded improvement and how the ICC's rate-making techniques resulted in perverse outcomes. The third section turns to Brandeis's alternative. I explain the principles of cultivational regulation and show how sliding-scale rate making and benchmarking were appropriate techniques to realize its ends.

LAW AND THE SCIENCE OF RATE MAKING

The controversy over railroad regulation paralleled the controversy over antitrust. Congress passed a populist law in 1887 that created the Interstate Commerce Commission and empowered it to regulate rate inequalities between shippers and excessively high rates. The courts demanded that the ICC set rates reasonably. And progressive economists devised a rate-making system that promised autonomy, objectivity, and legal legitimacy. This section explains the law and science of railroad rate making.

The Interstate Commerce Act outlawed two common monopolistic practices perpetrated by the railroads: rate discrimination and rate extortion. The first became important to Brandeis because debate over discrimination revealed faulty accounting practices and opened Brandeis's eyes to the engineers' alternative. The second became important to Brandeis because debate over how to regulate extortion revealed deep flaws in the dominant model of rate making and led him to consider a more effective alternative.

Section 4 of the Interstate Commerce Act, which outlawed the practice of charging more for a short haul than for a long haul over the same line, failed to resolve a controversy over rate making. Small and medium-sized cities throughout the nation had long complained that higher rates undermined their prosperity and biased economic development toward huge cities such as New York and Chicago. Congress redressed those grievances by forcing the railroads to treat all shippers alike. But railroad managers, economists, and judges criticized Section 4. The railroads complained that they were only responding to technological and market imperatives. They had little choice but to meet long-haul competition with lower rates; otherwise, the high fixed costs of corporate debt threatened bankruptcy. If the result was rate discrimination, it was not the fault of the carriers.[1]

[1] Gerald Berk, *Alternative Tracks: The Constitution of American Industrial Order, 1865–1917* (Baltimore: Johns Hopkins University Press, 1994), 88–112.

The economists agreed, because the science of marginalism provided a more precise theory to understand the carriers' dilemma. Railroads faced not only high fixed costs, but also "joint costs." As economist Frank Taussig explained, all classes of traffic – long and short haul, passenger and freight, and bulk and specialty freight – made simultaneous use of railroad track and rolling stock. Because most railroad costs were fixed (track and rolling stock), once a train was on its way, additional freight or passengers added little increase in per unit costs. (As Chapters 5 and 6 will show, the economists thought *all* mass-production industries had joint costs and so it was impossible to segregate the costs of diverse products in them as well.) The result was a counterintuitive, but efficient, rate structure. Railroads took a loss on competitive long-haul traffic by setting rates slightly above variable costs (fuel and labor), and made up the difference with higher rates on noncompetitive short-haul traffic. Although it offended short-haul shippers and Congress, the economists thought this rate structure was efficient. It maximized total traffic, decreased costs through scale economies, and made it possible for railroads to lower all rates, competitive and noncompetitive alike.[2]

The ICC's chief statistician and prominent economist, Henry Carter Adams, agreed with Taussig. Rate discrimination was inevitable and efficient. Adams told commissioners that joint costs made it impossible for his department to calculate the exact cost of any particular railroad service. Where different classes of service made the same use of track and rolling stock, it was impossible to segregate their costs. Therefore, it was also impossible to judge charges of rate discrimination according to differences in the cost of service. It made much more sense to use the "value of service" (or what the traffic would bear). Adams thought that railroads were justified in defending rate discrimination as a legitimate response to competition. Therefore, he directed ICC accountants to abandon all efforts to gather cost data on diverse classes of traffic. Because these cost data were impossible to measure in practice, he told the commissioners they were useless for rate making.[3]

[2] F. W. Taussig, "A Contribution to the Theory of Railway Rates," *Quarterly Journal of Economics* 5 (July 1891): 438–65; Herbert Hovencamp, *Enterprise and American Law, 1836–1937* (Cambridge, MA: Harvard University Press, 1991), 153–56.

[3] Paul J. Miranti Jr., "The Mind's Eye of Reform: The ICC's Bureau of Statistics and Accounts and a Vision of Regulation, 1887–1940," *Business History Review* 63 (Autumn 1989): 479–86; H. C. Adams, "A Bureau of Railway Statistics and Accounts," *The Independent* 44 (October 6, 1892): 1384–85.

In 1897, the Supreme Court endorsed the joint cost theory of rate discrimination. Like its ruling sixteen years later in *Standard Oil*, the Court declared that regulated rates must respect a *rule of reason*, which distinguished clearly the constitutional rights of the public from those of the corporation. Writing for the majority in *ICC v. Alabama Midland Railway*, Justice Shiras said that although the ICC had constitutional authority to regulate discriminatory rates in the public interest, it had no right to deprive private corporations of their right to respond to market imperatives. There must be a sharp distinction between the public's right to equal access to railroad service and the railroads' right to contract. Otherwise, private corporations with public purposes would perish. Therefore, competition was a sufficient reason to depart from the rule in Section 4. As long as railroads were responding to market imperatives, discrimination was reasonable. The theory of joint costs thus triumphed over Congress's desire for equal access.[4] But as influential as the theory of joint costs became, the following section will show how Brandeis and the engineers criticized it for inhibiting railroad efficiency and distorting regulation.

The courts also shaped ICC regulation practices by ruling on the Interstate Commerce Act's provisions against rate extortion. In 1895, the Supreme Court said that ICC efforts to rectify illegally high rates had to be reasonable. This meant the commission must distinguish, once again, the rights of the public to low rates against the rights of railroads to protect their property. In *Smyth v. Ames*, Justice Harlan ratified the ICC's obligation to rectify excessively high rates, but he also declared the railroad corporation a "natural person," whose property deserved protection before the law. Reasonable rates, Harlan added, must sit at the boundary of legitimate regulation and property confiscation.

"Reasonable rates," Harlan wrote, must realize a "fair return" on the "fair value" of "property being used ... for the convenience of the public." He admitted this was a challenging empirical problem, but not one beyond calculation. Fair value must include the cost of construction and improvement, the market value of stocks and bonds, present costs, earning capacity, and operating costs. Reasonable rates, in other words, must be set according to a fair return on private investment.[5]

[4] *Interstate Commerce Commission v. Alabama Midland Railway Co.*, 168 U.S. 172 (1897); Hovencamp, *Enterprise and American Law*, 149–68; Berk, *Alternative Tracks*, 107–8.

[5] *Smyth v. Ames*, 169 U.S. 466, 546 (1898). See also Berk, *Alternative Tracks*, 156–57.

Like antitrust, the progressive economists took up the Court's challenge to classify. Henry Carter Adams was especially sanguine about the ICC's capacity to set rates at the boundary between regulation and confiscation. Unlike joint costs, Adams thought it was necessary and possible for the Statistics Department to measure the fair value of railroad property. Indeed, "no tribunal," he wrote, "can pass satisfactory judgment upon the reasonableness of railway rates without taking into account the value of railroad property." No less than the ICC's authority itself depended on its capacity to measure objectively. Accurately gauged, railroad costs are the "*true records of administration,* and he who controls accounts, can in large measure control the policy of management."[6]

Unfortunately, ICC statistical capacity fell short at the outset of Adams's reign. Pressed into action in rate extortion cases, the Statistics Department estimated value from corporate securities. But Adams criticized this practice. He thought the "commercial value" of corporate securities had little to do with the "real value of railway property." And so, in 1903, he asked Congress to authorize and fund the Statistics Department to conduct a "physical valuation" of the entire U.S. railway net. Only then would the ICC have a "solid" base on which to evaluate rates by measuring the rate of return on the real value of railroad property.[7]

Adams captured a key component of the progressive mind: trust in numbers was necessary to resolve otherwise intractable political conflict. In the absence of objective measurement, there was no end to the conflict between regulation and confiscation. Railroads would always contest ICC rates as an unlawful taking of private property, if the commission was unable to demonstrate they earned a fair return on the value of their property. If commission government were to stand outside the fray, objective measurement necessitated cultural authority and those who conducted it necessitated social prestige.[8]

[6] Interstate Commerce Commission, *Annual Report, 1901* (Washington, DC: Government Printing Office, 1901), 26–27, emphasis added.

[7] Interstate Commerce Commission, *Report of the Statistics of Railways in the United States, 1888* (Washington, DC: Government Printing Office, 1889), 5–6. See also Adams to ICC Commissioner Wheelock G. Veazey (1893) quoted in Miranti, "The Mind's Eye of Reform," 478–79. On the role of science in making society "legible" to the modern state more generally, see James C. Scott, *Seeing Like a State: How Certain Schemes to Improve the Human Condition Have Failed* (New Haven, CT: Yale University Press, 1998).

[8] On this theme, see Theodore M. Porter, *Trust in Numbers: The Pursuit of Objectivity in Science and Public Life* (Princeton, NJ: Princeton University Press, 1995).

It took nearly a decade of annual requests before Congress granted the ICC authority and resources to measure railroad value. In 1912, Congress passed the Railway Valuation Act. Coupled with the Mann-Elkins Act, passed two years earlier, which empowered the ICC to set maximum rates, the commission now had statutory authority to realize the Court's directive in *Smyth v. Ames*.[9] For the first time, the commission could evaluate rates according to whether they provided the railroads with a fair rate of return on the real value of their investment. In principle, then, the Mann-Elkins Act and the Railway Valuation Act provided the ICC with the tools to locate the line between legitimate regulation and property confiscation and to finally set rates based on a scientific foundation.

THE ADVANCE RATE CASES

The promise to objectivity, legitimacy, and autonomy proved elusive. Instead of resolving conflict, the commission and carriers locked horns in a bitter stalemate after 1912. So paralyzed did regulation become that the Wilson administration nationalized the railroads for the duration of U.S. participation in World War I.

Brandeis participated in the crisis of railroad regulation first as a partisan, then as a consultant to the ICC. In three rate hearings between 1910 and 1913, he served as counsel to an association of shippers opposed to rate increases. In 1914, the commissioners asked him to help them review a fourth request from the railroads to increase rates. As in antitrust, Brandeis consulted engineers, not economists, on railroad rate regulation. They taught him about the flaws in railroad accounting practices, rate-of-return rate making, and the ICC's valuation project. They also provided techniques for an alternative. The next section recounts the trouble with the theory and practice of joint costs and rate-of-return rate making.

The Trouble with the High Fixed and Joint Cost Paradigm

In 1911, Brandeis sparked a national controversy over scientific management when he asked Harrington Emerson to testify in support of the shippers' opposition to an across-the-board rate increase. Emerson was an engineer and efficiency expert who had worked closely with Frederick

[9] Berk, *Alternative Tracks*, 158–68.

Taylor on early innovations in scientific management. He explained how he had saved the Atchison, Topeka, and Santa Fe Railroad (AT & SF) thousands of dollars by implementing scientific management in traffic management. Asked what scientific management could do for railroads more generally, Emerson estimated the carriers could save as much as a million dollars a day by implementing the techniques he and Taylor had pioneered in manufacturing. The press loved Brandeis's audacity in calling Emerson to the stand, and scientific management suddenly entered the popular lexicon.

Emerson raised challenging issues for the railroads and the ICC. Institutionalists and organizational historians have mistakenly seen his testimony as a publicity stunt. Acting for shippers before a weak commission, they argue, Brandeis hoped to mobilize public opinion in favor of his clients.[10] Brandeis's attention to the press is undeniable. But Emerson raised a much more fundamental issue, which dogged railroad regulation, antitrust, and trade regulation for the next two decades: Were high fixed and joint costs inexorable features of railroads and all mass-production industry, or were they merely artifacts of accounting custom? The answer to this seemingly prosaic question about bookkeeping determined *who* was accountable and to *what* standards. If it was the former, then railroads were correct to request rate increases to subsidize capital improvements. Efficiency was the result of volume and the larger the load railroads could handle, the lower the unit costs and the greater the mutual benefit to ratepayers and railroads. If it was the latter, then maybe railroads overvalued volume and underestimated other ways to realize efficiency. Hence, their claims to a rate increase might be unwarranted and the ICC ought to rethink the way it evaluated efficiency when making rate decisions. Emerson's work at the AT & SF showed the latter. By segregating traffic costs according to class of service and the department in which they were incurred, railroads could make incremental improvements, which added up to vast cost savings. If Emerson's experiments with one railroad were applicable more broadly, then the railroads and the economists were wrong. Joint costs were not an objective measure of transportation or a law of railroad economics. They were an artifact of accounting custom,

[10] Stephen Skowronek, *Building a New American State* (Cambridge: Cambridge University Press, 1982), 269–70; Albro Martin, *Enterprise Denied: Origins of the Decline of American Railroads, 1897–1917* (New York: Columbia University Press, 1971), 206–19; Thomas K. McCraw, *Prophets of Regulation* (Cambridge, MA: Harvard University Press, 1984), 91–94.

that is, a social convention, which circumscribed what managers, professionals, and regulators thought possible. As such, they could become the subject of creative deliberation, experimentation, and change.[11]

Drawing from Emerson's testimony, Brandeis told the commissioners and the railroads that the failure to segregate traffic costs resulted in two perverse consequences. First, the railroads fell behind manufacturing in "operating efficiency." Unaware of the costs of many operations, they gave no thought to reducing them. Brandeis pressed this point with the railroad managers: Do you evaluate particular classes of traffic according to the spread between costs and revenues? Do you break transportation processes down into their component parts and compare performance over time? When Brandeis asked the president of the Baltimore and Ohio Railroad the cost of locomotive repair, he answered in the aggregate, that is, in average annual costs per locomotive mile. "Just see how uncertain that factor is," Brandeis responded. "You are taking the average. [But] the only way you tell whether the work on any one of those cars was efficiently done, is it not, would be for you to know the particular thing that was done on that particular car?" But management, like the economists, saw little sense in disaggregating the costs of production and service. In an industry where most costs were perceived to be joint, it made sense to add service if it brought any additional revenue to service debt.[12] The result, Brandeis charged, was to restrict imagination and improvement.

The second perverse result of assuming joint costs was that railroads were unable to distinguish profitable from unprofitable services. "The traffic manager's success or failure is tested by the tonnage moved instead of the profit earned," Brandeis told the ICC. As a result, the carriers assumed, instead of tested, the principle that additional traffic always augmented revenues and reduced costs. Until they developed "reasonably

[11] For Emerson's testimony, see Louis D. Brandeis, *Scientific Management and Railroads: Being Part of a Brief Submitted to the Interstate Commerce Commission* (New York: The Engineering Magazine, 1912), 8–10, 15–17, 34–35, 44–45, 61, 67–71, 73–74, 77–78, and 83–88, where he recounts cost savings at the Atchison, Topeka, and Santa Fe Railroad.

[12] U.S. Congress, *Senate, Evidence in Matter of Proposed Advances in Freight Rates (1910–1911)*, 61st Cong., 3d sess., Sen. doc. no. 725, vol. 4 (Washington, DC: Government Printing Office, 1911), 2400–01. Hereafter cited as *Advance Rate Case.* Brandeis's complaints were not new. A similar critique of railroad costing practices underlay the long-standing charge of rate discrimination. Among the most articulate critics of the overemphasis on long-haul, high-volume traffic was the Chicago, Great Western Railroad's president, Alpheus Beede Stickney. See Berk, *Alternative Tracks*, 91–100, 116–49.

accurate knowledge of whether a particular service was rendered at a profit or a loss," Brandeis charged, the railroads would fail to realize their public duty to conserve "legitimate revenues" and their demands would ring hollow.[13] If the carriers were wanting for cash, it was more likely due to the "disastrous financial results" of their cost accounting practices, than it was to the ICC's failure to raise rates. Until the railroads demonstrated a sincere commitment to reducing costs, it made little sense for the ICC to raise rates. "If we are to travel in the vicious circle of meeting higher costs by ever higher costs, if the burden of increased rates and other burdens are to come upon the community, then where is the limit?" Brandeis asked the commission.[14]

Recent scholarship indicates Brandeis's critique of railroad accounting practices was correct. In a comprehensive survey of railroad costs, Gregory Thompson finds that between 1870 and 1940, 80–90 percent of all costs were variable (labor or materials). The widespread assumption that most costs were fixed or joint is incorrect. Thompson cites a study by Adams's successor in the ICC Statistics Department, Otto Lorenz, which demonstrated that railroads faced high fixed and joint costs only at lower levels of traffic density. Once they achieved the density typical of twentieth-century carriers in the East and the Midwest, average costs remained constant regardless of traffic density and almost 100 percent of operating expenses were variable. Although these conditions did not hold for lines with lower density in the South and the West, Lorenz concluded that even in those regions, most costs were variable. Like Brandeis, Thompson debunks the assumption of railroad managers, economists, and historians looking back. "The ability of a railroad to reduce operating expenses and adjust a supposedly fixed plant in the face of traffic reduction," he concludes, "is far greater than commonly thought.... The popular notion of a railroad line having unlimited capacity once it is put down is entirely inaccurate."[15]

Moreover, my study of the Chicago, Great Western Railway demonstrates there was another way to run a railroad. By paying careful attention to reducing the costs of mixing carload and less-than-carload and long-haul and short-haul freight, this regional carrier achieved productivity

[13] "Five Percent Rate Case, Brief of Louis Brandeis," 27 April 1914, 31 ICC 103–5, quoted in G. L. Thompson, "Misused Product Costing in the American Railroad Industry: Southern Pacific Passenger Service between the Wars," *Business History Review* 63 (Autumn 1989): 520.

[14] Quoted in Alpheus T. Mason, *Brandeis: A Free Man's Life* (New York: Viking, 1946), 325.

[15] Thompson, "Misused Product Costing," 522–32.

levels higher than many of the large national railroads, which prized high-volume, homogeneous, long-haul freight over all other ends.[16]

In sum, by importing tools from engineering into the rate controversy, Brandeis revealed the constructed nature of railroad costs and opened the door to alternative methods of measurement and management. He showed how the carriers assumed, rather than tested, the proposition that all additional traffic was profitable because it economized on high fixed and joint costs. This strategy was an artifact of accounting habits, not a rational response to technological or market constraints. Alter accounting techniques, Brandeis hypothesized, and new strategies for efficiency would become visible. Two techniques, which broke with the high fixed and joint costs paradigm, were available from cost accounting innovations in scientific management and manufacturing. In the first, Brandeis asked railroads to refine the measurements of their production costs: What is the cost of turning a wheel, loading a particular class of freight, or maintaining telegraph cable? In the second, he asked railroads to measure the costs of their diverse "products" or traffic services. Together, he thought the implementation of these techniques would demonstrate that the carriers had taken their public obligation to improve service, as well as private right to property, seriously. If profits still declined, then under the rules of *Smyth v. Ames* this would signal the need for a rate increase. Until then, Brandeis thought the carriers had not made a convincing case.

The Trouble with Rate-of-Return Regulation

Despite its assurance to autonomy, objectivity, and legitimacy, rate-of-return regulation came up short. The promise to fix a rate base through physical valuation and set rates according to a return on value failed to convince railroads, shippers, or the Wilson administration to defer to ICC autonomy. Instead, regulation became paralyzed in intractable conflict. The failure of rate regulation convinced Brandeis that the Court's doctrine in *Smyth v. Ames* was deeply flawed and so the ICC's efforts to put regulation into practice were doomed.

Brandeis was a partisan to the rate controversy, one who argued forcefully for shippers and consumers within the framework outlined in *Smyth v. Ames*. He told the commission it would be a "serious danger to the country" to establish the "principle" that every time the railroads

[16] See Berk, *Alternative Tracks*, 116–49.

claim they "need more money" they get a rate increase, instead of doing what every competitive business does, namely, to find ways to increase revenues by "reducing [their] costs." If the ICC raised rates every time the railroads complained of increased costs, it would violate the principle outlined in *Smyth v. Ames*. All the advantages would tip to the railroads, and the public's right to reasonable rates would be ignored.[17]

Although Brandeis argued within the parameters of *Smyth v. Ames*, as noted in the previous section, he thought it was deeply flawed. He criticized rate-of-return regulation for making false promises to resolve the conflict and for providing railroads with perverse incentives to enlarge their capitalization ("water their stock") instead of lowering costs. The more he consulted the engineers, the more he thought valuation was doomed to failure.

Brandeis found an alternative to valuation in the work of engineer F. Lincoln Hutchins: performance benchmarking. Part of Taylor's circle of scientific managers, Hutchins wrote extensively on railroad cost accounting and regulation. In 1912, he proposed the ICC scrap its valuation project and instead ask the carriers to measure their costs with the same methods and submit data to a central bureau, which would calculate useful benchmarks for evaluating the performance of individual carriers. The following year, Brandeis suggested the ICC create an efficiency bureau to implement benchmarking and hire Hutchins to run it.[18] Short of that, he asked the commissioners to read Hutchins's work on railroad regulation in *The Engineering Magazine*.

Valuation, Hutchins charged, was a false god, which made empty promises to solve the conflict between railroads, shippers, and the state. First, it raised insurmountable methodological problems. For example, it was impossible to recover the original costs of construction, capitalization, or real estate. Second, the relationship between value and rates was indeterminate. Suppose, Hutchins conjectured, it was possible to measure railroad value; even so, a million questions about rates remained. What basis could be used to set the rates of several roads running between the same points when there are large differences in physical property and capitalization? What should one do with a railroad, located in a region where it was expensive to build, whose costs have gone up over time? Should rates be set to permit the least advantageously situated road to realize an average return? If so, how should the ICC restrict the better

[17] Quoted in Mason, *Brandeis*, 325.
[18] Mason, *Brandeis*, 335.

situated from earning more? If, on the other hand, rates are set so that the most favorably situated carrier earns only an average return, what happens to those who cannot live up to that rate? Likewise, how would the ICC adjust rates between classes of passenger and merchandise traffic according to the Court's standards? These questions revealed the incoherence of the project itself. "The present attempt to fix return to capital invested in railroads, by means of physical valuation of the property, or in limiting the return upon its capitalization, has no scientific foundation and will lead to no satisfactory result either to the railroad capitalist, or to the community which is served."[19]

In a widely read critique of valuation published in 1920, legal realist Gerard Henderson looked back on the ICC's folly:

> The relation between the public utility and the community cannot be expressed in terms of a simple, quantitatively ascertainable fact, for the relation involves numerous and complex factors which depend on compromise and practical adjustment rather than deductive logic. The whole doctrine of *Smyth v. Ames* rests upon a gigantic illusion. The fact which for twenty years the court has been vainly trying to find does not exist. "Fair value" must be shelved among the great juristic myths of history, with the Law of Nature and the Social Contract. As a practical concept, from which practical conclusions can be drawn, it is valueless.[20]

Brandeis agreed with Henderson and Hutchins's critique of valuation and rate-of-return regulation. Valuation did not resolve the conflict between regulation and confiscation. Rate-of-return regulation was a failure. Progressives were wrong to cap profits. The public's interest is in better service at lower rates, not in profits that are "very high or very low." Moreover, the results of profit regulation were perverse. At best, they undermined the incentive to improve by placing a "limit on achievement." At worst, they gave managers incentives to act opportunistically. Instead of decreasing costs, managers increased capitalization, without augmenting productive assets, in order to justify higher rates. Costs went up instead of down and managers devoted their energies to gaming the system instead of to innovation and improvement. Instead of balancing

[19] F. Lincoln Hutchins, "The Railroad Problem: Rates, Unit Costs, and Efficiency," *The Engineering Magazine* 42 (January 1912): 489–90; F. Lincoln Hutchins, "The Railroad Problem: Capitalization and Regulation," *The Engineering Magazine* 43 (February 1912): 711 (quotation).

[20] G. Henderson, "Railway Valuation and the Courts," *Harvard Law Review* 33 (1920): 902–28, 1031–57. The quotation is on page 1051. For more on Henderson's place in the "legal realist" movement, as well as his critique of *Smyth v. Ames*, see Morton J. Horwitz, *The Transformation of American Law, 1870–1960* (Oxford: Oxford University Press, 1992), 104–5, 162–63.

public and private rights, *Smyth v. Ames* resulted in the steady deterioration of railroad service.[21]

"The public interest, as well as justice [for the carriers]," Brandeis told the Hadley railroad commission, "demands ... due appreciation of greater efficiency in management; and some method must be found of determining the degree of efficiency attained and of providing adequate rewards."[22] Brandeis proposed to jettison valuation and rate-of-return regulation altogether, and replace them with benchmarking and sliding-scale rate making.

CULTIVATIONAL REGULATION

Brandeis's proposal to reform railroad regulation was deep and detailed. Drawing on Hutchins, he proposed the ICC replace valuation with benchmarking. Drawing on his experience with artificial gas regulation in Massachusetts, he proposed to replace rate-of-return rate making with the British system of sliding scales. Like his approach to antitrust, Brandeis's design for railroad regulation expressed his republican experimentalism. He thought it possible to cultivate common ends between the ratepayers and the railroads and an experimentalist sensibility among managers and regulators.

I call Brandeis's approach to reform "cultivational regulation" for three reasons. The first is cultural. Brandeis hoped to change the way managers and regulators understood themselves and their relationship. Where judges and progressives assumed conflict between the commission and the carriers, Brandeis thought it possible to cultivate habits of collaborative reflection, inquiry, experimentation, and evaluation. This was not merely a matter of altering incentives to get railroads and regulators to cooperate, as today's game theorists and institutionalists suggest, or a matter of changing social norms. Instead, Brandeis recognized that information about how to improve railroad efficiency and service was elusive, and that managers and regulators could learn to work together to create better knowledge. The more managers and regulators saw their ends in this way, the more likely they were to align their private interests with a broader public interest in endless improvement.

21 "The Best Solution Is a Government Bureau" (statement before the Hadley Railroad Securities Commission, published in *The Engineering Magazine*, vol. 42 [October 1911]) in O. K. Fraenkel, ed., *The Curse of Bigness: Miscellaneous Papers of Louis D. Brandeis* (New York: Viking, 1934), 192–94.

22 Brandeis, "The Best Solution Is a Government Bureau," 192.

The second reason I call Brandeis's proposal cultivational was because it was meant to cultivate economic growth. Although judges and progressives turned their attention to distribution because they thought the problem of production had been solved,[23] Brandeis thought production remained the central problem. As he said, the goal of regulation was better service at cheaper rates.

The third reason I call Brandeis's proposal cultivational is scientific. He intended regulation to "improve" service by "labor, care, and study."[24] By instituting uniform cost accounting and a benchmarking system, the ICC would improve the capacity of railroad managers to set targets for improvement and evaluate their performance. In sum, Brandeis hoped to nurture civic personality, economic improvement, and scientific inquiry through cultivational regulation. Although these were ambitious goals, the means were creative, detailed, and apt.

Sliding Scales

Brandeis proposed to replace rate-of-return regulation with the English system of sliding scales, in which increases in corporate dividends were pegged to proportionate decreases in rates. In principle, ratepayers and railroads would share efficiency gains and the carriers would have an ongoing incentive to improve.

Brandeis learned about sliding-scale rate making during a controversy over Massachusetts artificial gas in 1906.[25] Massachusetts was an innovator in public utility regulation. In 1875, the legislature empowered the Boston Public Utility Commission to set rates on electricity and natural gas according to a fair rate of return on capital. Like railroad regulation forty years later, rate-of-return regulation failed in Boston. The gas companies eluded the commission's cap on profits by "stock watering" (issuing new securities without investing in additional productive assets). The higher the rate base, they realized, the larger their claim on net revenues would be.

In 1894, the state legislature passed a law against stock watering, but gas producers evaded this rule as well. In 1902, they convinced the

[23] On this point, see James Livingston, *Pragmatism and the Political Economy of Cultural Revolution, 1850–1940* (Chapel Hill: University of North Carolina Press, 1994), 24–56.

[24] See the definition of "cultivate" in *Webster's New Collegiate Dictionary* (Springfield, MA: G&C Merriam, 1977), 277.

[25] The narrative of Brandeis's involvement in the fight over the regulation of Massachusetts natural gas comes from Mason, *Brandeis*, 126–40.

legislature to incorporate Boston Consolidated, a merger of eight natural gas companies, with a combined capitalization nearly one-third higher than that of the independent companies. The Massachusetts Franchise League protested: incorporation violated the 1894 statute and so it should be held void.

A prominent member of the Franchise League, Brandeis proposed a compromise: allow Boston Consolidated to survive, its capitalization intact; empower the Utility Commission to regulate all new security issues; and abandon rate-of-return regulation for a system of sliding scales. In sliding-scale regulation, "the amount the company" receives in dividends depends "upon what was given to the community." For example, if Boston Consolidated lowered the price of gas by 25 percent it would be allowed a proportionate increase in its dividends.[26] Brandeis told the legislature:

> The proper aim of the public must not be to limit dividends, but to secure gas of good quality at low prices ... a limitation on dividends was desirable only when it conduced to that end; and ... under the proper conditions a reasonable assurance of the undisturbed enjoyment of large dividends might be the best method of attaining cheap gas.[27]

Although Brandeis's proposal met with skepticism from progressives in the Franchise League, who thought it gave too much to the corporations, and from Boston's investment bankers, who thought it gave too little, support from Governor Curtis Guild Jr. and Consolidated's president, James L. Richards, convinced the legislature to make it law. The 1906 statute empowered the Public Utility Commission to supervise securities, set rates on a sliding scale, and hold periodic hearings to revisit the ratio of rates to dividends. At the end of its first year of operation the volume of gas distributed increased by 16 percent, rates fell by 1 percent, and dividends increased by 1 percent. Only cities in natural gas–producing regions performed better.

Years later, Brandeis recounted the Massachusetts story to the Hadley Railroad Commission and the ICC. Progressives, he said, had been wrong about artificial gas regulation. Rate-of-return regulation turned the utilities into opportunists, increased conflict between the public and corporations, and reduced efficiency. In New York, where it remained, regulation

[26] Mason, *Brandeis*, 133.

[27] Louis D. Brandeis, "How Boston Solved the Gas Problem," *American Review of Reviews* (November 1907), reprinted in Louis D. Brandeis, *Business – a Profession* (Boston: Small, Maynard, 1925), 108.

became mired in litigation, stalemate, and poor performance. The lesson for railroad regulation was clear. On the one hand, the state must enable "adequate rewards" if it wanted improvement. On the other hand, regulated corporations were a "quasi public business" that owed endlessly better service to passengers and shippers. Thus, like Boston Consolidated, the railroads should receive compensation on a "sliding scale, so that the greater the service to the public, the greater the profit to those furnishing the service." Brandeis acknowledged that railroad rate making was more complex than artificial gas rate making. But he thought the profit-sharing principle was sound and technically adaptable to railroads.[28]

Thus, where progressives thought the conflict between ratepayers and railroads could be resolved through scientific rate making, Brandeis thought their interests could be aligned through sliding scales. The case of Massachusetts artificial gas demonstrated it was possible. It could not be worse than rate-of-return regulation, which had proved a failure. And so Brandeis encouraged the ICC and Congress to try.

Benchmarking

The second means to cultivational regulation, performance benchmarking, constructed knowledge about the nature and uses of measurement in a way radically different from valuation. Adams (the economist) thought it possible to locate objective value, whereas Hutchins (the engineer) thought effective measurement was mostly a matter of agreement over conventions. For Adams the problem was to devise measures that best mirrored nature, whereas for Hutchins the problem was to create a common language through measurement, which allowed comparison across diverse circumstances. The Supreme Court assumed the necessity of an objective rate base in order to solve distributive conflict, whereas Brandeis thought measurement should set standards by which business and government could compare performance over time or across firms and learn how to do things better. For Brandeis and the engineers, once sliding scales provided railroads with the incentive to improve, the ICC could turn its attention to providing valuable information about how to improve. Benchmarking was the means to that end.

Brandeis came to benchmarking through his critique of joint costs. He thought improvement stalled because the carriers failed to disaggregate

[28] Brandeis, "The Best Solution Is a Government Bureau," 193.

costs according to (1) their source in production or (2) the class of traffic in which they were incurred. Once the railroads learned to distinguish the costs of loading from unloading freight, carload freight, and less-than-carload freight, they would also learn to track performance over time and to set targets for the future. This was the main lesson Emerson drew from his experience at the AT & SF.[29] However, Brandeis and the engineers also thought there were limits to what could be learned from self-monitoring. Their inquiry into railroad accounting practices revealed how easy it was for management to become mired in custom. Brandeis and Hutchins proposed that the ICC create a system to make it possible to compare company performance publicly. Suppose, they said, all railroads adopted a uniform system of cost accounting and then submitted their data to an ICC efficiency bureau. The bureau could then calculate industry averages and distribute them back to the industry. The goal, Brandeis said, was not imitation, but to perturb habits. If managers learned they were higher than average on a particular operation (e.g., engine repair), they could ask what the reasons were. If they learned their costs were particularly high on one class of freight and low on another, they might conclude that it made more sense to specialize. In other words, benchmarking made it possible to pose intelligent questions that were otherwise unimaginable.[30]

Instead of the elusive search for objective value, Hutchins wrote that the railroads ought to agree to a set of yardsticks, or cost conventions, so they could compare performance over time and across firms. It made little difference exactly what those conventions were, as long as they made comparison possible. The ICC should acknowledge that efforts to root its authority in the objectivity of measurement were chimerical. It was better to hold railroads accountable to comparative measurements. But this meant that the ICC had to abandon its search for autonomy in the objectivity of economic science and descend into the messier world of engineering. Hutchins proposed a measurement "unit in which each kind of service [or operation] is equated to the same value. Like the engineer's

[29] On Emerson's use of "standard costs" to set targets for improvement at the Atchison, Topeka, and Santa Fe Railroad, see Louis D. Brandeis, *Scientific Management and Railroads: Being Part of a Brief Submitted to the Interstate Commerce Commission* (New York: *The Engineering Magazine*, 1912), 67–68.

[30] Brandeis's contemporary, John Dewey, wrote eloquently about the cultivation of "intelligent habits" in a democracy in ways that sounded much like Brandeis. See John Dewey, *Human Nature and Conduct* (Amherst, NY: Prometheus Books, 2002 [1922]).

'*benchmark*,'" he added, "it must serve as the base from which to measure the variation from any standard selected." To this end, Hutchins devised a single measure – the *service unit* – with which railroads could compare costs on a wide range of expenditures and types of traffic.[31] Once they submitted cost data to the ICC's efficiency bureau, the agency could convert it to "cost per service unit," calculate industry averages, and publish benchmarks in regular ICC reports.

Hutchins thought benchmarking was the beginning, not the end, of collective and individual inquiry. Unlike physical valuation, which promised an empirical answer to a metaphysical question – where is the line between private rights and public obligations? – benchmarking raised concrete questions about practice. Is comparatively high maintenance cost the result of inappropriate equipment, an inefficient repair shop, or poor materials? Do irregularities in unit costs over time reveal changing conditions or the fact that a carrier has "no settled policy" with regard to improvement or "fixed standard" to measure it? Does higher-than-average cost on a class of freight mean a carrier should specialize elsewhere or search for methods to reduce cost?[32]

The more railroads posed such questions, the more they would ratchet individual performance up to "the best ascertained practice" found in the industry.[33] In other words, benchmarking not only provided information about how to improve, it also provided nonmarket incentives to improve. As Brandeis put it, under the guidance of an efficiency bureau, costs could be "properly supervised, analyzed, classified, and compared, so that each railroad should have the benefit of knowing the lowest unit cost of each operation attained by any American railroad, and how it was attained."[34] Such knowledge would incite managers to surpass the "existing records" for every department, class of traffic, or operation.[35]

[31] F. Lincoln Hutchins, "Rates, Unit Costs, and Efficiency," 490–91.

[32] Hutchins, "Capitalization," 713.

[33] Hutchins, "Capitalization," 713.

[34] "The Best Solution Is a Government Bureau," 193.

[35] *Boston Evening Transcript*, November 21, 1910, quoted in Mason, *Brandeis*, 327. See also *Scientific Management*, 75, where Brandeis says that the ICC should require "each company [to] ascertain and report to it the simple ultimate unit costs of each operation in every department of the road. The further fact that the railroad business is largely noncompetitive makes it proper to publish these costs, and to give to each railroad the benefit of knowing the lowest elementary unit cost of each operation attained by any railroad, and how it was attained. The ascertainment of the ultimate unit cost is necessary before an instructive basis of comparison can be had.... What is needed as a basis for comparison are the ultimate unit costs; the cost of turning a wheel, the

In sum, progressive economists thought science could provide objective standards for an empirical solution to the conflict between regulation and confiscation, whereas Brandeis and the engineers thought statistical objectivity an elusive end. There were too many variables in play; physical measurements involved value judgments; and the value of statistics always depended upon the sorts of questions one wanted to ask. Instead, drawing on the work of F. Lincoln Hutchins, Brandeis proposed that the ICC establish a set of accounting conventions – agreed upon measurements – that would allow railroads to evaluate their own performance over time and compare themselves to industry averages. Where Adams thought statistical legibility was necessary for state control over industry, Brandeis thought the ICC could create a common language by which railroads could compare themselves across diverse conditions and learn how to improve.[36] And whereas the progressives thought physical valuation could overcome the railroad opportunism through more effective coercion, Brandeis thought benchmarking promised to channel management behavior from opportunism to inquiry, experimentation, and comparative evaluation.

Brandeis thought cultivational regulation would have salutary effects on railroad performance, but its likely effect on "social and individual development," he told the ICC, was "worth infinitely more than the financial gain." This was a civic enterprise. The Massachusetts experience demonstrated that a collaborative alternative to regulatory paralysis was possible. Instead of "standing always with shield and with sword to protect themselves against popular clamor and criticism, [railroad managers] could be looked upon as James L. Richards, of Boston, is looked upon to-day": a model "public servant," who raised Consolidated Natural Gas from a "state of inefficiency and scandal" to one of steady improvement in rates, service, and profits. "This possibility lies before the

cost of laying a tie or rail under particular conditions, and even that relatively simple operation must again be analyzed and separated into its ultimate simple elements."

[36] Benchmarking was not the only means by which the ICC could coordinate standard setting and economic learning. In addition to a Bureau of Railroad Efficiency, Brandeis also proposed that the ICC establish a series of experiment stations. Modeled on those run by the Department of Agriculture, the commission would "develop valuable inventions and discoveries" of its own. Perhaps of greater service, it would test inventions and methods devised by others and disseminate its findings. "There are undoubtedly in existence today hundreds of inventions ... which, if adopted, would enhance the efficiency of railroad operation..., but which are not known to the operating men because no adequate means exist for bringing them to their notice." Such demonstration projects, Brandeis, concluded were a "proper function of government," because they helped "raise the standards" of railroad safety and efficiency. See Brandeis, "The Best Solution Is a Government Bureau" in Fraenkel, ed., *The Curse of Bigness*, 194.

railroad men to-day. They may become in fact, as they are legally, public servants. They may secure the admiration and gratitude of the public as well as of their stockholders," Brandeis added. Or they can sustain the paralyzing discord that marked railroad regulation so far. Benchmarking and sliding scales offered a technical means to moral development and public/private collaboration, should government, the railroads, and the public muster the collective will to make them a reality.[37]

CONCLUSION

Brandeis had an ambivalent relationship with progressives. He shared their commitment to applied science, state building, wealth redistribution, trade unionism, and the welfare state. But he thought they reified economic power, overestimated the ability of science to overcome human fallibility in government and the economy, and underestimated the capacity of common people to achieve public ends. In antitrust, he thought the economist's formal categories – perfect competition and natural monopoly – underestimated the diversity of economic arrangements and their consequences. In railroad regulation, he thought that the economist's propensity to naturalize costs reified particular management customs as though they were economic law. The result not only slowed economic progress, but also impeded self-reflection among professionals, as well the imagination necessary for creative solutions to dilemmas of regulatory design. Whether in antitrust, public utility, or railroad regulation, the progressive's favored

[37] *Evidence Taken by the Interstate Commerce Commission in the Matter of Proposed Advances in Freight Rates by Carriers*, 61st Cong., 3d sess., Sen. doc. 725, vol. 8 (Washington, DC: Government Printing Office, 1911), 5277–78. Brandeis made similar arguments about the use of benchmarking and scientific management in industrial relations. Testifying before Congress on scientific management, he said human development in the age of factory work was elusive. Therefore, it necessitated a sense of "accomplishment," the realization that one can "do something better ... than before, or perhaps better than others do." He admitted that capitalism usually prodded competitors to evaluate performance in wins and losses. But the "joys of accomplishment" are also personal – learning to best an individual or group record and knowing that there is always the possibility for further "development." None of this was possible, Brandeis told the senators, without a standard – a benchmark – for measurement. Moreover, he thought a truly effective cost accounting or benchmarking was impossible without unions, not only because workers without protection were likely to subvert measurement. More important, he believed intimate knowledge of the shop floor was necessary for accurate measurement in the first instance. See Brandeis testimony before the U.S. Congress, Senate, Commission on Industrial Relations, Vol. XIX, 64th Cong., 1st sess., Sen. doc. 415, serial 6936, 1915, 994–97, 1003–6.

solution for a natural monopoly – an independent commission empowered to set prices according to a fair return on property – came up short. Experience showed that instead of closing off conflict and opportunism, rate-of-return regulation displaced them. Private corporations with public purposes proved endlessly inventive in finding ways to evade their obligations to consumers and the state. The progressive's promise to find a technocratic solution to the problem of coercion turned out to be hubris.

There was another way. Drawing on republican aspirations to cultural development and the techniques of scientific management, Brandeis outlined a cultivational design, which intended to achieve three ends: cultural refinement, economic growth, and scientific learning. Brandeis borrowed techniques from cost accounting, scientific management, and English utility regulation to outline a syncretic alternative to the progressive model of bureaucratic administration. Through product costing, benchmarking, and sliding-scale rate making, he hoped to lift railroad regulation from paralysis to incremental progress. Just as regulated competition in antitrust combined elements of rivalry and restraint, cultivational administration combined private incentives with public obligations to channel economic behavior from opportunism to improvement.

The ICC did not become a cultivational agency. Instead, Congress passed the Transportation Act of 1920 – an uneasy compromise between shippers and railroads, which looked more like a pluralist bargaining model than cultivational regulation. Nevertheless, Brandeis's experience with railroad regulation helped him to rethink antitrust. And as the various political factions in that debate came to agree over the need for a federal trade commission, Brandeis adapted his cultivational design to antitrust. We turn to that story next.

Chapter 4

The Origins of an Ambiguous Federal Trade Commission

On September 26, 1914, President Wilson signed the Federal Trade Commission Act into law. Not long before, it looked as though antitrust reform was dead, because populist Democrats and progressive Republicans disagreed over the commission's ends and its powers. But creative entrepreneurs in Congress overcame the conflict through legislative syncretism. They transcended the debate between a weak and a strong commission by introducing Brandeis's cultivational option. They combined failed Democratic and Republican proposals by turning progressive instruments to populist ends. And they created a majority coalition in favor of the statute by crafting a law with multiple meanings. Section 5 declared unfair competition illegal and licensed the commission to issue cease-and-desist orders against it. For Brandeisians and populists, this meant the FTC was empowered to prevent monopoly and set the nation back on the path to republican equality. For progressives, it meant the commission was empowered to countervail economic power and cut a new path from drift to mastery. Thus, the statute passed not because it was clear victory for anyone, a mere compromise, or a "common carrier" that served multiple interests.[1] The Federal Trade Commission Act passed because it had quite specific, yet different, meanings for its supporters.

[1] Charles Lindblom, *The Intelligence of Democracy* (New York: The Free Press, 1965). For a recent application of the concept of a common carrier to institutional change in Congress, see Eric Shickler, *Disjointed Pluralism: Institutional Innovation and Development in the U.S. Congress* (Princeton, NJ: Princeton University Press, 2001). Adapting the idea of a common carrier, one could see the Federal Trade Commission Act as a "discursive common carrier."

This chapter recounts a constructivist history of the Federal Trade Commission Act, which shows how its path to success generated more possibilities and involved more creativity, deliberation, and storytelling than is usually recognized. Only months before Wilson signed the bill into law, Congress rejected a Democratic proposal for a weak (informational) commission and a progressive proposal for a strong (regulatory) commission. It looked as though legislation was doomed. But creative syncretists reopened legislative channels, combined earlier failures into new possibilities, and reinterpreted their work to colleagues through broad cultural narratives.

Among the alternatives not usually recognized was Brandeis's third way. Neither a weak nor a strong commission, the cultivational agency that Brandeis proposed would prevent monopolies by upgrading competition through a combination of positive and coercive instruments. Drawing on his work at the Interstate Commerce Commission, he proposed to empower a commission to implement performance benchmarking and monitor business trade agreements. Although Congress rejected Brandeis's proposals in their written form, his intervention helped redirect the legislative process. When the Democrats reconvened to consider their options, Brandeis's idea for a commission, empowered to prevent monopoly, took hold because it provided a means of forging an alliance between progressive Republicans and populist Democrats. Democratic legislators reappropriated a progressive regulatory technique to realize populist ends. They proposed to empower a federal trade commission to regulate "unfair competition." Where progressives had proposed this instrument to protect the weak from the strong, Democrats explained it as a means to prevent inequality in the first place.

If "unfair competition" had a double meaning in the House, it looked as though it had no meaning at all in the Senate. Populists from both parties attacked it as an empty signifier that capitulated to corporate power. Instead of recrafting the House bill to meet objections, creative senators explained the bill with multiple frames. In the House, creative syncretists legislated; in the Senate, they interpreted. Two senators took up a bipartisan effort to explain the Federal Trade Commission bill: Francis Newlands (D-NV) and Albert Cummins (R-IA). As if to address skeptics from across the aisle, Cummins set the commission within a populist narrative, whereas Newlands told a progressive story about power, expertise, and mastery. A commission empowered to check unfair competition, Cummins said, would prevent monopolies before they resulted in inequality. Although antitrust remained necessary to destabilize power once in place, the commission would rechannel the future to egalitarian ends. The same commission, Newlands said, would ratify economic power when it was efficient, but ensure the strong did not abuse their power to dominate weak rivals or unorganized consumers. Creative interpretation proved sufficiently convincing to forge a bipartisan majority in the Senate.

This chapter applies the theory of creative syncretism to the legislative history of the Federal Trade Commission Act in four sections. The first section describes the impasse. The second section explains Brandeis's third way. The third section recounts the story of legislative syncretism in the House and the Senate. And the fourth section evaluates the political nature of the outcome. I show how no one got everything they wanted, but, more important, both Brandeisians and progressives claimed victory. Looking back, the meaning of the Federal Trade Commission Act remained contested. I conclude by showing how a constructivist account of this statute differs from an institutional one.

IMPASSE

When antitrust reform finally reached the legislative agenda in 1914, progressive Republicans and populist Democrats retreated to habitual positions. Despite Brandeis's best efforts, it looked like the only options were enforced competition or regulated monopoly. Populist Democrats introduced legislation to reverse the rule of reason, define antitrust violations more clearly, and create a weak federal trade commission to support the legal process. Progressive Republicans introduced a bill to create a strong trade commission, empowered to supervise and control monopoly power. The debate fell into well-worn grooves, a majority remained elusive, and antitrust reform hit an impasse.

In 1914, the Democrats controlled both houses of Congress, and the presidency for the first time in a generation seized the initiative. Party populists promised to strengthen state power to enforce competition, reverse corporate power, and return the United States to the path of free markets and republican democracy. They introduced four bills. The first would have overturned the rule of reason by changing the language in the Sherman Act. Every effort to "carry out restrictions in trade or acquire a monopoly," limit production or raise prices to prevent competition, or to make any agreement to prevent "free and unrestricted competition" was declared unlawful.[2] The second was a "trade relations bill" that identified

[2] Scott James, *Presidents, Parties and the State: A Party Perspective on Democratic Regulatory Choice, 1884–1936* (Cambridge: Cambridge University Press, 2000), 172–73.

and made unlawful particular predatory methods of competition and restraints of trade, including holding companies, tying contracts, and price discrimination. The third bill outlawed interlocking directorates. The fourth created a weak interstate trade commission with power to gather and publicize information. It could investigate violations of antitrust laws on its own initiative or under the directive of the Department of Justice; it was empowered to subpoena witnesses and corporate financial records, and produce detailed reports for public distribution. But it had no regulatory or enforcement powers.[3] The definitions bill imposed stiff criminal sanctions for corporations and their officers convicted of violations: a fine not exceeding $5,000 or imprisonment not exceeding one year, or by both punishments, at the discretion of the court.[4] Together, these bills would enforce competition by clarifying the Sherman Act, augmenting the capacity of the state to prosecute with a weak commission, and increasing the cost of violating the law.

Broadly denounced, the Democrats' package failed. The House Judiciary Committee heard harsh criticism from business, professionals, trade associationalists, and Republicans and Democrats alike. Corporate leaders attacked rules against interlocking directorates and intercorporate shareholding in industry and banking. Representatives of small business associations (e.g., druggists, merchants, grocers) and large manufacturers criticized the strict prohibitions against trade agreements to limit production or regulate prices. Businesspeople of every stripe attacked the criminal sanctions. So common were the practices proscribed that vast numbers of their class would find themselves behind bars. The Democrats, they complained, proposed nothing less than a "straight jacket" on U.S. enterprise.[5]

[3] James, *Presidents, Parties and the State,* 171–75. A fifth bill, seen as part of the package, empowered the Interstate Commerce Commission to regulate railroad securities.

[4] Thomas K. McCraw, *Prophets of Regulation* (Cambridge, MA: Harvard University Press, 1984), 119.

[5] Gabriel Kolko, *The Triumph of Conservatism* (New York: The Free Press, 1963), 261–62; McCraw, *Prophets of Regulation,* 118–22; Robert Wiebe, *Businessmen and Reform: A Study of the Progressive Movement* (Chicago: Quadrangle Books, 1962), 137–39; James Morison Russell, "Business and the Sherman Act, 1890–1914" (PhD diss., University of Iowa, 1966), 207–21, 228–38. On opposition from small business, who wanted legalized trade agreements, see the statement by a Mississippi businessman, who says, "I respectfully submit that while Big Business is the alleged aim of these drastic laws, they hurt small business far more.... We may not combine to save costs, may not agree to desist from trying to take away markets from each other, may not agree to hold our goods for prices fairly remunerative.... Really we are being governed to our undoing"; quoted in Russell, "Business and Sherman Act," 208.

Progressives gave voice to the widespread frustration with the populist proposals. They tagged the bills as "radical" and "incompetent." Roosevelt's commissioner of corporations, Herbert Knox Smith, spoke for many when he attacked the Democrats as nostalgic and irrational. These were crude policies, he charged, which promised to turn the U.S. economy back to the "the blacksmith forge, the grist mill, and the cobbler's bench," when "unbridled, aggressive competition" reigned. It was an endeavor proved futile by the great merger wave. Break up combinations and they will return all over again. In the meantime, Americans will sacrifice "efficiency in business" and gain little in equality. The only alternative was a regulatory commission, with sufficient authority to harness corporate efficiency to public ends.[6]

Progressives were not alone; even Wilson's advisers criticized the legislation. Attorney General James McReynolds told the president that the definitions bill would be hung up in court for years. Brandeis condemned the House Democrats for their blind faith in competitive markets. These were "not Administration bills," he told the U.S. Chamber of Commerce. The president does not support "free and unrestricted competition": he has always advocated "regulated competition." By the middle of February 1915, even the president distanced himself from House Democrats, when he announced his opposition to changes in the Sherman Act and tagged the remaining bills as first "drafts."[7]

Enforced competition was dead. President Wilson assuaged business anxieties, and urged the House to drop the definitions bill, consolidate the prohibitions in a single bill, and initiate hearings on a new trade commission bill in another committee.

Once they had gained the ear of prominent Democrats, progressive Republicans introduced legislation of their own. Victor Murdock (R-KS) initiated three bills in the House to create a strong federal trade commission empowered to distinguish natural from artificial monopoly and regulate the former. The first created a trade commission with power to subpoena information from corporations with annual gross receipts over $3 million; compel uniform financial accounting methods; publicize incidences of overcapitalization, unfair competition, and credit abuse; and assist the courts in dissolving monopolies. The second protected weak firms from their more "powerful" rivals by empowering the commission to issue restraining orders

[6] Quoted in James, *Presidents, Parties and the State,* 173. See also James, 186.

[7] James, *Presidents, Parties and the State,* 179. Evans Johnson, *Oscar W. Underwood: A Political Biography* (Baton Rouge: Louisiana State University Press, 1980), 211–12.

against "unfair competition." And the third empowered the commission to distinguish between natural and artificial monopolies and to suggest legislation to regulate the former or alterations in corporate form to dissolve the latter. (The bill defined *natural* monopoly as control over natural resources, terminal or transportation facilities, financial resources, or "any other economies inherent in the character of the industry.")[8] Thus, the progressive initiative proposed a strong commission with substantial coercive power over corporate discretion.

Murdock's bills failed to gain traction in the House and it looked as though antitrust reform would remain mired in a well-worn groove. But the progressive proposals tipped congressional attention to a commission and altered the basket of resources for legislative syncretism. Brandeis joined the deliberation with a third way to build a modern state.

BRANDEIS'S THIRD WAY

In March 1914, the editors of the progressive magazine *Collier's* declared Americans had but two options: enforce competition and turn back the clock on economic progress, or accept corporate capitalism and empower a government commission to regulate it. Brandeis disagreed. There was a third way: regulate competition by creating a cultivational commission, with the capacity to nurture civic mindedness, economic prosperity, and collaborative learning. Brandeis explained the republican experimentalist ends of cultivational administration to the House Interstate Commerce Committee. He hoped his proposal would excite progressives and populists alike.

The uppermost goal of a trade commission, Brandeis said, should be to foster business practices that made prosecution and coercion unnecessary. Neither a weak agency devoted to gathering information, nor a strong one devoted to supervision and coercion, Brandeis's FTC would be first and foremost positive and prophylactic. It should "create conditions which will render less likely the existence of restraints of trade and monopolies," not merely "correct them when they are discovered," Brandeis told Congress.[9]

[8] Victor Murdock, Prog. Kan., House Debate, 63d Cong., 2d sess., May 21, 1914, *Cong. Rec.* 51, 8978–81, in Earl W. Kintner, ed., *The Legislative History of Federal Antitrust Laws and Related Statutes,* part I, vol. 5 (New York: Chelsea House, 1978), 3824–26; James, *Presidents, Parties and the State,* 174.

[9] U.S. Congress, House, Committee on Interstate and Foreign Commerce, *Hearings on Interstate Trade Commission,* 63d Cong., 2d sess., January 30–February 16, 1914 (Washington, DC: Government Printing Office, 1914), 8–9. Hereafter cited as *Adamson Committee.*

> The important thing ... is to prescribe systems and rules which will prevent breaches of the law and not punish breaches of law. Our aim should be, in the aid of business and in aid of the community, to make resort to criminal law as infrequent as possible; ... *not to instill fear, but to so develop the commercial conditions that crime becomes unnatural.*[10]

The commission should prize "aid" over "restriction," because "industrial crime is not a cause, it is an effect; the effect of a bad system."[11] All too often, habit rewarded opportunism or predation over advances in productivity, product quality, or service. An effective trade commission would redirect self-interest from predation to production; cultivate the conditions for economic progress; and organize collective inquiry, experimentation, and knowledge diffusion. Brandeis outlined two techniques to realize these ends: cost accounting and trade agreement monitoring.

Although Brandeis agreed with the progressive economists that accounting was vital to advancing efficiency and state capacity, he disagreed with them over what the purpose and nature of accounting should be. Whereas the economists hoped to resolve distributive conflict through publicly supervised financial accounting, Brandeis hoped to foster economic improvement and collaborative learning between firms and between business and government through cost accounting.

As we saw in the conflict over railroad regulation, progressives wanted to regulate corporate "stock watering." They believed that the more corporations issued securities without real investment, the greater the burden on consumer prices. The trusts were able to abuse their power over investors and consumers because financial transactions were opaque. Thus, a commission empowered to force corporations to adopt public accounting standards and disclose information to investors would check the tendency to stock watering (overcapitalization) and reduce the pressure on prices. Although this power was far less than the ICC's power to regulate prices according to a fair return on corporate value, progressives thought it went a good distance toward making corporations public and a federal trade commission a utility regulator.

Brandeis thought stock watering was a red herring, because it diverted policy makers from the more important problems of economic power

[10] *Adamson Committee*, 89–90, emphasis added.
[11] *Adamson Committee*, 9.

and improvement.[12] Solve the problem of predatory competition and corporations would lose their power to water stock, cheat investors, and fleece consumers. It was more important to redirect business administration from deceit and opportunism to engineering, invention, and incremental improvement. The most positive thing the commission could do in this regard was foster improvements in business cost accounting. Brandeis's experience with the railroads was instructive. The engineers also taught him that far too few manufacturers knew precisely "what an operation costs, ... why it costs that amount, and why it does not cost less."[13] In a democratic nation, Brandeis told Congress, it was appropriate for government to educate business in the best accounting methods and provide incentives to adopt them.[14]

In addition to setting cost accounting standards, Brandeis asked Congress to empower the commission to classify business into comparable sectors and set uniform methods for all businesses in those categories. Uniformity, Brandeis said, was the basis for a common language, which made comparison – or benchmarking – across firms possible. It was not enough for managers to learn why an operation does not cost less; they should also know whether "somebody else [can] do it for less." Once firms had adopted uniform methods, they could submit their data to the commission, which would calculate detailed average costs for each industry participating and publicize them in annual reports.[15]

[12] For Brandeis's views of stock watering, see U.S. Congress, Senate, Committee on Interstate Commerce, *Hearings on Control of Corporations, Persons, and Firms Engaged in Interstate Commerce*, 62d Cong., pt. 16, Pursuant to S. Res. 98, December 14–16, 1911 (Washington, DC: Government Printing Office, 1912), 1246–47, 1284–85. Hereafter cited as *Clapp Committee*. Brandeis's approach to accounting also differed dramatically from that of Taft Republicans, who advocated a commission with powers to gather and publicize financial information. Where the latter thought financial disclosure would result in better-informed market decisions, Brandeis thought benchmarking would provide management with information unavailable from within the market or the firm about how to improve. Where progressive goals were coercive, and Taft Republican goals libertarian, Brandeis's were cultivational.

[13] *Adamson Committee,* 15.

[14] *Adamson Committee,* 15–16, 98–99.

[15] *Adamson Committee,* 6–8, 15. Brandeis testified twice before the House Committee on Interstate Commerce. As his first discussion came to a close, the committee asked him to draft an accounting amendment to its bill. He returned the following week with a proposal to grant the commission "broad" powers to periodically "classify" corporations, prescribe as "nearly as possible, a uniform system of accounts," and compel members of those groups to submit "truthful" information to the commission. For a full reproduction of Brandeis's amendment, see *Adamson Committee,* 89.

The goal of benchmarking was to increase the pace of invention and improvement by providing firms with detailed information about how their performance compared with that of their competitors. Brandeis thought information one means to this end. But he also believed benchmarking would cultivate professional deliberation. Like medicine and law, where debate over public information "enlarged" "honorable" rivalry, Brandeis thought open discussion of industry benchmarks would upgrade competition. With the FTC's help, businesspeople would learn to "talk as freely about the details of advances in ... efficiency as physicians now talk about ... new discoveries in aid of health." The commission's role was cultivational, that is, using benchmarking as a means to foster professionalization.[16]

The second means to cultivational regulation was trade agreement monitoring. Brandeis recommended that all trade agreements be registered with the commission, but stopped short of calling for licensing agreements or providing immunity from antitrust prosecution. He thought government knew too little about trade agreements to go that far. Some agreements, such as the German steel cartel's production quotas, upgraded competition, whereas others, such as United Shoe Machinery's tying contracts, suppressed it. The commission should have power to monitor, supervise, and learn. Brandeis recommended that all parties to a trade agreement be required to submit it to the commission. Upon doing so, they would be relieved of criminal liability for making the agreement in the past or continuing it into the future, as long they as ended participation after proper notice from the Department of Justice or the commission that an agreement contravened the law. This provision gave the commission power to monitor trade agreements and business an incentive to be candid. Brandeis thought that, in time, the commission would learn how to refine its monitoring capacities and suggest new powers to Congress. Meanwhile, submission, monitoring, and deliberation would go some distance toward channeling trade agreements from suppressing to upgrading competition.[17]

[16] *Adamson Committee,* 8, 15. See also Brandeis's 1912 commencement address at Brown University, where Brandeis says Americans should encourage the tendency for business to become more and more like the professions, in Louis D. Brandeis, *Business – a Profession* (Boston: Small, Maynard & Co.: 1914), 1–12. Note how similar Brandeis's ideas about publicity were to the ideas of the associationalist Arthur Eddy. See also Brandeis, *Business – a Profession,* 3, where he says, "The old idea of a good bargain was a transaction in which one man got the better of another. The new idea of a good contract is a transaction which is good for both parties to it."

[17] See Louis D. Brandeis, "The Solution of the Trust Problem," *Harper's Weekly,* November 8, 1913, 19; and *Adamson Committee,* 5.

Brandeis's design for a cultivational federal trade commission transcended the debate between populists and progressives. The ends of benchmarking and trade agreement monitoring were neither coercive nor informational. Weaker than the progressives' blueprint for an agency modeled on the Interstate Commerce Commission, Brandeis's design did not include coercive control over corporate finance, unfair methods of competition, or the pricing practices of natural monopolies. Stronger than the progressives' model, Brandeis's commission did not take business power as it found it. Instead, it assumed that a democratically empowered state could shape business organization to republican ends. Far more ambitious than the populist proposal for a commission to support government litigation, Brandeis's design aimed to reshape business custom and competitive practice. Cultivational administration was not merely a compromise between a regulatory and an informational agency: it was a third way.

LEGISLATIVE SYNCRETISM

With enforced competition on the ropes, the Democrats faced a political challenge. How could they court progressives without alienating populists in their own party? How could they regulate without capitulating to corporate power? Brandeis's proposal hinted at the answer.[18] Creative Democrats noticed that a prophylactic, if not a cultivational, commission could turn progressive techniques to populist ends, and they reappropriated Victor Murdock's proposal to regulate unfair competition to prevent, rather than restrain, monopoly power. But populists and progressives continued to disagree over ends; creative politicians also accorded the proposal multiple meanings. They told progressives a commission empowered to regulate unfair competition would protect the weak from the strong. They told populists it would prevent power before it became invincible. If skeptics from both factions were convinced to support the Federal Trade Commission Act, it was not merely because it combined populist and progressive features. Nor was it because the bill was sufficiently vague for politicians to avoid rebuke from the voters. It was because they accorded the statute precise, yet multiple, meanings.

[18] Congress rejected Brandeis's benchmarking proposal in April 1914 and never considered his proposal for trade agreement monitoring. Nonetheless, in time it adopted softer versions of both. See Allyn A. Young, "The Sherman Act and the New Antitrust Legislation: II," *Journal of Political Economy* 23, no. 4 (April 1915): 313; Kintner, *Legislative History of Federal Antitrust Laws,* part I, vol. 5, 3856–57.

This involved legislative syncretism in the House and creative interpretation in the Senate.

Creative Combination in the House

President Wilson took up the cause of syncretism during the summer of 1914, when he told Senator Henry Hollis (D-NH) the Democrats could secure a real advantage in the fall elections if they succeeded in forging a "combination of" populist and progressive "measures" in a single trade commission bill.[19] Brandeis agreed. The time was ripe to forge an alliance between "progressive Democrats" and "near Democrats."[20] Wilson enlisted party leaders to "facilitate" the "merger": James Covington (D-MD) and Raymond Stevens (D-NH) in the House and Francis Newlands in the Senate. He also asked Brandeis to assist drafting a bill that "harmonized" progressive and populist "principles and methods."[21] Preoccupied with railroad regulation, Brandeis sent his trusted colleague George Rublee instead. (Brandeis and Rublee had formed a close relationship during the "Pinchot-Ballinger" controversy over conservation and corruption at the Department of the Interior.)[22]

Working closely with Representative Stevens, Rublee proposed to reappropriate progressive means to populist ends. He had considered a variety of compromises to soften progressive regulatory measures, but each one seemed to undermine progressive commitments and populist goals. Instead, drawing on Victor Murdock's failed proposal, Section 5 of the Stevens bill declared unfair competition illegal and licensed the commission to issue cease-and-desist orders against it. It also included a weak version of Brandeis's benchmarking proposal, which empowered the FTC to classify business into comparable categories, establish standards for gathering information appropriate to those categories, and publicize such information when it was necessary to achieve the broader goals of the statute.[23]

[19] Quoted in James, *Presidents, Parties and the State*, 187.

[20] See Philippa Strum, *Louis D. Brandeis: Justice for the People* (Cambridge, MA: Harvard University Press, 1984), 211.

[21] *Congressional Record 51*, 63d Cong., 2d sess., 1914, pt. 13, 1286, quoted in James, 188; Francis Newlands Papers, Yale University, Letter Essay, Box 90, undated, page 7.

[22] See McCraw, *Prophets of Regulation*, 122–25; Strum, *Louis D. Brandeis*, 132–39; Mason, *Brandeis*, 255–82; George Rublee, "The Original Plan and Early History of the Federal Trade Commission," *Proceedings of the Academy of Political Science* 11, no. 4 (January 1926): 115.

[23] Rublee, "The Original Plan"; Marc Winerman, "The Origins of the FTC," *Antitrust Law Journal* 71 (2003): 62–68.

In June 1914, Rublee and Stevens assured President Wilson their proposal was a Democratic bill, whose goal was to prevent monopolies before they became invincible. In a dramatic reinterpretation of the Democrats' "New Freedom" platform from the election of 1912, Stevens said his bill fulfilled his party's promise to "regulate competition." Gone was the party's commitment to enforced competition: Democrats, Stevens said, have long known that "unregulated competition" always results in monopoly. Had the prophylactic commission been in place in 1890, Rublee added, it would have "frustrated" the trusts's "astonishingly successful" efforts to destroy competition. The Democratic idea, Stevens told his colleagues in Congress, is to destroy existing monopolies by supplementing the Sherman Act with a definitions bill and to prevent them in "the future" by empowering the federal trade commission to ensure "fair competition."[24] This was not a progressive bill. It reappropriated progressive techniques to Democratic ends.

Though initially cautious about coercive commission powers, Brandeis was pleased with the Stevens bill. He came to believe a coercive FTC was necessary to keep up with innovative predators. He was also pleased with the bill's deliberative features.

As Rublee explained, the commission's coercive powers were intended only for the "pirates of business," not the many instances where unfair methods of competition had become custom, which firms were unwilling to abandon for fear of losing a competitive advantage. Section 5 provided a deliberative procedure to discover and reconfigure destructive customs. It required the commission to review competitive methods with industry representatives before initiating a formal hearing to consider a cease-and-desist order. This provided competitors with ample opportunity to devise a collective alternative to unfair customs acceptable to the commission. Like Brandeis's proposal for trade agreement monitoring, Rublee's procedure gave business an incentive to forge agreements to upgrade competition and share them with the commission.[25]

[24] Although there is no transcript of the meeting, Rublee forwarded Wilson a detailed memo outlining their logic through Secretary of the Interior Franklin Lane. See Franklin Lane to Woodrow Wilson, July 10, 1914; and "Memorandum Concerning Section 5 of the Bill to Create a Federal Trade Commission," in *Woodrow Wilson Papers,* Microfilm, Series II, Reel 60, 5, U.S. Library of Congress. On Stevens's presentation to the House, see *Report of the House Committee on Interstate and Foreign Commerce (Minority Views),* HR 533, pt. 2, 63d Cong., 2d sess. April 20, 1914, in Kintner, *Legislative History,* part I, vol. 5, 3763–64.

[25] Rublee reported that the U.S. Chamber of Commerce, which would work closely with trade associations and the FTC to regulate competition through trade agreements, had heartily endorsed Section 5. Strum, *Louis D. Brandeis,* 215; Melvyn I. Urofsky, "Wilson, Brandeis and the Trust Issue, 1912–1914," *Mid-America* 49, no. 1 (January

Wilson was also enthusiastic about the Stevens bill. He told reluctant populists in his party that it was a "wise" and "feasible" combination of progressive and Democratic proposals. It empowered the commission to "regulate competition without making terms with monopoly." As such, it compromised with progressive technique, but did not waver from Democratic ends.[26]

When he was not preoccupied with his ailing wife or the war in Europe, Wilson lobbied for the Stevens bill during the summer of 1914. He defended it from critics who thought Section 5 too vague, too regulatory, or too deferent to business. He also enlisted Brandeis to lobby the Senate, where it looked like the Stevens bill would run aground.[27] If the Democrats were to complete the president's New Freedom before the midterm elections in the fall, Democratic senators had their work cut out for them. Their challenge, it turned out, was less legislative than interpretive.

Creative Interpretation in the Senate

When Democratic and Republican senators alike attacked the Stevens bill, creative legislators assuaged their worries and enlisted support by reinterpreting its provisions to populists and progressives. Francis Newlands, who managed the legislative process for the Democrats, reached across the aisle to progressive Republican Albert Cummins for help. Together, they amended the bill to meet objections by clarifying the relationship between FTC actions and antitrust prosecutions. But compromise, alone, failed to assuage the critics. And so, as if to speak to opponents across the aisle, Newlands told Republican progressives this was a bill to regulate monopoly, whereas Cummins told Democrats it was a bill to prevent it. By conferring two very different meanings to "unfair competition," they convinced enough skeptics to forge a majority.

1967): 25–28; Rublee, "The Original Plan;" McCraw, *Prophets of Regulation*, 122–25.

[26] WW to Rep. William C. Adamson, August 5, 1914. Woodrow Wilson Papers, Microfilm, Series III, Reel 138.

[27] Strum, *Louis D. Brandeis*, 215; Arthur S. Link, *Wilson: The New Freedom* (Princeton, NJ: Princeton University Press, 1956), 437–439. See also WW to Senator Charles Culberson, July 30, 1914, Wilson Papers, Microfilm, Series III, Reel 138, where Wilson expresses "very grave doubt" as to the advisability of attempting to define "unfair competition." Like "fraud," the term has ample meaning at law. It is "elasticity without real indefiniteness, so that we may adjust our regulation to actual conditions, local as well as national."

William Borah (R-ID) led the attack on the Senate version of the Stevens bill. Opening with a long quotation from William Jennings Bryan on the evils of monopoly, Borah charged the Democrats with duplicity. The bill would "dull the edge" of antitrust and undermine public confidence in the state's capacity to "destroy monopoly." The Democrats had abandoned all principle. Instead of clarifying antitrust after the *Standard Oil* decision, they offered the American people a hollow law. "Unfair competition" was an empty signifier, Borah complained, readily manipulated by powerful corporations. Five commissioners would be powerless against the trusts, who had amply proved their capacity to manipulate the law to their advantage. The trade commission would "shelter," not "destroy," the great combinations that threatened democracy.[28] Borah's attack was seconded by Moses Clapp and Knute Nelson (both R-MN), Thomas Sterling (R-SD), James Reed (D-MO), J. Hamilton Lewis (D-IL), John Shields (D-TN), Charles Thomas (D-CO), and Duncan Fletcher (D-FL). Newlands's bill, they said, did little to assuage their worries.[29]

Newlands and Cummins listened carefully to their critics. Drawing on Rublee's legal research, they explained the meaning of "unfair competition" in antitrust and common law. The FTC would have no more difficulty applying it than the courts or the Department of Justice, they assured their colleagues. They also added an amendment that severed the relationship between FTC decisions and antitrust. The commission would not undermine the government's ability to dissolve monopoly through antitrust. Its powers were "supplemental."

But accommodation and compromise were not enough. The senators continued to debate the meaning of Section 5 and the purposes of the Federal Trade Commission. Newlands responded patiently to progressive concerns about economic regression. He assured Republican progressives that the commission was intended to regulate, not destroy, large corporations. Cummins responded patiently to populist concerns about economic power. He assured them that the FTC was meant to prevent

[28] See Senate debate, 63d Cong., 2d sess, June 27, 1914, in Kintner, *Legislative History*, part I, vol. 5, 4007–25. See also Winerman, "Origins of the FTC," 73.

[29] Kintner, *Legislative History*, part I, vol. 5, 4026–30, 4129–31, 4200–3, 4259, 4334–41, 4410–12, 4471–72, 4497–4502, 4560–61. Conservative Republicans charged the opposite. The vagueness of Section 5 would result in a commission of "snoopers and spotters," who would undermine competition prosperity. See, for example, the speeches by Lippitt (Rhode Island) and Brandegee (Connecticut) in Kintner, *Legislative History of Antitrust Law*, part I, vol. 5, 4171. On the "strange coalition of conservative and radical" critics of the Stevens bill in the Senate, more generally, see Link, *Wilson: The New Freedom*, 438–39.

corporate power before it undermined economic initiative and democracy. Together, they turned the Federal Trade Commission Act into a law with multiple, yet precise, meanings.

Newlands assured progressives that his bill did not "wish to destroy" these "enormous corporations," it only meant to regulate them. "Large aggregations of wealth in the corporate form" are inevitable, efficient, and valuable. They also have constitutional rights that Congress must respect. The trouble was, once in place, great corporations were tempted to abuse their power over consumers and weaker competitors. There were only two solutions: either you "break up great combinations of capital" and "forbid" corporate organization, or you "disarm monopoly" so the "powerful cannot destroy the weak." Thirty years of experience with antitrust and railroad regulation revealed that only the second option was a viable one. Although antitrust failed to prevent corporate combination, the ICC learned to tame railroad power. Railroad regulation was an excellent model for the FTC.[30]

When Congress created the Interstate Commerce Commission in 1887, Newlands said, it placed the state between powerful railroads and weak shippers. Now Congress must act again to countervail economic with state power and create an agency with the capacity to protect small business from powerful corporations. Newlands proceeded with the analogy. In 1887, Congress recognized the need for broad powers, so it licensed the ICC to regulate unfair "rate discrimination" – a term that had plain legal meaning. Today, we recognize that the Federal Trade Commission must have equally broad powers. Thus, it is necessary to license it to regulate "unfair competition" – another term with a clear and durable legal meaning. When "large corporations" use predatory "practices for the purpose of destroying their pygmy competitors," Newlands told his critics, this was "unfair competition." To be sure, every time Congress attempted to augment the ICC's powers, it raised controversy. But having done so, "almost every transportation question has been settled." Newlands admitted that the Federal Trade Commission bill was "imperfect" and Congress would have to amend its powers down the line. But it was a good start and, with time and experience, it would protect the weak from the strong.[31]

[30] For another account of Newlands, see Winerman, "Origins of the FTC," 76–79.

[31] Kintner, *Legislative History*, part I, vol. 5, 3960, 4012–13, 4092–93. On protecting the weak from the strong, see also Kintner, *Legislative History*, part I, vol. 5, 4096, 4127. On railroad regulation, see Kintner, *Legislative History*, part I, vol. 5, 4012–13. Note

Meanwhile, Cummins took a different tack to explaining Newlands's bill. Monopoly, he said, was not inevitable. Section 5 was designed to prevent it. Railroad regulation was not a good model. The bill under consideration would create a prophylactic, not a countervailing, commission.[32]

Americans, Cummins said, should not accept on "economic faith" the principle that "great corporations" can produce goods more cheaply than "small concerns." We still do not know whether the trusts would have amassed so much power had they been unable to employ unfair methods of competition. Think of Section 5 as an experiment, Cummins told the Senate. It licensed the state to arbitrate the debate over scale economies by precluding predatory means to bigness. Antitrust proved unable to resolve the debate, because it could only reach unreasonable "restraints of trade" once they were in place. To be sure, Cummins made his own hypothesis clear. Had Congress created a commission to prevent unfair competition in 1890, "we would not be plagued with the great combinations, the monopolistic aggregations of which we are now complaining." History demonstrated the necessity to "seize the offender before his ravages" destroyed competition and democracy.[33]

"My friend from Nevada" [Newlands] was wrong about the ICC, Cummins added. It is a poor model for the trade commission. Railroads are common carriers, and are obliged to serve all shippers equally. Therefore, it was appropriate for Congress to regulate "public commerce" by licensing a commission to protect weak shippers from powerful railroad corporations. The FTC, by contrast, is designed to reshape "private commerce," by setting and enforcing rules of fair competition. Its goal is to prevent, not regulate, monopoly. Therefore, it necessitated different powers.[34]

Thus, as Newlands assured his colleagues that monopoly was inevitable, Cummins assured them that it was not. Newlands explained Section 5 as a countervailing power to protect the weak from the strong, whereas Cummins explained it as a prophylactic power to prevent inequality in the first place. Newlands, the Democrat, told Republican progressives

also how Oregon Democrat Harry Lane joins Newlands in his assessment that it is impossible to turn back the clock on consolidation. In this sense, Lane, like Newlands, confounds his party and sectional status. See Elizabeth Sanders, *Roots of Reform: Farmers, Workers, and the American State, 1877–1917* (Chicago: University of Chicago Press, 1999): 480–n72.

32 On Cummins, see also Winerman, "Origins of the FTC," 81–88.

33 Kintner, *Legislative History,* part I, vol. 5, 4237–38, 4467. Cummins was joined by New Hampshire Democrat Henry Hollis who also defended Section 5 as a progressive means to a Democratic end. See Kintner, *Legislative History,* part I, vol. 5, 4131–49.

34 Kintner, *Legislative History,* part I, vol. 5, 4256–57.

the bill was theirs. Cummins, the Republican, told populist Democrats it was theirs. Together, they turned the Federal Trade Commission bill into a text with multiple, yet precise, meanings.

On August 5, 1914, the Senate passed the Act to Create a Trade Commission, 63 in favor and 16 opposed (27 not voting). Twelve Republicans voted for the bill, 14 voted against.[35] Enacted with Section 5 intact, the statute declared unfair competition in commerce unlawful and empowered the commission to issue cease-and-desist orders when it detected such practices. All commission orders could be appealed in U.S. District Court, which could review matters of law, not fact. The law also licensed the commission to gather and compile information; to periodically classify corporations at its own discretion, and make rules and regulations with reference to classified groups in order to carry out the act; to investigate potential antitrust or trade violations on its own initiative or the initiative of Congress or the president; and to publicize all information deemed in the public interest. It also included Cummins's amendment ensuring that FTC actions and powers would not prevent or interfere with the enforcement of other antitrust laws.[36]

The Federal Trade Commission Act

The Senate forwarded its trade commission bill to a conference committee, where the House changed the wording of Section 5 to unfair "methods" of competition and left the commission's regulatory powers intact. House conferees agreed to Cummins's amendment on judicial review, but added a clause that sent all trade commission cases directly to circuit court to save time and minimize conflicting decisions in lower, district courts. The conference committee also added a provision that permitted the commission to refuse to investigate alleged unfair methods of competition if it appeared the public good would not be served. There was little disagreement over the commission's powers of investigation, because House and Senate bills were roughly the same on this issue.[37]

On September 26, 1914, Woodrow Wilson signed the Federal Trade Commission Act into law. The statute created an agency with five commissioners, appointed by the president with the advice and consent of the

[35] Young, "The Sherman Act," 316; Kintner, *Legislative History,* part I, vol. 5, 4678–79; Link, *Wilson,* 440–41.

[36] Young, "The Sherman Act," 315; Kintner, *Legislative History,* part I, vol. 5, 4680–86.

[37] Young, "The Sherman Act," 316; Link, *Wilson,* 441–42.

Senate. No more than three commissioners were to come from the same party. Section 5 read "unfair methods of competition in commerce are hereby declared unlawful." It empowered the commission, upon a full airing of its charges at a hearing, to issue a cease-and-desist order against an unfair method of competition in the event it was found unlawful. The commission was also granted broad powers to investigate alleged antitrust violations at the request of the president, the attorney general, and Congress or on its own initiative. It was empowered to require, by general or special order, corporations to file with the commission in such form as the commission may prescribe annual or special reports. It was also licensed to "classify corporations and to make rules and regulations for the purpose of carrying out the provisions of [the] Act"; to publicize information (except trade secrets and customers); to monitor corporations, subject to judicial antitrust decrees; to require information by subpoena; and to impose penalties on corporations or persons failing to provide information or providing untruthful information.[38]

STRATEGIC AMBIGUITIES OF REFORM

Who got what from the antitrust reforms of 1914? Progressives got a regulatory commission, empowered to regulate unfair methods of competition. In addition to a commission empowered to gather and publicize information, populist Democrats got the Clayton Act, which outlawed specific violations of antitrust law, such as interlocking directorates and tying contracts. Gone, however, was the progressive inclination to public utility regulation. The commission had no authority to distinguish natural from artificial monopolies or to regulate securities or prices when they found the former. Also gone was the populist proposal to reverse the rule of reason by amending the Sherman Act. Brandeis also got some of what he wanted from the 1914 legislation. Ever since the *Standard Oil* decision, he had advocated a law to clarify the rule of reason by outlawing particularly pernicious restraints, such as tying contracts, interlocking directorates, and predatory pricing. Though weaker than the legislation Brandeis drafted for Senator LaFollette in 1911, the Clayton Act realized most of these goals.

Although Congress rejected Brandeis's proposals for benchmarking and trade agreement monitoring, it granted the commission a number of general powers appropriate to cultivational administration. The

[38] *Federal Trade Commission Act*, September 26, 1914, ch. 311, 38 stat. 717.

commission was licensed, at its discretion, to require "uniform reporting and public business information, classify corporations, and write rules and regulations for the purpose of carrying out the act." Whether the agency turned these broad powers to cultivational techniques (e.g., performance benchmarking and monitoring trade agreements) remained to be seen.

Posing the material question – *who got what?* – provides a partial and, in one sense, misleading evaluation of the antitrust reforms of 1914. It assumes that one can evaluate the outcome by matching the instruments in first proposals against the provisions enacted into law. But the meaning of those instruments changed during the legislative process. Therefore, it is necessary to ask the following constructivist question: Who *thought* they got what? It reveals a very different answer, because both progressives and Democrats claimed victory. Like Cummins and Newlands in the Senate, they interpreted the Federal Trade Commission Act through different frames. Progressives maintained that the Democrats succumbed to their pressure. Cowed by charges of economic mismanagement, the Democrats feared losing their fragile majority in the midterm elections. Bryan populists not only abandoned their efforts to reverse the rule of reason, they also reluctantly accepted a regulatory commission. As the leading progressive intellectual, Roosevelt adviser, and editor of the *New Republic*, Herbert Croly, wrote, "The Trade Commission Act represents a totally different approach [from the Democratic program], a spirit strangely contradictory to the campaign theories of the President.... It seems to contradict every principle of the party which enacted it" and to embody the principles and proposals long advocated by Theodore Roosevelt and the Progressive Party.[39] Satisfied that Congress had created a regulatory commission sufficiently powerful to control monopoly power, Croly believed a tenacious vanguard wore down its opposition.

But Wilson claimed victory for the Democrats. These laws, he wrote, "kill monopoly in the seed." Before them, it was possible to fragment power once formed. "But there was no law to check the process [by which it was formed] ... until the tree was full grown and its fruit developed." We have seen the power of monopoly exhibited, Wilson went on,

[39] Quoted in Scott C. James, "Building a Democratic Majority: The Progressive Party Vote and the Federal Trade Commission," *Studies in American Political Development* 9, no. 2 (Fall 1995): 331. For Croly's critique of antimonopolism and proposal to repeal the Sherman Act, see Herbert Croly, *The Promise of American Life* (Cambridge, MA: Harvard University Press, 1965 [1909]), 343–81.

and we know it is "more apt to control government than be controlled by it." With this legislation, the Democrats repeated their commitment to freedom: "we will not consent that an ungovernable giant should be reared to full stature in the very household of government itself." The New Freedom had been realized.[40]

Looking back in 1921, Brandeis agreed:

> [In 1914] there was general agreement that further legislation was desirable. But there was a clear division of opinion as to what its character should be. Many believed that concentration ... was inevitable and desirable; and these desired that concentration should be recognized by law and be regulated. Others believed that concentration was a source of evil; that existing combinations could be disintegrated, if only the judicial machinery were perfected; and that further concentration could be averted by providing additional remedies, and particularly through regulating competition. The latter view prevailed in the Sixty-Third Congress.... The Federal Trade Commission Act created an administrative tribunal, largely with a view to regulating competition.[41]

Both sides took credit for the antitrust reforms of 1914. Like Cummins and Newlands in the Senate, Brandeis and Croly claimed victory for regulated monopoly and regulated competition. Rublee and Stevens forged a successful coalition with the general term "unfair competition" not because it compromised earlier proposals or let strategic legislators off the hook with voters, but because it had precise, if very different, meaning for the factions supporting it.

CONCLUSION

The birth of the Federal Trade Commission was a triply creative act. It transcended the debate between a weak and a strong commission by opening the field to cultivational and prophylactic options. It combined failed proposals by turning progressive means to populist ends. And its sponsors interpreted the law through multiple frames. Moreover, although the legislative process eliminated one option (enforced competition), it did not resolve the struggle over capitalism and regulation. It did, however, alter the terrain on which that contest took place and the

40 WW to Oscar Wilder Underwood, October 17, 1914, Link, ed., *The Papers of Woodrow Wilson,* vol. 31, 168–74. Link notes that this letter was published widely during the campaign of 1914. See 174n1.

41 See Brandeis's dissenting opinion in Federal Trade Commission v. Graz et al., 253 U.S. 421 at 433, 1920.

resources creative actors brought to it. The Federal Trade Commission Act licensed multiple projects and created new debates.

Institutionalists have missed Brandeis's third way and the discursive ambiguity of the Federal Trade Commission Act. Instead, they recount a struggle between advocates of a weak commission and a strong commission and debate who won what and why. For Elizabeth Sanders, the Federal Trade Commission Act was a compromise between sectional economic interests.[42] For Martin Sklar, it was a victory for the corporate liberals, who outflanked progressives by forging an intraclass compromise between big business and small.[43] For Scott James, it was partisan compromise, in which Democrats maintained power in return for abandoning their principles and Republican progressives exploited their electoral leverage to gain a regulatory commission.[44] This chapter draws liberally from their insights. The Federal Trade Commission Act was stronger than populists from the periphery initially wanted and weaker than northeastern progressives thought it should be. It empowered Democrats by portending the New Deal alliance between Democratic populists and Republican progressives. And, instead of empowering the FTC to regulate corporations (e.g., public utilities) as many progressives wanted, it left price and securities regulation to the market.

But the Federal Trade Commission Act was not a mere compromise between interests, whether considered in class, sectional, or partisan terms. Its ambiguities were intentional and they necessitated interpretation. Creative legislators told their colleagues different stories about how the trade commission would redirect a gloomy past into a hopeful future. And looking back on the commission's birth, creative actors reinterpreted the gift of legislation differently. The Federal Trade Commission Act is better seen as an act of creative syncretism than a sectional, class, or party compromise. It decomposed technical principles and cultural tropes and recombined them in a statute with multiple meanings. Legislators gazed on the words "unfair methods of competition" and saw actions with various intentions and consequences. The trade commission law turned out to be sufficiently meaningful to legislators, who narrated corporate capitalism differently, to make a law.

[42] Sanders, *Roots of Reform.*

[43] Martin J. Sklar, *The Corporate Reconstruction of American Capitalism, 1890–1916* (Cambridge: Cambridge University Press, 1988).

[44] Scott, *Presidents, Parties and the State.*

The Federal Trade Commission Act did not resolve the debate over corporate capitalism or regulation, as some have argued.[45] Neither, as others have written, was it "stillborn" in confusion.[46] Instead, it provided fresh resources to actors with diverse ideas and intentions. Creative syncretists inside of the trade commission seized those resources for multiple projects, among them cultivational administration. The next chapter recounts their story. Creative syncretists outside the commission seized those resources for multiple projects, among them regulated competition. Subsequent chapters tell their story. But, neither cultivational administration at the FTC nor regulated competition in the economy ever became completely secure. As Chapter 8 will show, the dispute over multiple meanings endured.

[45] Sklar, *Corporate Reconstruction of American Capitalism;* James, *Presidents, Parties and the State.*

[46] McCraw, *Prophets of Regulation.*

PART II

REGULATED COMPETITION IN PRACTICE

Chapter 5

Cultivational Governance at the Federal Trade Commission

Between 1915 and 1932, creative syncretists at the Federal Trade Commission were remarkably successful in realizing Brandeis's proposal for cultivational governance. While they lacked the capacity to carry out cost accounting or to monitor trade agreements on their own, they found resources in civil society to construct institutions devoted to regulated competition. Deliberating regularly with cost accountants, trade associations, and the U.S. Chamber of Commerce, creative administrators renarrated the causes of cutthroat competition. Like Brandeis's engineers, they hypothesized that it was the result of cost conventions that overvalued volume. By doing so, they opened new avenues to policy experimentation and institutional design. They launched a Cost Division, published two cost accounting manuals, encouraged trade associations to design cost systems of their own, and assembled industries in deliberative conferences. Building on these initiatives, creative administrators reconceptualized the commission's role in steering competition from predation to improvement. By 1926, they had institutionalized a deliberative structure for defining standards of fair competition and reviewing associational cost accounting initiatives. In doing so, creative syncretists invented a novel form of regulatory organization, which proved effective in collaborating with professional and business associations to respond effectively to economic uncertainty, diversity, and change.

Students of state building in the 1920s do not usually recognize policy innovation at the FTC, because they see the commission's formative context as inhospitable to autonomy and policy planning. A vague mandate, meager resources, judicial meddling, internal conflict, fragmented organization, diverse objects of regulation, and intimate ties to industry conspired to undermine bureaucratic autonomy and capacity. The FTC is not unique in the institutionalist narrative. Like the ICC before it, the trade commission came late to a field crowded with corporations, a jealous judiciary, and a legislature beholden to patronage parties. Early experiments in federal regulation were not especially successful in the United States.

But institutionalists conflate explanations of the impossible with the possible. Although the conditions for Weberian bureaucracy were absent at the FTC, the result was not "confusion," "stillbirth," "incongruous layers" of authority, or "ad hocracy" – an agency, that is, incapable of setting or realizing policy goals. Institutionalists underestimate the diversity of possibilities, the creativity of U.S. state builders, and the resources available for non-Weberian forms of governance.[1]

Some federal trade commissioners found resources where institutionalists see only constraints. From the commissioners' point of view, a contested mandate provided the opportunity for debate, mobilization, and policy experimentation. Meager funding and ties to civil society provided the opportunity to cultivate learning and standard setting capacities in professional, peak business, and trade associations – what political theorists Joshua Cohen and Charles Sabel call "directly-deliberative polyarchy."[2] And diversity in the objects of regulation provided a wide range of experiences from which to compare and learn.

But opportunity and resources do not constitute action for a new agency. It is not enough, as institutionalists suggest, to understand the

[1] On the Weberian features of the modern state, see Theda Skocpol, "Bringing the State Back In," in Theda Skocpol, Peter Evans, and Dietrich Reuschemeyer, eds., *Bringing the State Back In* (New York: Cambridge University Press, 1985); Richard Franklin Bensel, *Yankee Leviathan: The Origins of Central State Authority in America, 1859–1877* (Cambridge: Cambridge University Press), 106–16; Karen Orren and Steven Skowronek, *The Search for American Political Development* (Cambridge: Cambridge University Press, 2005), 177; Daniel P. Carpenter, *The Forging of Bureaucratic Autonomy* (Princeton, NJ: Princeton University Press, 2001), 18–25; Marc Allen Eisner, *From Warfare State to Welfare State* (State College: University of Pennsylvania Press, 2000), 2, 7, 12, 27–30, 37, 41. On the absence of those features in the FTC in particular and the U.S. state more generally, see Carpenter, *Forging*, 7–11; Theodore Lowi, *The End of Liberalism: The Second Republic of the United States* (New York: Norton, 1979), 97, 101, 111–12; Kenneth Finegold and Theda Skocpol, *State and Party in America's New Deal* (Madison: University of Wisconsin Press, 1995), 53–57; Thomas K. McCraw, *Prophets of Regulation* (Cambridge, MA: Harvard University Press, 1984), 81, 125–28; Thomas Lane Moore III, "The Establishment of a 'New Freedom' Policy: The Federal Trade Commission, 1912–1918" (PhD diss., University of Illinois, 1980).

[2] See Joshua Cohen and Charles Sabel, "Directly-Deliberative Polyarchy," *European Law Journal*, 3: 4 (December 1997): 313–42.

structural conditions into which the FTC was born to make sense of its actions. In a constructivist account, such conditions and resources always necessitate active interpretation, experimentation, and institutional design. Viewed from the perspective of republican experimentalism, reflexive state builders at the FTC turned the background conditions hostile to Weberian bureaucracy into the raw materials for cultivational governance.

To be sure, institutionalists have recognized examples of cultivational governance as a weak substitute for administrative autonomy. Given the weakness of commission government, this story goes, the state had little choice but to work through associations in World War I and the 1920s.[3] But the "associative state" was too weak, incoherent, and unsustainable to solve the fundamental economic problem of the era: overcapacity. As much as the FTC tried, it was unable to enforce association agreements or make them accountable, because it lacked credentialed professionals, monitoring capacity, corporate culture, hierarchical organization, and autonomy from industry.

This chapter shows how creative administrators at the FTC valued different ends and organizational resources. Instead of trying to regulate overcapacity, they attempted to reconfigure destructive habits and open alternative paths to profit and productivity. Instead of Weberian features, they valued porous boundaries between state and society, economically embedded professionals, an argumentative culture, learning by benchmarking, and what sociologist David Stark calls "heterarchical organization." Where

[3] The pioneering works on associationalism in World War I and 1920s are Robert Cuff, *The War Industries Board; Business-Government Relations during World War I* (Baltimore: Johns Hopkins University Press, 1973); Robert F. Himmelberg, *The Origins of the National Recovery Administration: Business, Government and the Trade Association Issue, 1921–1933* (New York: Fordham University Press, 1976); and Ellis W. Hawley, "Herbert Hoover and American Corporatism, 1929–1933," in Martin L. Fausold and George T. Mazuzan, eds., *The Hoover Presidency: A Reappraisal* (Albany: State University of New York Press, 1974), 101–19; Ellis W. Hawley, "Herbert Hoover, the Commerce Secretariat, and the Vision of an 'Associative State,' 1921–1928," *Journal of American History* 61 (1974): 116–40; Ellis W. Hawley, "Three Facets of Hooverian Associationalism: Lumber, Aviation, and Movies, 1921–1930," in Thomas K. McCraw, ed., *Regulation in Perspective* (Cambridge, MA: Harvard Business School Press, 1981). Building on their work, a more recent group of political scientists and historians interprets business associationalism in the 1920s as a weak substitute for a strong state linked to corporatist organizations. See, for example, Colin Gordon, *New Deals: Business, Labor, and Politics in America, 1920–1935* (Cambridge: Cambridge University Press, 1994), 5–86, 128–65; Mark Allen Eisner, *From Warfare State to Welfare State* (University Park: Pennsylvania State University Press, 2000), 89–138; Finegold and Skocpol, *State and Party in America's New Deal*, 4–12, 92–103.

Weberian bureaucracy differentiated functions among divisions and integrated their tasks through hierarchical management, the heterarchical FTC multiplied functions within divisions, encouraged interdependence and lateral communication between departments, and engaged top managers in policy implementation. Bureaucratic hierarchies assume clear goals, a limited range of means, and relatively homogeneous objects of regulation, whereas the FTC turned general goals, imprecise means, and diverse objects of regulation into assets by creating an organization that valued experimentation, dialogue, and collaborative learning.[4]

This chapter tells the story of cultivational governance at the FTC through a matrix of programs and people. I focus on two programs – cost accounting and trade practice conferences – and three commissioners: Edward Hurley, Nelson Gaskill, and William Humphrey. Together, Hurley, Gaskill, and Humphrey realized much in Brandeis's proposal for cultivational governance. These commissioners enlisted allies to cultivational governance by actively reinterpreting the FTC's possibilities in the history of antitrust. Like Brandeis, they explained how state-sponsored cost accounting could channel rivalry from destructive pricing to incremental improvements in products and production processes. Once they enlisted the support of trade associations, cost accountants, and the U.S. Chamber of Commerce, they established an institutional infrastructure to make regulated competition possible. Under Hurley's guidance, the FTC created a model cost system, enlisted trade associations to cost work and benchmarking services, and reviewed association cost systems for approval. Under Gaskill's guidance, the FTC's trade practice conference program deepened Hurley's efforts to link the FTC to organizations in civil society. And under Humphrey's guidance, the FTC combined cost accounting and trade practice conferences in a new division.

POLICY INNOVATION IN A CONSTITUENCY COMMISSION

In 1915, Wilson yielded to the many factions who claimed victory in the Federal Trade Commission Act and appointed a constituency commission.[5] For progressives, he named Will Parry and Brandeis's ally George

4 David Stark, "Heterarchy: Distributing Authority and Organizing Diversity," in John H. Clippinger Jr., ed., *The Biology of Business* (San Francisco: Josey-Bass, 1999), 153–80.

5 I adapt the term "constituency commission" from Lowi's concept "constituent party." Theodore Lowi, "Party, Policy and Constitution in America," in William Nisbet and

Rublee. For southern Democrats, he named Georgia politician William Harris, who would use the position as a stepping-stone to the Senate. For business, Wilson appointed a successful Chicago entrepreneur and head of the Illinois Manufacturers' Association, Edward Hurley. And for professional state builders and neoclassical economists, he named Bureau of Corporations chief, Joseph Davies. Rublee served only sixteen months as an unconfirmed commissioner when his formal appointment was undermined by his home-state senator, Jacob Gallinger (R-NH). Rublee and Gallinger had crossed swords in the election of 1914. Wilson replaced Rublee with another progressive, Senator Victor Murdock (R-KS).[6]

It is not surprising that, given their diverse backgrounds, the commissioners quarreled. Davies and Rublee especially clashed over resale price maintenance, on whether business should receive "advance advice" on the legality of their trade agreements, and on the meaning of "unfair competition." Like the economists, Davies thought resale price maintenance was a form of price fixing, which should be counted as an unfair method of competition and proscribed by the commission. He favored advance advice because he thought economic models had become sufficiently precise for the commission to apply them to trade agreements ex ante. Like Brandeis, Rublee thought resale price maintenance was a productive restraint that protected manufacturers from retailers who priced below cost by using trademarked products as "loss leaders." He also thought trade agreements were too diverse and uncertain to rule on ex ante.

But discord resulted in creative action, not paralysis, at the FTC. Rublee and Davies agreed to declare *both* resale price maintenance *and* loss leaders unfair methods of competition, thereby minimizing the motivation for fixing resale prices. The debate over advance advice generated experiments with trade practice conferences, where the FTC assembled industries to set codes of fair competition under its guidance. And the commission's second chair, Edward Hurley, circumvented other conflicts by forging a consensus over cost accounting. In short, discord in a constituency commission stimulated two policy innovations: trade practice conferences and cost accounting.

Walter Dean Burnham, eds., *The American Party System* (New York: Oxford University Press, 1975).

6 See Moore, "The Establishment of a 'New Freedom' Policy," 51–2, and 70–72 on Rublee's trials in the Senate.

BRANDEIS'S SECOND CHANCE

In March 1915, Brandeis addressed the FTC on cost accounting and trade practice rules. Invited by Commissioner Hurley, Brandeis arrived a day early to discuss the commission's future. He found a kindred spirit. A successful manufacturer with republican sensibilities, Hurley shared Brandeis's passion for engineering and civic development. Hurley made a fortune in pneumatic tools and then turned his attention to Democratic politics and trade associations. As president of the Illinois Manufacturer's Association, he had observed how poor cost accounting impaired productivity and demoralized competition. As the second chair of the FTC, he championed cost education. In addition to cost accounting, Brandeis and Hurley found they shared commitments to trade associations, regulated competition, and business–government collaboration.[7]

Recall Brandeis's proposal for cultivational governance. In 1914, he asked Congress to grant the FTC authority to order uniform cost accounting, provide benchmarking services, and supervise trade agreements. Uniform cost accounting held the promise of upgrading competition by making production and pricing decisions more intelligent. Benchmarking could reconcile the state's need for performance data with business efforts to learn how to produce better products at lower costs. Supervision of trade agreements by the FTC could reconcile learning and monitoring. Because trade agreements were so ambiguous and diverse, Brandeis thought dialogue between the state and business necessary to assess their legality and economic consequences. Congress rejected Brandeis's proposals for uniform cost accounting, benchmarking, and trade agreement supervision. In 1915, he welcomed the second chance to propose them to the FTC.

Brandeis told Hurley's colleagues that the FTC could be a great positive force in U.S. industry if it took its cultivational mandate seriously. In addition to its regulatory task, the commission was uniquely situated to cultivate individual development and economic improvement. At once "sympathetic" to business and "detached" from the rigors of competition, the FTC could devise an infrastructure for economic learning and serve as a business consultant on the effects of competitive strategy on profitability and efficiency. Business vision, he said, was inevitably "small" and "self-interested." The FTC, by contrast, could observe business troubles sympathetically, draw inductive generalizations and analogies, and gather and publicize information unavailable to firms. The commission should

[7] On Hurley, see *The Nation's Business*, March 15, 1915, 3.

prod business to share information, discuss its problems, and think more carefully about the relationship between individual action and destructive competition. In short, Brandeis repeated his republican teaching to Congress: by cultivating the conditions for economic intelligence, the FTC could reduce business violations of antitrust law.

Brandeis lectured briefly on trade agreements and extensively on cost accounting. Asked whether he supported the practice of giving advance advice on the legality of a trade agreement, he said it was impossible to review the relevant facts ex ante. They depended far too much on the particular history, context, and competitive practices in an industry. It made more sense to open lines of communication between the FTC and the associations who brokered trade agreements, and then to monitor their progress in channeling competition from predation to improvement.[8]

Brandeis applauded Hurley's cost accounting plans. The FTC was well situated to provide two services: education and benchmarking. These were exceptionally powerful tools, because they regulated competition through individual development instead of coercion, exhortation, or signaling. Brandeis predicted that the effects of cost education would be "deep" and "far reaching." It will teach a "man" not merely the techniques of efficiency analysis, but, more important, to "understand his own individual power" to alter competitive conditions. Teach the many businessmen, who have "never done any close thinking before," to analyze their costs, Brandeis said, and you will "eliminate five-sixths of all cut-throat competition, and, ultimately, the desire for combination." Rivalry will turn less on poaching market share by slashing prices and more on genuine productivity advantages and better products. Individual development will have social consequences.[9]

Brandeis also told the commissioners that socialized information would inevitably have positive individual consequences. The FTC was well situated to construct and publicize social information by benchmarking costs for all manufacturing industries. It should gather data from individual participants, calculate useful industry benchmarks, and distribute them widely. By showing every manager how his expenses compare with others, "you will be educating men to do business constantly better." By this point, Brandeis had abandoned his proposal for mandatory participation. Apparently, he

[8] Louis D. Brandeis, "Disseminating the Facts of Industry," from a statement before the Federal Trade Commission (April 30, 1915) in Alfred Lief, ed., *The Social and Economic Views of Mr. Justice Brandeis* (New York: Vanguard Press, 1930), 411–12.

[9] Brandeis, "Disseminating the Facts of Industry," 412–13.

thought it was politically impossible after the fight in Congress over the formation of the FTC. Instead, he encouraged the commission to mobilize voluntary participation by exploiting its capacity to disseminate large amounts of information while maintaining confidentiality. The more businessmen learned to rely on comparison with others to devise their own best plans, they more they would learn to "play the game with cards right up on the table." Coupled with cost education, benchmarking would go far toward "mending" the "terrible competition" that inevitably drove men into "improper company" and conflict with the state.[10]

Thus, Brandeis outlined three techniques of cultivational governance: trade agreement supervision, cost education, and benchmarking. The first promised to foster ongoing dialogue between business and government over competitive standards; the second to channel competition from cutthroat pricing to improvement in products and production processes; and the third to upgrade competition by providing business with information unavailable from the market or the firm about how to improve. In practice, cultivational governance also promised to reduce mutual suspicion between state and industry by engaging the FTC and business in practical collaboration over the design, implementation, and evaluation of techniques to upgrade competition.

COST ACCOUNTING

Commissioner Hurley was delighted with Brandeis's visit and asked him to draft legislation to authorize the FTC to implement his proposal for benchmarking. Brandeis declined, because he was in the midst of a controversial appointment to the Supreme Court. (It is also likely he thought it would fail.)[11] The statist option closed, Hurley found other resources to cultivate accounting and benchmarking capacity in civil society. He convinced his fellow commissioners to create a Cost Division; mobilized cost accountants, trade associations, the U.S. Chamber of Commerce, Congress, and the president in support of his project; launched work on a model cost system; opened discussion with bankers and the Federal

[10] Brandeis, "Disseminating the Facts of Industry," 412–13.

[11] Brandeis to E. N. Hurley, 2/8/16, in Melvyn I. Urofsky and David W. Levy, eds., *Letters of Louis D. Brandeis, vol. 3* (Albany: State University of New York Press, 1973), 680–81; Philippa Strum, *Louis D. Brandeis* (Cambridge, MA: Harvard University Press, 1984), 291–99.

Reserve Board over inducements to adopt accounting standards; and initiated a process to review and approve trade association cost systems.

The Cost Division

With Brandeis's help, Hurley convinced his fellow commissioners to create a new department devoted to cost accounting. He hired an experienced accountant to head the division, and launched an initiative to publish a model cost system.

Drawing on his midwestern manufacturing networks, Hurley hired Cleveland cost accountant Robert Belt to head the Department of Cost Accounting. A specialist in metalworking, Belt had written a cost primer for the malleable castings industry. When he left the FTC in 1917, he became president of the American Malleable Castings Association and, like many in his profession, offered his accounting services to several trade associations. He also became active in the movement for trade association cost accounting (see Chapter 6).[12]

Although he was an independent professional, not a company employee, when he came to the FTC, Belt's expertise was largely practical and inductive, derived as much from drawing analogies between his clients as from academic training. He was typical of the embedded cost accountants, who saw themselves as consultants to firms, associations, and government. As Chapter 6 will show, Belt and his colleagues at the National Association of Cost Accountants rejected the orthodox techniques of professionalization – government licensing, behavioral monitoring, and coercion. Instead, they organized cost accountants to deliberate, share information, and educate one another in the best practices in their profession.

Compare Belt to the ICC's Henry Carter Adams or the FTC's own chief economist, Francis Walker. Belt was what might be called an embedded professional, whereas Adams and Walker were typical of a new class of

[12] See Moore, "The Establishment of a 'New Freedom' Policy," 110–12. See also *FTC Minutes: The Early Years*, April 29, 1915, http://www.ftc.gov/os/minutes/index.shtm (accessed December 30, 2008), where the commission authorizes Hurley to confer with Dean Gray of Harvard Business School on uniform cost accounting. On Belt, see U.S. Chamber of Commerce, Fabricated Production Department, *Proceedings of Uniform Cost Accounting Conference,* Chicago, October 25, 1923, U.S. Chamber of Commerce Papers, Hagley Museum and Library, Acc. 1960, 2 (hereafter cited as *Chicago Cost Conference*, October 1923); *The Accountant's Directory and Who's Who, 1925* (New York: Prentice Hall, 1925), 376; Robert E. Belt, *Foundry Cost Accounting; Practice and Procedure* (Cleveland: Pentor Press, 1919).

autonomous economists. Belt's cost accounting was practical, inductive, and analogical science, whereas Adams and Walker practiced an increasingly deductive and positivistic science. By the time the FTC was created in 1914, professional economists had already set their sites on colonizing the space between university professorships and expert service to the state. A contemporary of Adams's, Walker's father, Francis Amasa Walker, served as president of the American Economics Association and the American Statistics Association. Francis Junior was trained in economics at MIT and served as deputy commissioner of the Bureau of Corporations under Joseph Davies. After 1914, he spent the remainder of his career at the FTC. Like Adams at the ICC, Walker provided the FTC with credentialed status and expertise in modern statistics and economics.[13] In short, Adams and Walker drew their status from prestigious training, deductive reasoning, and professional credentials, whereas Belt drew his from the depth and breadth of his practical experience.

In the summer of 1915, Belt and Hurley reviewed their options and decided to proceed on four fronts. First, they administered a cost accounting questionnaire to a sample of manufacturers and retailers. Second, they enlisted the American Association of Public Accountants (AAPA) to work with Belt to devise a model cost system. If the FTC could not mandate uniform cost accounting, they reasoned, it could provide industry and trade associations with a standard for discussion and comparison. Third, Hurley mobilized support from accountants, trade associations, and politicians by providing a public justification for the FTC's cost program. Finally, the Cost Division initiated procedures to review trade association cost systems.

Creative Conceptualization

Hurley scheduled an ambitious speaking tour in 1916, which included visits to the U.S. Chamber of Commerce, the American Iron and Steel Institute, numerous city commercial clubs and sectoral trade associations, and the National Wholesale Grocers' Association. He placed his speeches in the *Congressional Record;* penned a book on cost accounting, associationalism, and business–government relations; wrote extensively for FTC

[13] On Adams, see the discussion of the rise of the economics profession and the marginalist revolution in Chapter 2. On Francis Walker Jr., see "FTC Commemorates 100th Anniversary of Predecessor, Bureau of Corporations," February 14, 2003, http://www.ftc.gov/opa/2003/02/bcorp.shtm (accessed December 30, 2008).

annual reports to Congress; and corresponded with President Wilson. Like Brandeis, Hurley's goal was to incite reflexivity in his audience by tackling taken-for-granted assumptions and renarrating the causes of industrial concentration. Destructive competition, unlawful combination, and the conflict between business and the state, Hurley hypothesized, were not ineluctable facts of industrial society. More often than not, they were artifacts of faulty accounting customs. Alter accounting techniques, he hypothesized, and business would find better ways to compete.

For the first time since the Sherman Act of 1890 the Federal Trade Commission Act made business–government cooperation possible in antitrust, Hurley wrote. But cooperation necessitated mutual adjustment. The commission must transcend its "police" powers for "constructive work," whereas business must reflect on the causes of destructive competition. Together, they could invent alternatives to cartelization, concentration, and business–government conflict. After two decades of discord over antitrust, the trade commission act provided business and government with a common interest in "intelligent competition." But cooperation necessitated a return to "first principles" of effective management. For Hurley this meant cost accounting.

Two aspects of weak (or nonexistent) accounting resulted in "reckless competition": undervaluing costs and faulty assumptions about volume and joint costs. The first caused business to price too low. The second caused it to make the wrong products.

Hurley explained how the FTC's questionnaire revealed that fewer than 10 percent of respondents included charges for depreciation of plant and equipment or overhead costs. As a result, banks overextended credit, and firms rushed into production, overestimated profits, and priced too low. To be sure, weak accounting might be inconsequential if competition ensured that good practices drove out bad. But the opposite was usually the case. Well-managed companies usually had little choice but to meet "reckless" pricing by cannibalizing their assets and undermining their capacity to innovate. Otherwise, they would lose business. Not only business, Hurley concluded, but also labor, lenders, and consumers suffered under the weight of undervaluing costs. This was all the result of human conventions that naturalized technology and truncated business imagination.[14]

The second cause of destructive competition derived from faulty ideas about volume. Like Brandeis's critique of the railroads, Hurley charged

[14] Edward N. Hurley, Chairman, Federal Trade Commission, *Awakening of Business* (New York: Doubleday, 1917), 1–17.

manufacturers with assuming, rather than testing, the idea that volume always lowered per unit costs. Therefore they measured commodity costs in the aggregate instead of segregating them by product classes. Fruit juice manufacturers kept no independent record of the costs and revenues of jams and jellies; iron and steel manufacturers failed to segregate the costs of coke and pig iron; and many firms evaluated salespeople according to the volume, rather than the profitability, of sales. The result was not merely to limit efficiency, but also to cause cutthroat price competition, as manufacturers slashed prices in pursuit of volume and market share. Reconstruct costs, Hurley told trade association audiences, and your members will rethink competitive strategy. Carefully segregating costs and profits by product would unlock other options. Firms would learn to specialize on strong lines and competition would turn more on product quality and productivity than on volume.[15]

Hurley assured business, trade associations, and Congress that cost accounting would remain voluntary and decentralized. The FTC planned to work with accountants to devise general standards and encourage trade associations to work out systems appropriate to their industries. He was particularly enthusiastic about the prospects for trade association benchmarking services. He expected that associations would learn to benchmark detailed product and process costs, so that manufacturers could compare their performance to one another and adjust. The more managers learned to use benchmarking information to make incremental improvements in production and specialize on their most profitable business, the "more intelligent" Hurley thought competition would become.[16]

[15] On the segregation of product costs, see Hurley, *Awakening*, 18–19, 180–81; Edward N. Hurley, "Address before the Boston Commercial Club," March 28, 1916, FTC Library, 5–6; Edward N. Hurley, "Address before the Tenth Annual Meeting of the National Wholesale Grocers' Association of the United States," June 15, 1916, FTC Library, 1–2; Edward N. Hurley, "Government and Business," Address before the Associated Advertising Clubs of the World, June 29, 1916, FTC Library, 23–24. On evaluating sales according to profit not volume, see Hurley, *Awakening*, 28–29. The similarity between Brandeis and Hurley on the importance of segregating product costs is also evident in Hurley's exchange with an executive of Gulf Oil Corporation during an FTC investigation of gasoline prices. Like Brandeis's questions to railroad executives, Hurley was surprised that managers in the oil industry could not recount the costs of various classes of products. See Moore, "The Establishment of a 'New Freedom' Policy," 89–91. Unaware of the debate between economists and accountants over this issue, Moore incorrectly concludes that Hurley's questions indicated his ignorance.

[16] Hurley, *Awakening*, 50–63. Like Brandeis, Hurley wrote favorably of German trade associations. See *Awakening*, 64–72.

In summary, Hurley took up where Brandeis left off. Although he acknowledged the commission's regulatory function – he promised to treat harshly those who exploited FTC cooperation opportunistically – Hurley thought the commission would have broader and deeper effects on competition by reconfiguring the way manufacturers thought about costs. Far more "insidious" than individual acts of unfair competition, he repeatedly said, was "ignorant competition." The FTC could do no more important work than to create an infrastructure for reflexivity and learning through better cost accounting.

In the spring of 1916, Hurley sent President Wilson a transcript of an elaborate speech on cost accounting, requesting comments and approval. The president obliged. In a letter, which Hurley circulated widely, Wilson applauded Hurley's work. When organized for the "purpose of improving conditions in their particular industry, such as unifying cost accounting and bookkeeping methods," Wilson wrote, trade associations should "meet with the approval of every man interested in the business progress of the country.... I am very anxious to see you continue to cooperate with ... business men ... along the[se] lines." Delighted with the endorsement, Hurley quoted generously from Wilson's letter in his communications with fellow commissioners, Congress, business, and accountants.[17]

FTC Cost Manuals

The Cost Division and the accountants completed their work on a model cost system in the fall of 1916. The FTC published two manuals, one for manufacturing and the other for retail.[18] The model systems were significant in two respects. First, they provided a focal point for public

[17] Wilson to Hurley, May 12, 1916, reprinted in Hurley, *Awakening*, i–ii. See also Edward N. Hurley, "Cooperation and Efficiency in Developing Our Foreign Trade," Address delivered before the American Iron and Steel Institute, May 26, 1916, reprinted in U.S. Congress, 64th Cong., 1st sess. Sen. doc. no. 459 (Washington, DC: Government Printing Office, 1916), 9–10; and Edward N. Hurley, "Address before the Tenth Annual Meeting of the National Wholesale Grocers' Association of the United States," Boston, June 15, 1916, FTC Library; Brandeis to Hurley 11/28/15, in Urofksy and Levy, eds., *Letters of Louis D. Brandeis*, vol. 3, 680–81.

[18] U.S. Federal Trade Commission, *Fundamentals of a Cost System for Manufacturers* (Washington, DC: Government Printing Office, 1916), 6; U.S. Congress, House, *A System of Accounts for Retail Merchants*, H 1355, 64th Cong., 1st sess. 1916, serial no. 7099; Thomas C. Blaisdell, *The Federal Trade Commission: An Experiment in the Control of Business* (New York: Columbia University Press, 1932), 116–17.

debate and diffusion. (Chapter 6 will describe that process.) Second, like Brandeis and Hurley, the FTC's cost manuals criticized the accounting assumptions of mass production and outlined an alternative.

Like Brandeis and Hurley, the cost manual for manufacturers criticized two accounting conventions that led manufacturers to prize volume over all other ends: (1) the failure to segregate costs and revenues according to product line (or the assumption of joint costs), and (2) the failure to distribute overhead to the products and processes where it was incurred (the assumption of fixed costs). The first led manufacturers (like the railroads) to cross-subsidize losses on competitive products with inflated prices on noncompetitive products – all in pursuit of greater volume. The second led them to underestimate remunerative prices on all products, and thus remain oblivious to the consequences of slashing prices in pursuit of volume. The results not only truncated the capacity of individual manufacturers to reduce costs, they also "seriously disturbed" competitive conditions for industries as a whole. Thus, read the cost manual, every manufacturer must "know on what article he is making a profit and on what he is incurring a loss"; and to "see that every article manufactured bears its proper share of ... overhead" costs.[19]

The Cost Division recomposed accounting conventions by outlining three techniques to realize these ends: (1) departmentalization, (2) overhead distribution, and (3) product costing. The first broke production costs into departments or "cost centers," where labor, fuel, rent, and capital costs could be measured in detail. The second provided principles for distributing overhead costs to particular jobs or product lines. The third invited management to segregate the costs of particular jobs or product lines and to calculate their profitability independently. (Chapters 6 and 7 will show how these techniques worked in practice.)

Together, the cost manual explained, these techniques made it possible to turn the assumption that volume reduced costs and provided a competitive advantage into a testable hypothesis. Manufacturers could learn whether cross-subsidizing multiple products was genuinely profitable and whether it was possible to adjust management and production

[19] U.S. Federal Trade Commission, *Fundamentals of a Cost System,* 6, where it reads, "It is necessary to-day for the business man's success that he knows on what articles he is making a profit and on what he is incurring a loss. Competitive conditions are seriously disturbed where losses on one or more articles are recovered by profits on other articles. It is obvious that a manufacturer should not only know the cost of each article he manufactures but that he should see that every article manufactured bears its proper share of factory and general overhead."

to reduce overhead (or "fixed") costs. From the commission's perspective, the *Cost Manual for Manufacturers* was not merely an educational tool to improve individual productivity and profits. It was also a means to upgrading competition from cutthroat battles over market share to product diversity and quality and nonvolume forms of productivity. Thus, by recomposing private management assumptions about the relationship among costs, volume, and profits, the FTC also realized its public mandate to regulate competition.

The commission distributed the cost manuals widely. Hurley wrote to every member of Congress, requesting the names and addresses of firms in their districts. The Cost Division publicized the manuals in scores of trade journals and association publications. By December 1916, the FTC had distributed 230,000 copies and Hurley penned a long letter to President Wilson on the commission's progress.

From System Review to Trade Practice Conference

In the spring of 1916, Hurley and Belt began to review trade association cost systems for approval. Unlike their other activities, this one caused a controversy that threatened to kill the program. But it proved an impermanent setback. Subsequent commissioners kept the program alive. And by 1927, the FTC restored system reviews under its trade practice conference program.

Under Hurley's guidance, the FTC cultivated capacity for cost accounting in trade associations and hoped it would filter down to firms. But, as vanguard associations passed from system design to diffusion, the commission's challenge changed. The more Hurley and Belt consulted with association executives, the more they learned the commission had an important role to play in convincing manufacturers to adopt standard cost systems. So, the Cost Division launched a review process that promised an informal credential for trade association cost systems.

In May 1916, Hurley sought legal counsel on system reviews from the House author of the Federal Trade Commission Act, Raymond Stevens (D-NH). As long as the FTC did not license association plans and take it upon itself to strip associations of the privilege of state approval, Stevens replied, reviews were legal. Hurley asked Belt to enlist the American Institute of Accountants to assist the commission and proceeded to solicit cost systems. By the fall of 1916, Hurley had issued letters of approval to associations in commercial printing, lithography, union-made garments, and pulp and paper.

The reviews were controversial among the commissioners, some of whom saw cost accounting through the lens of economics instead of engineering. Commissioner Davies objected: FTC approval was license to price fixing. With the commission's imprimatur, trade associations would establish not merely standard methods of cost accounting, but standard costs as well, which members would use to set prices and lock in monopoly. Davies demanded all reviews pass before a full commission vote. But this did not settle the matter. When Hurley requested $100,000 from Congress to expand the accounting program, he found the door closed: Davies had apparently mobilized Department of Commerce secretary William Redfield to block the commission's request. A former Democratic representative in the House, Redfield remained influential. Like Davies, Redfield thought the FTC's warrant was regulatory. Hurley's cultivational project belonged in a promotional agency, such as the Department of Commerce, where it would be used to educate individual businesses, instead of providing trade associations with the tools to monopolize their industries. Hurley objected and, in a last-ditch effort to maintain FTC cost accounting, suggested the FTC merge with the Department of Commerce. But Davies's alliance with Redfield proved too powerful and as 1916 came to a close, the FTC's Cost Division was transferred to the Department of Commerce. Within three months, Hurley resigned.[20]

Despite this setback, Hurley's project survived. The commission became the state's cost accountant during the war; subsequent commissioners linked cost accounting more directly to the FTC's regulatory project and deepened the commission's ties to trade associations; and in 1925, the FTC revived cost system review within the Trade Practice Conference Division.

Not long after Hurley's resignation, President Wilson asked the FTC to become the state's cost accountant to the war effort. (Apparently, the president was more confident in the FTC than in the Department of Commerce.)[21]

[20] Moore, "Establishment of 'New Freedom' Policy," 93, 110–15.

[21] The FTC conducted cost reviews for the War Department, the Navy, the War Industries Board, the Fuel Administration, the Shipping Board and Emergency Fleet Corporation, the Railroad Administration, the Department of Agriculture, the Department of Justice, the Post Office, and the Government Printing Office. For a complete list of cost reports submitted by the commission during the year 1918–1919, see *Annual Report of the Federal Trade Commission 1919* (Washington, DC: Government Printing Office, 1919), 38–42.

Wartime cost accounting was led by the commission's third chair, William Colver. In 1917, he hired 180 accountants, who conducted studies for no fewer than 10,000 sectors, with an aggregate investment of nearly $20 billion.[22] The war studies, Colver explained, corroborated the FTC's earlier findings. Investigators found cost conventions that overvalued volume and managers who rarely stopped to question compulsive routine. Like Brandeis and Hurley, Colver complained that the failure to adequately account for product costs demoralized competition. Far too few manufacturers track "unit costs and profits by products," Colver told the American Academy of Social and Political Science – a practice, he emphasized, which was "essential ... to the safe conduct of industry." Nonetheless, Colver tagged the FTC's wartime cost work a success, which sparked widespread Deweyan deliberation and experimentation. Accountants for the FTC engaged a "full and frank discussion of costs, methods and products" with thousands of businesspeople. They helped "revise" weak systems and "install" new ones, and they reviewed trade association cost work. And they recombined the best practices in proposals for uniform industry cost systems. There was still much to do, Colver added. At the very least, the FTC should encourage trade associations to "assemble and distribute ... reliable information," without being suspected of facilitating "price fixing or restraints of trade."[23]

As the war came to a close, another cost accounting enthusiast joined the FTC. Fresh from his tenure as New Jersey attorney general, where he was responsible for implementing Woodrow Wilson's state-level antitrust reforms, Nelson Gaskill became the FTC's leading architect of cultivational governance between 1920 and 1925. Gaskill renovated FTC cost accounting by linking it to the commission's regulatory, and cultivational, mission. He recomposed Hurley's ties to civil society and resurrected the system review within trade practice conference procedures.

Thus, despite its setbacks, the commission established an impressive record in cost accounting by 1920. Under Hurley's guidance, the FTC mobilized embedded professionals, designed a model cost system, encouraged trade associations to take up cost work, reviewed cost systems for approval, and forged links to civil society. By doing so, the

[22] Blaisdell, *The Federal Trade Commission*, 118.

[23] William B. Colver, "Lessons of War Cost-Finding," Address before the American Academy of Social and Political Science, Philadelphia, December 21, 1918, FTC Library, *Annual Report of the Federal Trade Commission 1917* (Washington, DC: Government Printing Office, 1917), 3–4.

commission focused careful reflection on the limits of mass (or volume) production and outlined techniques to reconcile the three main goals of antitrust: economic decentralization, productive competition, and steady improvement in products and production processes. In short, even though Brandeis's original statist proposal for mandatory cost accounting and FTC benchmarking services proved impossible, creative syncretists at the FTC mobilized and recombined resources from civil society to achieve considerable progress toward his cultivational ideal during the commission's first five years.

TRADE PRACTICE CONFERENCES

In 1919, the FTC took up Brandeis's second proposal for cultivational governance: state supervision of trade agreements. Like the commission's cost program, this one deviated considerably from Brandeis's legislative initiative. Brandeis proposed trade agreement registration, whereas the commission organized industry deliberation and rule making. And Brandeis proposed legal immunity until FTC lawyers or the Department of Justice found otherwise, whereas the commission classified all trade practice rules according to their legality. Despite these differences, trade practice conferences realized much in Brandeis's outline for cultivational governance. They upgraded rivalry by sparking reflection and experimentation through discussions, which focused on efforts to distinguish constructive from destructive practices.

Like the commission's cost work, its trade practice program was the result of creative syncretism. It took place in three stages: experimentation, conceptualization, and institutionalization. Faced with meager resources, a contested mission, and a bewildering diversity of industries to regulate, creative commissioners experimented with deliberation. But experimentation alone did not constitute state building – bureaucratic or cultivational. This step involved creative conceptualization, mobilization, and design. Between 1920 and 1925, Nelson Gaskill took up this task. Like Hurley, Gaskill wrote and lectured extensively in an effort to explain cultivational governance and mobilize allies and participants. His successor, William Humphrey, led the third step: institutionalization. Under his leadership, the FTC created a Trade Practice Conference Division and formalized its relationship with other parts of the agency.

The resulting form was heterarchical. It multiplied functions within the Trade Practice, Economics, and Legal divisions; valued interdependence between and lateral communication across divisions; and dropped top management down the organizational hierarchy into the practical matters of administering trade conferences.

Experimentation

While the commissioners debated advance advice, subordinates within the FTC responded to the continuing pressures for consultation on trade agreements by experimenting with trade practice conferences. Although discord stymied policy innovation at the top in 1915, the Economics Division stumbled on a solution when it assembled fertilizer manufacturers to review a research report on their industry. To the division's surprise, the manufacturers worked out a successful code of fair competition. Their discovery lay fallow until the armistice in 1918, when the creative administrators reflected on the fertilizer industry's code, surveyed its resources in civil society, and launched a full-scale trade practice conference program.

From the moment the FTC opened its doors in 1915, the Legal Division heard multiple complaints against the same unfair practices, which caused them to reflect on whether they could issue industry-wide rulings. Typewriter manufacturers protested competitors who passed off rebuilt equipment as new. Varnish manufacturers, coffee roasters, and tea packers complained of widespread commercial bribery to secure and retain customers. Oil companies charged their competitors with slander, false representation of products, and free provision of tanks and pumps. Lumber and building materials dealers charged price discrimination. The list went on, as did the pressures for broader action on industry trade agreements.[24]

The pressure to act also came from associations, who requested informal meetings to make sense of FTC policy toward trade agreements. Among the hundreds of informal discussions the commissioners held with businesspeople, attorneys, academics, bankers, and accountants during

[24] *Annual Report of the Federal Trade Commission 1917* (Washington, DC: Government Printing Office, 1917), 10–12, 46–58; *Annual Report of the Federal Trade Commission 1918* (Washington, DC: Government Printing Office, 1918), 56–74; *Annual Report of the Federal Trade Commission 1920* (Washington, DC: Government Printing Office, 1920), 44, 46. On multiple complaints, see also Hunker, *Trade Practice Conferences,* 31–32; Sumner S. Kittelle and Elmer Mostow, "A Review of the Trade Practice Conferences of the Federal Trade Commission," *George Washington Law Review* 8, no. 3 (January–February 1940): 427; *Annual Report of the Federal Trade Commission 1927* (Washington, DC: Government Printing Office, 1927), 7.

their first two years, nearly a third were with trade association officers seeking guidance on trade agreements. The commissioners heard from regional and national associations in lumber; coal mining; hardware; printing; button manufacturing; sheet metal; jewelry; sewer pipes and tiles; retail dry goods, hardware, and groceries; shoe and leather; silk; motion pictures; newsprint; printing; chemistry; and more.[25]

Unable to resolve the legal debate over advance advice, the idea for trade practice conferences came not from FTC lawyers, but from its economists. Early in 1916, the Economics Division convened an informal conference of fertilizer manufacturers. To their surprise, most of the industry showed up and agreed to abandon a substantial list of destructive practices. Researchers had not planned the conference. But, when they circulated a draft report, the manufacturers requested a conference, where they agreed to end unfair methods of competition. Subsequent research revealed substantial compliance. For example, the division found that the widespread practice of using bogus independents to drive competitors from selective markets had disappeared. Perhaps the fertilizer producers feared FTC coercion. The record is unclear. But it is also possible that, like the famous Hawthorne experiments in worker productivity, the Economics Division found that once it named destructive practices, firms began to reflect on the consequences of industry custom. Either way, the fertilizer conference garnered a good deal of approbation.

The division's discovery might have remained obscure in a larger agency with a clearer division of labor between regulation and research. It might have also been ignored in an agency committed to Weberian bureaucracy and command and control regulation. But the FTC was still a tiny organization in 1916, housed in a cramped corner of the Department of Commerce. For all its weakness, however, economists, lawyers, and the commissioners found themselves in daily conversation. The commissioners discussed the fertilizer conference at their daily meetings and highlighted its success in their 1916 annual report.[26] However, absent a broader perspective on the social nature of competition and the process by which customs were constructed and changed, the lessons of the fertilizer conference might have escaped the commissioners. Drawing on the republican experimentalist dispositions he shared with Brandeis, Hurley generalized. When "bad

[25] *FTC Minutes: The Early Years*. See also meeting with Arthur Jerome Eddy in *FTC Minutes*, April 17, 1915.

[26] *Annual Report of the Federal Trade Commission 1916* (Washington, DC: Government Printing Office, 1916), 23–24; *FTC Minutes*, December 20, 1915.

practices have such a grip on some industries that no individual manufacturer can abandon them without placing himself at a serious disadvantage," he said, it made more sense to assemble firms for a frank and open discussion of competitive standards than to use coercion.[27] But trade practice conferences would have to wait until the end of the war, when the commissioners convened members of the creamery, jewelry, and typewriter industries.[28]

Creative Conceptualization

Trade practice conferences might have been a transitory response to a pressing problem. But, by 1927, the commission had institutionalized them. What happened? Creative conceptualization was a critical step in the process from experimentation to institutionalization. No individual did more to naturalize the state's role in the process of trade custom development, and thereby accord trade practice conferences an obvious and authoritative role, than Nelson Gaskill. Like Hurley, he scheduled an ambitious writing and lecturing schedule to convince Congress, cabinet members, fellow commissioners, trade associations, cost accountants, bankers, social scientists, the U.S. Chamber of Commerce, and the general public that the state had a crucial role to play in steering business from predatory to productive habits.

Gaskill conceptualized a foundation for trade practice conferences by reconstructing competition from a process of individual market exchange, as it was understood by the courts and the marginalist economists, into a social process. Like Brandeis, John Dewey, and many institutional economists of his time, Gaskill told audiences that economic action was a social affair, in which coordination occurred when individuals settled on habits or "customs." Sometimes, however, customs became destructive and economic agents needed outside intervention to perturb habits and unearth alternatives. Trade practice conferences served that role.[29]

27 Hurley, *Awakening*, 61.

28 Kittelle and Mostow, "A Review of the Trade Practice Conferences," 429–31; Robert James Hunker, "*Trade Practice Conferences*" (master's thesis, Ohio State University, 1949), 31–37.

29 See John Dewey, *Human Nature and Conduct* (Amherst, NY: Prometheus Books, 2002 [1922]). On pragmatism's influence on institutional economists and their differences with the marginalists, see Yuval P. Yonay, *The Struggle over the Soul of*

Unlike the marginalist economists, Gaskill thought competition was not easily abstracted from history and context. The state of rivalry in any trade, he wrote, is determined by a social "process of tender, acceptance and rejection of ideas, methods, [and] customs" that produce "mass conformity of customs, rules and habits of business conduct." Customs, like Deweyan habits, were necessary for economic coordination and effective action. They were provisional solutions to collectively defined problems. But they could also turn destructive, as the conditions around them inevitably changed.[30]

In Gaskill's view, there were three characteristic responses to dysfunctional customs. The first, like Dewey's account of "deliberation," was visionary. "Clear thinking, [and] forward looking," some businesspeople chart a new course through experimentation, observation, and adjustment. "This is American business at its best," he told the Southern Wholesale Grocers' Association. With sufficient "cooperation" and "support" from the state, it "can accomplish ... what an army could never do." The second response was predatory. The "pirate" exploits dysfunctional customs to perpetrate fraud, theft, and opportunism. A monopolist-in-the-making, he warrants the "policeman's club." The third response was habit or Deweyan "routine." Most businesspeople "blindly accept conditions, customs, practices as they are and find justifications in long usage. Inclined toward things past rather than things to come," they perpetuate destructive competition. Reluctant to reflect on the consequences of habit or to change when they do, they become unwitting allies to the pirate. Trade practice conferences were designed for them. With FTC "encouragement," "explanation," and "advice," they might learn to "amalgamate" with the visionary instead of the predator.[31] Thus, as Gaskill saw it, the collective

Economics: Institutionalist and Neoclassical Economists in America between the Wars (Princeton, NJ: Princeton University Press, 1998).

[30] Nelson Gaskill, "Public Interest versus Private Interest in the Federal Trade Commission Act," *Proceedings of the Academy of Political Science* 11, no. 4 (January 1926): 124–25. See also Gaskill, *Price Control in the Public Interest* (Washington, D.C.: Washington Bureau of Sales Management Magazine, 1931), 85, where he writes, "The state of competition, in any trade or industry, is the compound of all the forces set in motion by the methods and practices of each and all its units. This compound sets the terms under which each unit operates. For unless it be of greatly superior strength or is lifted above the general competitive level by some special circumstance, each unit in the industry will meet method and practice in the terms or their equivalent. So the accustomed methods and practices of an industry shake down to some common denominators."

[31] Nelson B. Gaskill, Chairman, Federal Trade Commission, "Business and the Law," An Address Delivered before the Southern Wholesale Grocers' Association, in Convention at St. Louis, Missouri [*sic*], May 11, 1922, FTC Library, 8–10. See *Annual Report of*

action problem was born of a failure of social imagination, not, as many institutionalists suggest, the mutual suspicion that collaborators will cheat on agreements to change.

The FTC had discovered many examples of destructive habit, but none more far reaching than pricing below cost – a practice that grew out of dysfunctional assumptions about the relationship between prices and costs. Although lawmakers and the public focused on the most notorious examples, such as Duke's "fighting brands" or Rockefeller's railroad rebates, there were many homely examples. In perfumes, tire sales, groceries, and many other trades, manufacturers and retailers slashed prices below costs in anticipation of scale economies and bigger market share. The mania for volume, Gaskill said, made sense in the nineteenth century, when markets were growing rapidly and were less crowded with rivals. But it became an "illusion" in the twentieth century, when it resulted in "displacement competition" instead of productivity or profit. Unreflective about the individual or collective consequences of their actions, firms slashed prices in pursuit of market share. The result was cutthroat competition or profitless prosperity, of which so many businesses complained in the 1920s.[32]

The FTC's and the Justice Department's coercive powers were well suited to policing the most obvious and visible predatory forms of pricing below cost: "fighting brands," railroad rebates, loss leaders, and price discrimination. But destructive habit necessitated another approach. Outside intervention was often necessary to perturb habits, make deliberation possible, and reveal alternatives. Gaskill applauded the cost accountants, trade associations, and Hurley's FTC for their good work in deconstructing the "volume illusion" and providing methods to measure performance in costs and profits instead of market share. Trade practice conferences provided a venue to assemble business to reflect on the

the Federal Trade Commission 1920 (Washington, DC: Government Printing Office, 1920), 43–44.

32 Nelson B. Gaskill, "The Reason for Cost Accounting," *National Association of Cost Accountants, Year Book, 1926* (New York: NACA, 1926), 21–24; Nelson B. Gaskill, Chairman, Federal Trade Commission, "Some Aspects of Price Cutting," Address to the National Wholesale Grocers, 8 June, 1922, 3, FTC Library; Nelson B. Gaskill, "The Larger Business," Address to the American Specialty Manufacturers' Association, November 16, 1922, FTC Library; Nelson B. Gaskill, "Looking Forward," Address to the Common Brick Manufacturers' Association of America, February 9, 1933, FTC Library ("volume illusion," p. 4); Nelson B. Gaskill, "Setting Sound Prices," Address to the Boston Chapter of the National Association of Cost Accountants, February 15, 1933, FTC Library ("displacement competition," p. 2).

relationship between accounting conventions, volume assumptions, and pricing practices. Gaskill looked forward to the day when the Conference Division made association cost system reviews a part of its evaluation of trade practice rules.

Thus, like Brandeis, Gaskill thought the goal of trade practice conferences was civic as well as economic.[33] Deliberation could enlarge business vision, so that managers might reflect more effectively on the social causes and consequences of their actions. Gaskill explained that the trade practice conferences implies a

> ... transition from the accepted conventions of free competition, a lessening of individual and personal antagonisms, a willingness to surrender somewhat of individual liberty for the benefit of the whole. It recognizes the individual self-interest as bound up in a community of interest. It translates the stated concepts of unfair competition out of the status of private rights and wrongs and makes them general rules of group public policy.... In last analysis it ... sees competition as a systematized method of expressing individual actions rather than as a confused struggle in the dark.[34]

This did not mean the FTC would reinvent human nature, turning businesspeople from profit maximizers into civic altruists. Trade practice conferences were premised on the assumption that it was often difficult for individuals to make sense of the social causes and consequences of their actions. Deliberation among practitioners and between them and a less interested, but knowledgeable, Federal Trade Commission promised new insights and possibilities. This was a good reason to institutionalize trade practice conferences, Gaskill told businesspeople, trade associations, social scientists, Congress, and his fellow commissioners, who he hoped would all envision a place for themselves in this deliberative order.

Trade Practice Submittals

Under Gaskill's leadership, the commissioners cobbled together trade practice conferences from existing resources. They gave them an official name, conveyed their legal status to Congress, clarified procedure, and

[33] On Gaskill's civic republicanism more generally, see Nelson B. Gaskill, Chairman, Federal Trade Commission, "The Larger Business," Address to the American Specialty Manufacturers' Association delivered November 16, 1922, 1–2; Nelson B. Gaskill, *Price Control in the Public Interest* (Washington, DC: Washington Bureau of *Sales Management Magazine*, 1931), 58–60.

[34] Nelson B. Gaskill, *The Regulation of Competition* (New York: Harper & Brothers, 1936), 11.

reported the outcome of each conference to the public. But they stopped short of institutionalizing trade practice conferences.

In recognition of their uncertain legal authority, the FTC named the conferences "trade practice submittals." Organized by the legal department, conferees were expected to submit principles of fair competition to its attorneys for consideration in FTC rule making. As the commission told participants and Congress, a commission "stamp of approval" had no legal authority. It implied neither immunity from antitrust nor a promise to enforce. The FTC promised to consult submittals only in the event they proved relevant to a formal complaint of unfair competition. In short, trade practice submittals were thoroughly voluntary affairs.[35]

The commission also drew on existing legal procedures to outline a procedure for trade practice conferences. The FTC or a body representing the industry could initiate a conference. Conferences were to be scheduled at a convenient location and administered by an FTC commissioner, whose role was to convene, observe, and serve as a consultant. Anything else would contravene the commission's statutory authority. The goal was to achieve consensus on standards of fair competition. The commission acknowledged, however, this was often impossible. Hence, "near unanimity" was sufficient for submission.

Between 1919 and 1925, the FTC held seventeen conferences, which resulted in trade practice rules of roughly two sorts. The first involved product quality, brand name, and advertising standards. For example, trade practice submittals declared unfair the practice of passing off rebuilt typewriters as though they were new, branding plastics with misleading names such as "ivory" or "tortoise shell," underfilling boxes of macaroni, or mislabeling the precious metal content of jewelry or the wood content of furniture. The second category involved rules against widespread competitive practices, which a majority felt demoralized trade. Examples in this category included commercial bribery, providing free products or services, price discrimination, or secretly paying salespeople to push some products over others.[36]

[35] FTC, *Trade Practice Submittals*, 1925, 1; FTC, *Annual Report for 1920*, 43. See also Hurley, *Awakening of Business*, 61; and Gerard C. Henderson, *The Federal Trade Commission: A Study in Administrative Law and Procedure* (New Haven, CT: Yale University Press, 1924), 78–83; Robert James Hunker, "*Trade Practice Conferences*" (master's thesis, Ohio State University, 1949), 35–38.

[36] See Federal Trade Commission, *Trade Practice Conferences* (Washington, DC: Government Printing Office, 1929), 5–54 (hereafter cited as *FTC, Trade Practice Conference, 1929*); Kittelle and Mostow, "A Review of the Trade Practice Conferences," 430–31.

Despite its progress in trade practice submittals, Gaskill wanted the commission to deepen its commitment to cultivational governance. In his final months at the FTC, Gaskill penned a white paper outlining a plan. Looking back on the FTC's first decade, he noted a brewing administrative crisis. Although the commission's caseload was thirteen times larger than it had been a decade earlier, its resources had remained nearly constant. The maximum time from an initial complaint of unfair competition to a final disposition had grown from two weeks to six months – in easy cases. Difficult cases took as long as a year. In 1916, five cases were carried over to the following year; by 1924 the number of cases that had to be carried over had grown to 264.[37] Because Congress had shown little inclination to increase the FTC's budget, Gaskill proposed it delegate two additional powers to the commission: "stipulation" authority and authority to sanction and enforce trade conference rules. In the first, when the FTC found a practice plainly illegal and its perpetrator agreed to abandon it, the commission would ask that person to sign a legally binding stipulation indicating as much. In the second, once an industry majority agreed to a code of fair competition, the FTC would review it for legality and enforce the rules meeting that standard. Gaskill predicted two positive results from the second proposal. It would reduce administrative costs and place the FTC in its proper relationship with business, that is, perturbing destructive habits, cooperating with the most forward-looking firms, elaborating successful experiments, and providing incentives to raise the plane of competition toward "common ideals."[38]

President Coolidge and the Republican Congress ignored Gaskill's plea. Nonetheless, Coolidge appointed a replacement commissioner, who made it his mission to implement Gaskill's proposals. Within five years, he had raised the status of deliberation, launched a Trade Practice Conference Division, and clarified the legal status of trade practice rules to distinguish the merely voluntary from the enforceable.

Institutionalization

The man Coolidge chose to succeed Gaskill was William Humphrey. A conservative Republican and Washington State attorney with deep ties

[37] Commissioner Gaskill, "The Federal Trade Commission: Supplemental Report," December 5, 1924, FTC Library, 1–5.

[38] Nelson B. Gaskill, "Supplemental Report," December 5, 1924, 8–9, FTC Library; "Reforms in Federal Trade Commission Championed by Gaskill," *Lumber World Review*, December 25, 1924, FTC Library.

to the lumber industry, Humphrey was a critic of business regulation. Before Coolidge appointed him to the FTC, he served two terms in the House, where he denounced the commission's "socialistic" investigations into the meatpacking, house furnishing, and lumber industries. He joined the FTC promising regulatory reform. Despite his bellicose rhetoric, Humphrey was not a revolutionary. Under his leadership, the commission scaled back on investigations and maintained confidentiality during those underway, initiated stipulations, and institutionalized trade practice conferences. The cultivational portion of his project had deep roots in the work of Brandeis, Hurley, Colver, and Gaskill.[39]

Under Humphrey's leadership, the FTC created a Trade Practice Conference Division, multiplied the number of conferences, and specified the legal status of trade practice rules. At first blush, these reforms look Weberian, because they increased the functional division of labor and subjected conferences to formal rules. But a closer look reveals they deviated from bureaucratic hierarchy. This section describes Humphrey's reforms; the next shows how they resulted in heterarchy.

Humphrey's first step was to signal a change in status by changing the name from Trade Practice Submittal to Trade Practice Conference. Although the former had no legal status, Humphrey promised that, after careful review, some trade practice rules would be enforceable under Section 5 of the Federal Trade Commission Act. His second step was to place a motion before his fellow commissioners to move trade practice conferences from the Legal Division into a new department devoted solely to administering conferences and reviewing trade practice rules. It passed unanimously. Administered by a director and an assistant director, the Trade Practice Conference Division was to investigate conditions warranting requests for a conference and make recommendations to the commissioners. Once they voted to proceed, the division was to administer a conference, solicit assent from nonparticipants for trade practice rules, monitor compliance, and suggest action against violators.[40]

[39] For an interpretation of Humphrey's term at the FTC as the triumph of conservative over progressive regulation, or business capture, see George Cullom Davis, "The Federal Trade Commission: Promise and Practice in Regulating Business, 1900–1929" (PhD diss., University of Illinois, 1969), 237–39; G. Cullom Davis, "The Transformation of the Federal Trade Commission, 1914–1929," *Mississippi Valley Historical Review* 49 (December 1962): 417–55. See also E. Pendleton Herring, *Public Administration and the Public Interest* (New York: McGraw-Hill, 1936), 125; and Blaisdell, *The Federal Trade Commission,* 80–81.

[40] See *Annual Report of the Federal Trade Commission 1926* (Washington, DC: Government Printing Office), 47–50.

With the new division in place, Humphrey's third step was to set all three FTC divisions – law, economics, and conference – to deliberate over the legal status of trade practice rules. In 1927 the FTC announced a classification scheme. *Group I* rules were those found consistent with existing antitrust and administrative case law. As such, the commission would consider them "mandatory requirements," enforceable under Section 5 of the Federal Trade Commission Act.[41] Among the many Group I rules that the commission promised to enforce were provisions against pricing below cost, interlocking directorates, price discrimination, patent infringement, inducing a breach of contract, and using false trademarks. By contrast, *Group II* rules were "advisory and optional provisions," deemed by the industry to represent "sound" business practice. Although unenforceable at law, the commission promised to review them for informal approval. Typical Group II rules involved recommendations to adopt a trade association's standard contract, bill of lading, or cost accounting system. While Group II rules were voluntary, Gaskill's social theory of trade custom formation provided Humphrey with confidence in their merit.[42]

Humphrey's fourth innovation was to resurrect FTC cost system reviews. Among the many Group II rules that the Trade Practice Conference Division reviewed after 1926 were provisions encouraging businesses to adopt their trade association's standard cost system. In the course of reviewing such rules, the division requested the cost systems themselves. By 1932, the FTC had reviewed 44 cost systems. Of the

[41] U.S. Congress, Senate, 76th Cong., 3d sess., Investigation of Concentration of Economic Power, Temporary National Economic Committee Report, *Control of Unfair Competitive Practices through Trade Practice Conference Procedure of the Federal Trade Commission*, Monograph no. 34 (Washington, DC: Government Printing Office, 1941), 4–5 (hereafter cited as TNEC, *Control*). For an earlier statement, see summary of Commissioner McCullough before the Hickory-Handle Branch, Woodturning Industry, July 18, 1928, in *FTC, Trade Practice Conferences, 1929*, 136, where he says in passing on resolutions adopted at trade practice conferences, the commission determines "whether the things which the industry condemns are really unlawful, and if they are found to be so such rules will be approved and will be enforced by the commission against every concern who may violate them." On the other hand, the commission recognizes that trade practice conferences concern themselves with practices that are not "strictly unlawful," but which participants determine to be "good business rules and sound methods of doing business." The commission doesn't approve or disapprove of the latter, but accepts "such rules as expressions of the trade."

[42] *Annual Report of the Federal Trade Commission 1928* (Washington, DC: Government Printing Office, 1928), 8–10, 13; TNEC, *Control*, 4–6; Kittelle and Mostow, "A Review," 434–37; Hunker, *Trade Practice Conferences*, 39–40, 77–80.

125 conferences whose rules were approved between 1926 and 1932, 31 percent included Group II rules advocating adoption of a trade association cost system. Thus, after a nine-year hiatus, the FTC reinstated cost system reviews.[43]

By 1928 the FTC had institutionalized trade practice conferences. Under Humphrey's guidance, it established a Trade Practice Conference Division, clarified the legal and policy status of trade practice rules, and increased the number of conferences from an average of three per year to seventeen.

HETERARCHY

Once it institutionalized trade practice conferences, the FTC created a unique organization, whose success depended upon its ability to respond to economic uncertainty, diversity, and change. At first blush, Humphrey's accomplishments look Weberian, because the commission proliferated specialties, drew a sharp distinction between rule formation and execution, and integrated the division of labor through hierarchical monitoring and control. However, FTC practice belied bureaucratic rationality. The commission multiplied functions within its divisions. In addition to running conferences and reviewing rules, the Trade Practice Conference Division conducted research and interpreted the law. Top administrators descended the organizational hierarchy to participate in trade practice conferences. And the Legal and Trade Practice Conference divisions engaged in routine horizontal communication. In practice, FTC organization is better understood as heterarchical.

Heterarchy occurred because of design and adaptation, intention and context. Although I have argued that the FTC's formative context was inhospitable to state autonomy and bureaucratic hierarchy, cultivational governance was not a matter of functional adaptation. It necessitated interpretation and creative action. The same was true for the commission's internal organization. Heterarchy was not a functional response to external constraints. There were any number of possibilities, including stalemate and paralysis. At the same time, once Hurley, Gaskill, and Humphrey tagged some qualities in the commission's context as

[43] S. P. Kaidanovsky, *Trade-Practice Conference Rules of the Federal Trade Commission (1919–1936): A Classification for Comparison with the Trade-Practice Provisions of the NRA Codes,* Office of National Recovery Administration, Division of Review, Trade Practice Studies Section, March, 1936, Work Materials no. 54, Table 10-A.

resources and committed the FTC to cultivational governance, some organizational features became more workable than others. Two aspects of the FTC's formative context became particularly salient to heterarchy: its general mandate and the diversity of its regulatory objects.

Section 5 of the Federal Trade Commission Act outlined a vague goal: the commission was to regulate "unfair methods of competition." Section 6 outlined equally general procedural powers: the commission was empowered to "make rules and regulations for the purposes of carrying out the provisions of this Act." As we have seen, the commissioners fought over advance advice (a procedural matter) because they disagreed over what, precisely, the act told them to do about trade agreements (substance). Nor did they agree over method. Some, such as Hurley, applied Brandeisian principles of regulated competition. Others, such as Davies, applied principles of marginalist economics. These conditions made it difficult for top managers to set clear rules to guide subordinates. Institutionalists tend to see such confusions as signs of disarray. Seen instead from a constructivist perspective, we find commissioners who were attuned to the value of republican and scientific deliberation. They turned these challenges into resources by expanding the scope of internal problem solving to include subordinates and by involving themselves in policy implementation.

Charged to regulate the whole U.S. economy, the FTC faced a bewildering variety of industries and problems, which were inhospitable to bureaucratic monitoring and control. Between 1920 and 1932, the FTC held conferences in 143 different industries. Participants came from custom, specialty, batch, and continuous process or mass-production sectors, such as construction, jewelry, knit goods, and paper, respectively.[44] Beyond manufacturing, the commission held conferences in the service trades (e.g., cleaning, dyeing), and the wholesale and retail trades (e.g., groceries, furniture, hardware). Some industries, such as photoengraving, were populated by a large number of small proprietorships, whereas

[44] This classification comes from business historian Philip Scranton, "Diversity in Diversity: Flexible Production and American Industrialization, 1880–1930," *Business History Review* 65 (Spring 1991): 27–90. The FTC held conferences in custom sectors, such as construction, furs, and cotton printing; specialty sectors, such as jewelry, photoengraving, and furniture; batch sectors, such as silverware, knit goods, baby chicks, and butter; and mass-production sectors, such as paper, edible oils, and petroleum. Beyond manufacturing, the commission held conferences in the service trades, such as cleaning, dyeing, and correspondence schools; and in wholesale and retail groceries, furniture, hardware, waste paper, drugs, and school supplies.

others, such as petroleum, were concentrated in large-scale corporations. A mixture of firm sizes and legal forms populated most sectors. Thus, measured by production characteristics, concentration, and legal form, the field of trade regulation was incredibly diverse.[45]

The content of trade practice conferences was equally diverse. A 1934 study found that the FTC approved 291 different trade practice rules between 1919 and 1933. Among them were rules governing advertising, bidding, commercial bribery, customer coercion, pricing, espionage, packing and shipping, contracts, credit, dispute resolution with customers, product grading, wholesaling, warehousing, product leasing, design piracy, ancillary services, and lawsuits.[46] Nor were trade practice rules or industry problems static. As Brandeis and Gaskill pointed out, no sooner were trade customs established, than innovators and opportunists invented new competitive tactics. The problem of unfair competition was diverse and ever changing.

From the institutionalist perspective of command and control regulation, general rules and diverse objects of regulation put strict constraints on organizational hierarchy. From the perspective of cultivational governance, however, they became resources for organizational innovation. As the FTC elaborated cost accounting and trade practice conferences in response to its general mandate and diversity in regulatory objects, it multiplied overlapping functions within its divisions, flattened its hierarchy, and promoted horizontal communication between departments.

Consider first the division of labor between FTC departments. By 1927, the FTC had four major departments, each with a different function: administration, law, economics, and trade practice conferences. Although the Trade Practice Conference Division specialized, it also took on critical legal and research functions. Conferences inevitably discovered new forms of unfair competition, refined the commission's understanding of the conditions under which competition became predatory, and redefined legal distinctions. For example, the Legal and Trade Practice Conference divisions were initially skeptical about Gaskill's proposal to declare pricing below cost an unfair method of competition, because it could be understood as FTC approval for price fixing. Therefore, the Trade Practice Conference Division classified industry rules against the practice in Group II. However, as evidence accumulated from a large number of diverse conferences, the division reclassified pricing below cost as

[45] Kaidanovsky, *Trade-Practice Conference Rules*, 60–65.
[46] Kaidanovsky, *Trade-Practice Conference Rules*, 46–65.

an unfair method of competition and placed conference rules against it in Group I. Drawing on the Trade Practice Conference Division's "research," the Legal Division adjusted its understanding of the practice as well. In the first scholarly study of the commission, Gerard Henderson found conference proceedings had become a successful venue for rule making and research. "Imbued with [a] scientific spirit," he wrote, commissioners and businesspeople "honestly search for the truth" in trade practice conferences. Thus, the Trade Practice Conference Division multiplied functions within its jurisdiction. In addition to running conferences and evaluating trade practice rules, it conducted research and refined administrative law.

The Trade Practice Conference Division also blurred the sharp distinction between top and middle management, or its corollary functions, between plan and execution. Although division administrators were supposed to run conferences, the commissioners did it. In good bureaucratic design, the commissioners delegated administrative power to the chief and assistant directors of the Trade Practice Conference Division, and set rules to ensure accountability. Among those directives was a provision instructing them to preside over conferences. In practice, however, the commissioners traveled all over the country to run industry forums. This involved a significant commitment of FTC resources. By 1925, the division held more than seventeen conferences per year. Moreover, many were in distant locations. Between 1926 and 1930, the commissioners traveled by train to St. Paul; Chicago; New York; Cleveland; Minneapolis; Philadelphia; St. Louis; Pittsburgh; San Francisco; Omaha; Biloxi; Memphis; French Lick, Indiana; and more.[47]

Why would the commissioners devote so much time to running trade conferences? In the absence of fixed categories of unfair competition or an agreed upon theory to assess diverse facts, the commissioners were hard pressed to provide the Trade Practice Conference Division with detailed criteria to judge industry codes. Because the legal distinction between fair and unfair competition, or Group I and Group II rules, was in flux, the commissioners chose to participate in conference deliberations. As Commissioner Humphrey put it, there would be no need for trade practice conferences if the rules of fair competition could be "standardized" and fully articulated ex ante. The FTC could simply publish a rulebook, "mail" it to every firm in the United States, and close the Trade

[47] Federal Trade Commission, *Trade Practice Conferences,* June 30, 1933 (Washington, DC: Government Printing Office, 1933).

Practice Conference Division. Of course, this would mean an end to the "benefit of collective discussion and collective experience," as the commission substituted its "guidance," "intelligence," and practical wisdom for a "two cent stamp."[48] Thus, unlike a Weberian bureaucracy, the FTC flattened its organizational hierarchy and narrowed the sharp distinction between plan and execution. Top managers participated directly in the implementation of policy.

The third feature of FTC organization that deviated from bureaucracy involved communication. Where communication in Weberian organization tends to be vertical, the Trade Practice Conference and Legal divisions engaged in regular lateral communication. Although the commissioners held all departments accountable to FTC goals through vertical communication, the process of reviewing and revising trade practice rules necessitated constant horizontal discussion between the Legal and Trade Practice Conference divisions.

Trade Practice Conference Division administrators consulted FTC counsel in reviewing, classifying, and revising trade rules.[49] And the more the lawyers learned from conference deliberations, the more they consulted the Trade Practice Conference Division when investigating complaints of unfair competition.[50] The commissioners acknowledged the interdependence of the departments when they reworked FTC procedural rules in 1926 to require horizontal communication. Should the lawyers suspect systematic, rather than discrete, acts of unfair competition, they were to report them to the Trade Practice Conference Division for consideration. Should the Trade Practice Conference Division suspect a violation of a settled Group I rule, it was to report it to the Legal Division for investigation and possible enforcement.[51] Thus, like overlapping functions and participatory administration, cultivational governance valued horizontal communication between specialized divisions.

To be sure, the commission's formative context might have resulted in confusion, "ad hocracy," or paralysis. However, by interpreting its general mandate and diverse objects of regulation through a cultivational

48 "Statement of Commissioner Humphrey Regarding the Standardization of Trade Practice Rules," FTC Library, no. 39, 2.

49 Humphrey, "The Standardization of Trade Practice Rules."

50 On the superior quality of information produced through trade practice conferences, instead of adversarial legal proceedings, see Blaisdell, *The Federal Trade Commission*, 243–44.

51 See *Annual Report of the Federal Trade Commission 1926* (Washington, DC: Government Printing Office), 47–50.

or republican experimentalist lens, Gaskill and Humphrey uncovered resources for policy innovation and organizational design. Harnessed to investigation, deliberation, and standard setting, the commission seized economic diversity as an opportunity for inductive learning or reasoning by analogy. Once committed to this process, some organizational features worked better than others. Instead of adopting principles of bureaucratic hierarchy, the commissioners improvised heterarchy.

CONCLUSION

Creative syncretists at the Federal Trade Commission made a great deal of progress in cultivational governance during the commission's first two decades. In addition to regulation and research, they developed an infrastructure to cultivate deliberative polyarchy in trade, professional, and peak business associations. Although decidedly less statist than Brandeis imagined, the FTC realized his proposals for trade agreement supervision and cost accounting. Brandeis hoped to empower the commission to mandate uniform cost accounting and provide benchmarking services, whereas the FTC cultivated those capacities in trade associations. Nevertheless, by providing a forum for setting standards of fair competition and effective cost accounting, the commission helped realize Brandeis's goal of regulated competition.

Cultivational governance was born of context and conviction. On the one hand, the FTC was born into a context hostile to Weberian state building: a general and contested mandate, meager finances, and diverse objects of regulation. However, where historical institutionalists looking back see only the conditions for confusion, paralysis, or capture, a constructivist perspective sensitizes us to reflexive state builders, who saw opportunities in the same conditions for policy innovation and institutional design. Under Brandeis's influence or drawing from a common cultural and technical well, Hurley, Gaskill, and Humphrey surveyed FTC possibilities with a republican experimentalist outlook. Hurley and Gaskill saw in the stalemate over advance advice an opportunity for consensus over cost accounting and trade practice submittals. Humphrey and Gaskill saw in the FTC's meager resources and ties to trade associations opportunities to institutionalize trade practice conferences. All three of these republican experimentalists saw opportunities for inductive learning and analogical reasoning in the commission's diverse objects of regulation, opportunities for cultivational governance.

Once Hurley, Gaskill, and Humphrey committed the FTC to cultivational governance, some organizational features proved more effective than others. Instead of bureaucratic hierarchy, the commissioners found heterarchy more appropriate to the process of setting, evaluating, and revising rules of fair competition. Although a strict division of labor, a hierarchical distinction between policy planning and execution, and vertical communication might have served an agency with a clear mandate and relatively homogeneous objects of regulation, the FTC found divisions with multiple functions, participatory administration, and lateral communication more effective to setting and revising rules in the face of diversity. Heterarchy was not a matter of functional adaptation to the structural conditions the FTC faced. Like cultivational governance, it was born of conviction and context, creativity and opportunity.

Did the FTC accomplish civic mindedness, economic growth, and collaborative learning? Two provisional conclusions are possible. First, the commission succeeded in establishing an infrastructure for republican experimentalism. It provided a forum for business, accountants, trade associations, peak associations, and the state to enlarge their sense of self-interest and to probe alternatives to destructive competition. Second, this forum succeeded in altering public discussion about the *causes* of destructive competition. By establishing a relationship between cost accounting and competition, the commission renarrated the causes of competition from technology to accounting custom. Instead of technologically induced overcapacity causing cutthroat price competition, Gaskill spoke for the commission and its interlocutors when he said the "volume illusion" caused "displacement competition," that is, a zero-sum rivalry for market share. The former implied an unalterable constraint (witness the language of *fixed* costs), whereas the latter opened management practice to collective imagination, experimentation, and evaluation. Change accounting customs, the commission and its accountants said, and business will begin to see novel opportunities to compete over productivity and product diversity. In 1916, the FTC's model cost system had identified the problem and outlined the means to upgrade competition. By 1932, the Trade Practice Conference Division had reviewed and approved more than fifty cost systems that shared those principles. Whether FTC-sponsored discussion succeeded in altering the terrain of civil society or actually improved business conditions is the subject of the next two chapters.

Chapter 6

Deliberative Polyarchy and Developmental Associations

The Federal Trade Commission's efforts to cultivate deliberative polyarchy bore fruit in creative action in civil society. The cost accountants took up the commission's challenge to work with trade associations to upgrade competition through cost work and benchmarking. Many trade associations took up the FTC's challenge, and in doing so, they made the transition from cartel to developmental association. In 1918, the U.S. Chamber of Commerce took up where the FTC left off in 1916 and assembled cost accountants, trade associations, and managers to conceptualize developmental associations and make the form more widely available. By 1925, at least 25 percent of all trade associations, in 15 percent of all manufacturing industries, had participated in crafting developmental associations, with up to half that number instituting its features in whole or in part.

This chapter recounts the progress of developmental associations in manufacturing and deliberative polyarchy in peak and professional associations. It shows how trade associations, cost accountants, and the U.S. Chamber of Commerce discovered cost accounting and conceptualized developmental associations. Trade associations created cost accounting and collaborative learning from their efforts to share price information. Cost accountants discovered developmental associations after a battle with financial accountants and after they failed to impose methods of scientific management on their clients. The U.S. Chamber of Commerce was introduced to developmental associations by the state. Once in the game, the National Association of Cost Accountants (NACA) and the Chamber of Commerce assembled trade association officials, accountants, business managers, and state officials to conceptualize developmental associations. By 1924, they had established an ideal type with four defining features: a common language, collective deliberation, benchmarking, and price stabilization. By conceptualizing developmental associations publicly, they hoped to make them available for adaptation, adoption, and policy debate.

Students of associationalism in the 1920s miss – or mischaracterize – deliberative polyarchy and developmental associations. In search of liberal corporatism, they find organizations too weak to overcome collective action problems, forge consensus, represent encompassing interests, or enforce rules. Like the FTC, peak business, professional, and trade associations were insufficiently bureaucratic and authoritative to resolve overcapacity problems or negotiate wage and price policy. Professional accountants were too divided before the New Deal to set and enforce ethics, accounting, and certification rules. Peak business associations were too internally diverse and insufficiently encompassing to represent class interests effectively in politics. And, hobbled by antitrust, trade associations were so weak that even modest efforts to coordinate collective action through information sharing proved impossible. The result, according to the conventional view, was experimentation, hand waving, and partisan dogma. However much Republicans embraced associational governance in the 1920s, it had little lasting economic or institutional significance.[1]

But if economic and institutional conditions were inhospitable to corporatism, they were not bereft of possibilities for creative experimentation. Background conditions alone cannot explain action or organizational results. The theory of creative syncretism asks us to look,

[1] The most recent versions of this history are Colin Gordon, *New Deals: Business, Labor, and Politics in America, 1920–1935* (Cambridge: Cambridge University Press, 1994), 35–86, 128–65; Kenneth Finegold and Theda Skocpol, *State and Party in America's New Deal* (Madison: University of Wisconsin Press, 1995); Stephen Skowronek, *Building a New American State* (Cambridge: Cambridge University Press, 1982), 267–71; and Mark Allen Eisner, *From Warfare State to Welfare State* (University Park: Pennsylvania State University Press, 2000), 89–138. See also Robert Himmelberg, *The Origins of the National Recovery Administration* (New York: Fordham University Press, 1976); Robert H. Salisbury, "Why No Corporatism in the United States," in Philippe Schmitter and Gerhard Lembruch, eds., *Trends toward Corporatist Intermediation* (Beverly Hills, CA: Sage, 1972), 213–30. On the divisions among accountants before the New Deal and the role of the Securities and Exchange Commission in the development of the profession, see Paul Miranti, *Accountancy Comes of Age: The Development of an American Profession, 1886–1940* (Chapel Hill: University of North Carolina Press, 1990); and Thomas K. McCraw, *Prophets of Regulation* (Cambridge, MA: Harvard University Press, 1984), 189–92. On corporatism more generally, see Oscar Molina and Martin Rhodes, "Corporatism: The Past, Present, and Future of a Concept," *Annual Review of Political Science* 5 (2002): 305–31.

instead, at how actors in civil society perceived the institutional landscape and recomposed its resources to experiment with novel institutional forms. Like reflexive state builders at the FTC, creative professionals and associationalists perceived their opportunities and constraints through a lens akin to Brandeis's republican experimentalism. They scanned the institutional landscape for resources to build associations capable of organizing deliberation, information pooling, and inductive learning. The architecture of their vision was remarkably different from the one economists, financial accounts, and corporatists mobilized to build associations devoted to professional autonomy, deductive standard setting, and discipline. Hence, they saw opportunities where corporatists and their historians saw only constraints.

When trade associations tried to build corporatist organizations by circumventing antitrust and sharing price information, they found it was also necessary to compare costs. Those who were receptive to alternative ways of conceptualizing organizational goals found that this opened the door to Deweyan deliberation – reflexive discussions about competition, productivity, and accounting customs – and made it possible to recompose cartels into developmental associations. When cost accountants developed accounting systems that failed to satisfy their customers, they saw an opportunity to rethink their professional identity, their clients' role in designing cost systems, and the nature of useful knowledge. By doing so, they invented a professional association devoted to deliberation and inductive learning, instead of autonomy, deductive standard setting, and discipline. When U.S. Chamber of Commerce executives failed to exercise authority over their diverse members on major policy issues, they reconceptualized the organization from a corporatist peak association, devoted to representing class interests in politics, to a deliberative service organization, devoted to improving business performance. In doing so, they found resources in their institutional environment to create a Manufacturing Division, which dedicated itself to the progress of developmental associations.

This chapter is organized in four sections: discovery, institutions, creative conceptualization, and the demography of developmental associations. The first section explains how trade associations, the U.S. Chamber of Commerce, and cost accountants discovered developmental associations. The second section describes the three mediating institutions that organized the creative conceptualization of developmental associations: the National Association of Cost Accountants, the U.S. Chamber of Commerce, and the American Trade Association Executives. The third section outlines the theory of developmental associations as the cost accountants and associationalists conceptualized it. Finally, the fourth section surveys the demography of developmental associations.

DISCOVERY

Trade Associations

In 1910, Brandeis's tutor on trade associations, Arthur Jerome Eddy, launched his first "open price association." He told an assembly of the Structural Bridge Builders' Society that the industry had suffered too long from an asymmetry of information between buyers and sellers. Clients secured bids, "peddled" them to contractors, and, in their ignorance, the bridge builders chipped away at their prices until every profit disappeared. Suppose that "instead of acting as jealous and independent units," contractors tried an experiment. What if they disclosed and freely discussed their costs, work in hand, prospective work, all bids actually made, and the general conditions in the industry? Eddy asked.[2]

> Competing in the open with full knowledge of all the conditions influencing others, no man would make a ruinously low price or an arbitrarily high one. The competition would be real, keen, and healthful. Prices would vary but they would not vary widely; ... in dull times prices would approach cost, but the educational value of the association would tend to deter ruinous bidding; open criticism of work inefficiently done would expose the tricky bidder.[3]

While institutionalists have noticed Eddy's experiments, they interpret them as failed efforts to solve collective action problems, and thus amenable to analysis with the tools of game theory. In these accounts, "open price associations" (as they came to be called) turned to tacit price coordination through information sharing after repeated failures to enforce cartels and antitrust suits.[4] These were, in effect, new institutional

[2] Milton Nels Nelson, "Open Price Associations," *University of Illinois Studies in the Social Sciences* 10, no. 2 (June 1922): 24–25.

[3] Arthur Jerome Eddy, *The New Competition* (New York: Appleton, 1912), 100–101.

[4] See John R. Bowman, "The Politics of the Market: Economic Competition and the Organization of Capitalists," *Political Power and Social Theory* 5 (1985): 51, where he writes, "When direct communication among competitors is impossible [because of antitrust], trade associations or similar institutions can perform a clearing house function and collect and disseminate 'average' past prices or current prices, which, with very little imagination, can be transformed into current minimum prices. The same end can be achieved through the circulation of studies, which calculate 'average' or 'typical' costs. A more subtle method of communicating cost (and price) data among

solutions to the problem of coordinating preferences or solving prisoners' dilemmas associated with overcapacity problems. Information cartels, in this view, did little better than their parents at stabilizing prices, because they fostered cooperation only under restrictive conditions: small numbers of firms, homogeneous products, and high entry barriers. But open price associations were in precisely the wrong industries. Construction, cotton printing, and hardware were custom or batch sectors, where firms were small and plentiful and entry was easy. Moreover, contrary to conventional accounts, these associations did not collapse at the first sign of opportunism. Instead, creative actors in open price associations taught their members how to play a new game. Through incremental trial and error, they transformed open price associations from competition-suppressing cartels into developmental associations devoted to collaborative learning.

As Eddy explained, information sharing was controversial, so it was necessary to enlist participation deliberately. Everyone assumed their competitors would take advantage of them if they revealed their prices. They mistrusted one another and no one trusted Eddy. So he tried an experiment to mobilize participants and spark collective deliberation about the causes of their distress. He asked the bridge builders to submit prices to the society during the bidding process and then discuss outcomes afterward. "The open price policy means not only open prices," Eddy wrote, "but open discussions." Once bids were revealed, the bridge builders inevitably raised questions about the circumstances under which winners secured contracts and in doing so, they reflected upon habitual methods of evaluating efficiency and competitive strategy. Did the

competing firms is through 'cost education' – making sure that capitalists know all of their costs and circulating rules of thumb that tend to equalize costs (at a relatively high level) throughout an industry." See also John R. Bowman, *Capitalist Collective Action: Competition, Cooperation and Conflict in the Coal Industry* (Cambridge: Cambridge University Press, 1989); Gordon, *New Deals*, 15–20; Peter Swenson, *Capitalists against Markets: The Making of Labor Markets and Welfare States in the United States and Sweden* (Oxford: Oxford University Press, 2002), 22–24. For a more general institutionalist appeal to use game theory to conceptualize business associations as mechanisms to thicken expectations and solve coordination problems through information pooling, see Peter A. Hall and David Soskice, "An Introduction to Varieties of Capitalism," in Peter A. Hall and David Soskice, eds., *Varieties* of *Capitalism: The Institutional Foundations of Comparative Advantage* (Oxford: Oxford University Press, 2001), 9–12; Pepper D. Culpepper, "Employers, Public Policy, and the Politics of Decentralized Cooperation in Germany and France," in Hall and Soskice, eds., *Varieties of Capitalism*, 275–307; and Pepper D. Culpepper, *Creating Cooperation: How States Develop Human Capital in Europe* (Ithaca, NY: Cornell University Press, 2003).

winners have the genuinely lowest costs? they asked. Or did they use shoddy materials, sweat their workers, or make false promises? Everyone agreed that none of these questions could be answered without better knowledge of costs and sufficient uniformity to compare across firms.

Discussion of prices, in other words, inevitably led to discussion of efficiency, competitive strategy, and costs. And when firms met to discuss costs, Eddy reported, debate became heated: "*no two agreed upon all the items that should be charged against a given piece of work. ...* Differences of opinion and practices developed in the discussion were so surprising that a competent committee was appointed to work out a cost system applicable to the industry."[5] Thus, Eddy's experiment in pooling price information succeeded in generating Deweyan deliberation: it perturbed habits, sparked spontaneous discussion, and formalized that discussion in a committee to reconfigure costs.

The standing committee's "comprehensive and scientific cost system" accomplished three goals. First, it provided small and medium-sized firms with access to expertise only the largest corporations could afford. Second, in a custom goods industry (e.g., construction), it developed a uniform "cost blank" for the purposes of bidding. Once "every item of cost entering into a piece of work" was included, prices would stabilize without agreement. Finally, once a uniform system of cost accounting was joined with open cost reporting, industry members had a yardstick to compare their own progress in cost reduction with others in their industry.[6] Thus, what began as monitoring for tacit price coordination became information sharing for deliberation and collaborative learning. Open price cartels, which were devoted to suppressing competition, became developmental associations, devoted to upgrading competition through improved cost accounting, information pooling, and collective deliberation.

Other industries abandoned corporatist strategies for collaborative learning more directly. Caught in the profit squeeze of rising wage costs and cutthroat price competition, associations in printing, tanning, paint and varnish, drugs, silk, malleable castings, biscuits, stoves and furnaces, plywood, and millwork also experimented with open cost work. Like Eddy, association officials in these industries learned how deliberation aroused interest. Many attempted to mobilize membership with a cost experiment. Each firm was asked to estimate the cost of a standard product,

[5] Eddy, *The New Competition,* 148, emphasis original.
[6] Eddy, *The New Competition,* 148.

such as business cards, soda crackers, a "16-inch taffeta," or a simple steel casting. The variations were dramatic, ranging from 15 percent in steam-fitting products, to 60 percent in metal casting, 125 percent in silk, 139 percent in printing, and 250 percent in drug manufacture.[7] It took little reflection to realize the differences flowed from differences in cost accounting methods, not productivity. In fact, participants were often startled by the results, and opened broader discussions about the relationship between cost accounting and productivity. In short, these experiments taught firms to turn cost assumptions into hypotheses and open new lines of inquiry. At a minimum, everyone learned "the great need for us to speak the same language," said Harry Green of the Biscuit and Cracker Association. "If we were all to get down to ... calling the same things by the same names, about seventy-five per cent of our troubles would be eliminated."[8] Or as the commissioner of the Plywood Manufacturers' Association put it, the key task for associations in the new century was to develop a common "cost lexicon."[9]

In summary, the same structural conditions that institutionalists argue precluded price coordination through information pooling made developmental associations possible. After repeated failures to enforce price cartels or coordinate cooperation over price fixing, creative syncretists in custom, batch, and specialty industries tried something different. Where large numbers, easy entry, and economic diversity were constraints on price coordination, associationalists learned to treat them as assets in mobilization. Drawing on the "natural curiosity" for comparison across diverse circumstances, reflexive associationalists persuaded reluctant businesspeople to discuss their costs. In doing so, they shifted the challenge

[7] See J. H. Foy, *Uniform Cost Accounting Conference, Chamber of Commerce of the United States*, New York City, March 25–26, 1924, U.S. Chamber of Commerce Papers, Hagley Museum and Library, Acc. 1960, 84–87 (hereafter cited as CofC, March, 1924); Robert Belt, "Benefits Secured from Uniform Methods of Cost Accounting," *Proceedings of the Chicago Cost Conference of the Chamber of Commerce*, U.S.A., October 23, 1923, U.S. Chamber of Commerce Papers, Acc. 1960, 4–5 (hereafter cited as CofC, October, 1923); Austin Cheney, CofC, March, 1924, 91–92; Howard Coonley, "The Executives' Use of Costs," *National Association of Cost Accountants, Year Book, 1926, 7th International Cost Conference* (New York: National Association of Cost Accountants, 1926), 34; George N. Voorhees, "The Story of Production Records," *Typothetae Bulletin* 21, no. 17 (July 27, 1925): 281.

[8] *National Association of Cost Accountants, Year Book, 1921* (New York: NACA, 1921), 163–64 (hereafter cited as *NACA, Year Book, 1921*).

[9] *Uniform Cost Accounting Conference* held at Congress Hotel, Chicago, Illinois, October 28–29, 1924, 81, Hagley Museum and Library, Papers of the U.S. Chamber of Commerce, Acc. 1960 (hereafter cited as CofC, October, 1924).

of association from collective action to collaborative learning and reinvented cartels as developmental associations.

Cost Accountants

Three experiences led the cost accountants to discover developmental associations: a divorce from financial accountants, their relationship with the FTC, and the failures of scientific management. The first pushed cost accountants away from corporate clients toward trade associations. The second deepened the relationship between cost accountants and associations by giving costing accounting a public, as well as a private, purpose. And the third taught cost accountants about the need for deliberation in creating practical cost systems.

In 1913, American accountants squared off on a seemingly obscure issue, which raised fundamental questions about narrative identity: whether to include interest on debt as a cost. Although technically resoluble, this fight was so divisive it resulted in divorce. Cost accountants and financial accountants squared off on fundamental issues of principle, social location, and narrative legitimacy. In 1918 cost accountants bolted the American Institute of Accountants (AIA) to form their own association, the National Association of Cost Accountants (NACA).[10]

In the financial accountants' story line, including interest as a cost in balance sheets and income statements undermined the legitimacy of their profession by making it appear they had no autonomy from their clients' interests. Having spent much of the previous decade valuing assets for corporate mergers, financial accountants came to see themselves as autonomous professionals in a world of self-interested clients. They valued accounts according to their probity, their clients' trust in numbers, and the public legitimacy they conferred upon the profession. From this perspective, interest looked like an "anticipated profit." To include it as a cost on a financial statement would be to inflate assets or profits, misrepresent

[10] For good secondary accounts of this contest, see Stephen A. Zeff, "Some Junctures in the Evolution of the Process of Establishing Accounting Principles in the U.S.A.: 1917–1972," *Accounting Review* 59 (1984): 448–50; Gary John Previts and Barbara D. Merino, *A History of Accounting in America: A Historical Interpretation of the Cultural Significance of Accounting* (New York: Wiley, 1979), 169–85; H. Thomas Johnson and Robert S. Kaplan, *Relevance Lost: The Rise and Fall of Management Accounting* (Cambridge, MA: Harvard Business School Press, 1991), 130–41; S. Paul Garner, *Evolution of Cost Accounting to 1925* (Tuscaloosa: University of Alabama Press, 1954, reprint 1976), 142–61.

corporate accounts to interested clients, and undermine the fragile legitimacy of this immature profession. In short, the technical problem of how to treat interest on debt in financial accounts raised thorny matters of principle, narrative identity, and social position. As the financial accountants saw it, the nature of accounts determined the accountability of the profession.[11]

In the cost accountants' story line, costs were engineering tools, which enhanced management capacity to improve products and production processes. It was necessary to include interest because it provided critical information for technical decisions. How could manufacturers decide whether to make or buy a component, calculate the most profitable mix of products, or compare productivity across departments without including the cost of capital in their calculations?[12] Like the FTC's Robert Belt, most cost accountants were trained in the factory, and saw themselves more as "management engineers" than simply accountants. As business historian Christopher McKenna writes, cost accountants of the 1920s invented the profession of business consulting in the United States.[13] Thus, like their financial counterparts, cost accountants saw the debate over interest as a matter of principle, narrative identity, and social position. As they saw it, the nature of accounts revealed indispensable stories about products and production.[14]

[11] For good examples of the financial accountants' understanding of how to treat interest, see J. P. Joplin, "Interest Does Not Enter into the Cost of Production," *Journal of Accountancy* 15 (1913): 334–35; J. E. Sterrett, "Interest Not a Part of the Cost of Production," *Journal of Accountancy* 15 (1913): 241–44. On Sterret and others who took this position aganst inclusion, see Paul J. Miranti, *Accountancy Comes of Age: The Development of an American Profession, 1886–1940* (Chapel Hill: University of North Carolina Press, 1990), 41, 73, 76.

[12] For the cost accountants view, see C. H. Scovell, "Interest on Investment as a Factor in Manufacturing Cost," *The American Association of University Instructors in Accounting* 3 (1919), *Papers and Proceedings of the Third Annual Meeting* (1918). Reprinted as *Papers and Proceedings of the American Association of University Instructors in Accounting* (New York: Arno, 1980), 12–32; William Morse Cole, "Interest on Investment in Equipment," *Journal of Accountancy,* 15 (April 1913): 232–36.

[13] Christopher D. McKenna, "The Origins of Modern Management Consulting," *Business and Economic History* 24, no. 1 (Fall 1995): 51–58; Christopher D. McKenna, "The World's Newest Profession: Management Consulting in the Twentieth Century," *Enterprise & Society* 2, no. 4 (December 2001): 673–79; Christopher D. McKenna, *The World's Newest Profession: Management Consulting in the Twentieth Century* (Cambridge: Cambridge University Press, 2006).

[14] On the distinction between "management" and "financial" accounting more generally, see Johnson and Kaplan, *Relevance Lost.*

In 1917, the AIA appointed a committee to resolve the dispute. The leading cost accountant, A. Hamilton Church, proposed a compromise: create two sets of books – one for investors with interest excluded as a cost, a second for management with it included.[15] The committee rejected Church's compromise. Dominated by financial accountants, it declared interest's objective status. It is not an "expenditure for production ... but ... an anticipation of profits. ... As such, [it] has no logical standing in the computation of production cost. ... Inclusion results in...false statements of assets and income." Given this truth, Church's proposal met ridicule. It was "artificial," redundant, and "absurd," not unlike the famous nursery rhyme involving the "hillside exploits of the 'Gallant Duke of York' and his famous ten thousand men," who marched them up to the top of the hill and marched them down again.[16] In the nascent corporate economy, where trust in numbers remained fragile, the financial accountants insisted that probity and professional autonomy trumped management capacity and embedded expertise.

Cost accountants were not orphaned by defeat; they created their own association. As the AIA distributed its report on interest in 1918, hundreds of cost accountants signed on to help with the FTC's wartime cost work, where they deepened their relationship with the commission and with trade associations. Coupled with Commissioner Hurley's efforts to enlist cost accountants to FTC's cost work in 1916, their experience in the war gave the cost accountants a sense of public, as well as private, purpose. When the war ended, they convened a meeting in Buffalo – the heart of industrial, not financial, New York – to launch the National Association of Cost Accountants (NACA). Within eight years, there were thousands of members in twenty-seven chapters from Boston to Hawaii.[17] As the next section will show, NACA became as important to developmental associations as it was to professional development.

A third experience led cost accountants to developmental associations: the limits of scientific objectivity and professional autonomy. No less than financial accountants or economists, cost accountants aspired

[15] A. Hamilton Church, "On the Inclusion of Interest in Manufacturing Costs," *Journal of Accountancy* 15 (April 1913): 236–40.

[16] American Institute of Accountants (AIA), *1918 Year-Book of the Institute of Accountants In the United States of America* (Including the American Association of Public Accountants) (Brooklyn, NY: American Institute of Accountants, 1919), 110–12.

[17] *National Association of Cost Accountants, Year Book, 1926*, 3–13.

to autonomy and objectivity. Followers of Frederick Taylor, many saw cost accounting as a vital means to scientific management's goal of optimal efficiency. But a disposition toward other ways of thinking about the nature and use of measurement and experience taught otherwise. More often than not, early efforts to implement scientific cost systems failed.[18] As NACA's second president, J. P. Jordan, told a gathering of trade association executives, the history of cost accounting showed that methods flawless in theory proved unworkable in practice. Nineteenth-century cost accounting was primitive. Among the few manufacturers who experimented with it, most guessed at depreciation and overhead. Then "along came a beautiful breed of efficiency engineers, of which I happened to be one myself." We designed theoretically elegant methods and attempted to "ramrod" them down our clients' "throats." The results were disastrous. The "best" cost systems languished on shelves – too complex, impractical, and costly to put into practice.[19]

The failures of scientific objectivity, Jordan went on, demonstrated the necessity of building cost systems from the bottom up. Cost accountants learned to "bring together" practitioners to "talk with one another."[20] Luckily, they found trade associations that had already begun to broach the subject. The result was a natural alliance between cost accountants and associations, which had grown into a broad movement for uniform cost accounting by the early 1920s. Thus, from the cost accountants' perspective, scientific management was not a unified system with tightly linked parts. When it failed, they creatively decomposed it into parts, jettisoned some, kept others, and granted what was left a novel meaning. Whereas scientific management once meant objectivity and autonomy, now it meant practicality and collaboration.

When Jordan talked about the shift in clients from firms to trade associations, he spoke from experience. His firm – Stevenson, Jordan, and Harrison – reorganized itself into two divisions to reflect its growing clientele among trade associations as well as individual firms. Like the FTC's Robert

[18] On the influence of scientific management over cost accounting, see Marc Jay Epstein, "The Effect of Scientific Management on the Development of the Standard Cost System" (PhD diss., Department of Accounting and Quantitative Methods, University of Oregon, 1973). On the spotty success of scientific management more generally, see Robert Kanigel, *The One Best Way: Frederick Winslow Taylor and the Enigma of Efficiency* (London: Little, Brown, 1997); Daniel Nelson, "Scientific Management in Retrospect," in Daniel Nelson, ed., *A Mental Revolution: Scientific Management Since Taylor* (Columbus: Ohio State University Press, 1992), 5–39.

[19] CofC, March, 1924, 51–57.

[20] CofC, March, 1924, 56–57.

Belt, who served several trade associations in metal casting, Jordan's partner, Charles Stevenson, became secretary of the National Envelope Association and the Fibre Box Association.[21] Many other cost accountants followed their lead, serving as salaried cost accountants to associations, associational executives, or presidents of industry cost associations. By the mid-1920s, cost accountants and trade associations had forged a common project.

In summary, the cost accountants discovered developmental associations as a result of their split with financial accountants, their relationship with the state, and the failures of scientific management. In doing so, they redefined the value of accounts according to their use in production and themselves as embedded professionals, whose success depended upon their capacity to guide the deliberations of practitioners toward better management.

The U.S. Chamber of Commerce

The U.S. Chamber of Commerce was born in 1912 in the midst of the struggle over antitrust reform. A peak business association, its goal was to mold business opinion and convey it to the state, or as historian Colin Gordon puts it, to unify and represent class interests in democratic politics. The U.S. Chamber of Commerce administered regular referenda and published their results. But, as institutionalists point out, its membership was too diverse to speak with one voice and its leadership was too weak to impose uniformity on complex policy issues such as antitrust. It was a weak corporatist organization. As a result, the U.S. Chamber of Commerce was slow to respond to the FTC's cultivational challenge. Although its president, Harry Wheeler, applauded Commissioner Hurley's efforts and initiated a cost committee in response, it lay fallow for nearly three years.[22]

[21] On Stevenson, see *National Association of Cost Accountants Year Book, 1927, Proceedings of the Eighth International Cost Conference* (New York: National Association of Cost Accountants, 1927), 20.

[22] On the U.S. Chamber's close ties with the FTC, see "The New Umpires of American Business," and "The National Chamber Appoints a Cooperating Committee," *The Nation's Business,* April 15, 1915, 7–8; and "Report of the Federal Trade Committee," U.S. Chamber of Commerce, Minutes of the Fourth Annual Meeting, 1916, 138, Hagley Museum and Library, Acc. 1960, Box 2. On the U.S. Chamber's criticism of the FTC, see George Cullom Davis, "The Federal Trade Commission: Promise and Practice in Regulating Business, 1900–1929" (PhD diss., University of Illinois, 1969), 197–200, 208–11, 233–34.

World War I changed the U.S. Chamber's relationship to its membership and the state and in doing so led its executives to recompose organizational resources to realize new ends. In 1917, the War Industries Board enlisted the association's help in forming industry-planning committees. Government planners asked the U.S. Chamber to tap its rich trade association membership for participation and to communicate the War Industries Board's policies and progress to American business.[23] When the association emerged from the war, creative executives reconfigured the U.S. Chamber of Commerce from a corporatist peak association into a service organization devoted to working more closely with trade associations and the state. In 1918, they mobilized trade association guidance and support to launch twelve industry-based service divisions.[24] At the FTC's prodding, the U.S. Chamber also resurrected its cost committee at the 1918 annual convention. In a concurrent meeting, more than 160 participants heard speeches from NACA officers; technical papers; and a series of lively debates over the relationship between cost accounting, trade associations, and government policy. As the meeting came to a close, creative syncretists in the newly formed Manufacturing Division announced their intention to take up trade association cost work. Over the next six years, the division became a national forum for the many creative actors who wanted to conceptualize developmental associations and make them more broadly available to American industry.[25]

The U.S. Chamber of Commerce's weak hierarchy and internal diversity proved to be assets to the FTC's cultivational project. Unable to forge a unified class opinion on antitrust, chamber executives recomposed organizational resources to create decentralized member services and committed its Manufacturing Division to FTC cost accounting. Like the FTC, it found resources where institutionalists see only constraints.[26]

[23] Robert D. Cuff, *The War Industries Board: Business-Government Relations during World War I* (Baltimore: Johns Hopkins University Press, 1973), 23–24, 155–58, 185–95, 201–2.

[24] Donald C. Blaisdell, *Economic Power and Political Pressures,* Temporary National Economic Committee, 66th Cong., 3d sess., Investigation of Concentration of Economic Power, Monograph no. 26 (Washington, DC: Government Printing Office, 1941), 25–37.

[25] *Proceedings of the Eighth Annual Meeting of the United States Chamber of Commerce*, "Group III – Cost Accounting," Box 3, Hagley Museum and Library, Acc. 1960, 324–93. The vast majority of participants came from manufacturing companies (39), industry trade associations (37), and state or local manufacturers associations (6). Other participants included cost accountants; representatives of local chambers of commerce; and educators from business, agricultural, and correspondence schools.

[26] Gordon, *New Deals,* 144–47.

Although internal diversity and weak hierarchy prevented the U.S. Chamber of Commerce from becoming a corporatist peak business association, they made it an excellent candidate for an organization devoted to deliberative polyarchy.

INSTITUTIONS OF DELIBERATIVE POLYARCHY

Three organizations took up the task of assembling trade associations, cost accountants, and managers to conceptualize developmental associations: the National Association of Cost Accountants (NACA), the U.S. Chamber of Commerce, and the American Trade Association Executives (ATAE). Each had an unorthodox, nonbureaucratic structure.

National Association of Cost Accountants

The National Association of Cost Accountants (NACA) was a deliberative association of embedded professionals. Like the creative administrators at the FTC, NACA's architects designed the association heterarchically in order to foster lateral communication between its departments and among members.

Contrast NACA's heterarchical organization with the bureaucratic hierarchy of the American Institute of Accountants (AIA). Led by financial accountants from the nation's most prestigious firms, the AIA set conventional professional goals: autonomy, objectivity, and trust among clients. The means to these ends were standard setting, restrictive licensing, and enforcement. The AIA's internal divisions were devoted to setting rules for ethics, auditing, and education, and enlisted the coercive power of state governments for licensing and enforcement. In short, like lawyers and physicians, financial accountants built bureaucratic capacity in their professional association to set standards, monitor behavior, enforce rules, and lobby government.[27]

The first president of NACA, William Lybrand, outlined three goals for the association: educate business about the relationship between cost accounting and good management, standardize cost techniques, and cooperate with trade associations.[28] The means to these ends were experimentation, discussion, and comparison. As NACA secretary Stuart McCleod put it, "we have dealt up to the present time almost entirely with principles

[27] Miranti, *Accountancy Comes of Age*, 7.

[28] *NACA, Year Book, 1921*, 12.

and methods." Now it was time to share and evaluate their experiences. NACA's goal was to facilitate learning about "'How we do it,' more than about 'How it ought to be done.'"[29]

NACA devised four divisions to realize these goals: research, education, publications, and chapters. Unlike the AIA, which separated functions, each NACA division shared functions and communicated with the other. The Department of Research took the lead. Instead of a division of experts, who conducted independent research on accounting standards and practice, the department became a clearinghouse for communication, deliberation, and education among its members. Its first chair, J. P. Jordan, implored members to "flood the ... Department with inquiries, suggestions, references to useful articles, and valuable stunts." It should be "remembered by all" that a vexing problem for one practitioner may be old hat for another. Therefore, the more the department can match question and answer, inexperience and experience, the greater the "tangible benefit to everyone."[30]

Under Jordan's creative guidance, the Department of Research formalized the "co-operative exchange of ideas" in a "vocational index." Because the "available literature" was silent on many practical questions and the department had limited resources, it classified members according to "experience" in an index and then referred inquiries to appropriate practitioners. Jordan praised curiosity as much as expertise. The more questions NACA fielded, the greater was its impact on managerial practice. By 1922, the Department of Research processed an average of twenty-five letters a day.[31]

The Research Division also fostered learning by compiling trade association cost systems. During its first five years, the department gathered more than one hundred manuals. Many were works in progress. Nonetheless, they "constitute[d] a mine of information" for firms and associations in the midst of the design process.[32] The Department of Research worked closely with the Publications Department to publish association systems in the association's monthly journal, *The NACA Bulletin*, and the proceedings of its annual meetings.[33]

[29] *National Association of Cost Accountants, Year Book, 1923* (New York: National Association of Cost Accountants, 1923), 14, 19–20.

[30] *NACA, Year Book, 1921*, 41–42.

[31] *NACA, Year Book, 1921*, 41; *NACA, Year Book, 1923*, 14.

[32] *NACA, Year Book, 1921*, 39.

[33] *NACA, Year Book, 1922*, 16.

The Education Department and the Chapters Department collaborated on another deliberative learning project. In 1922, they initiated a process of "rotating papers" among NACA's chapters, which fostered collective deliberation and learning among diverse participants. The Education Department organized a committee to write a series of "master papers" on a variety of topics. Hoping to exploit the specialized knowledge of local practitioners, the Chapters Division circulated the papers in sequence, asking each chapter for comments, revisions, and amendments. In the end, the papers were returned to the national office in New York, where the Education Department edited and compiled them into a "digest" that distilled "the best" practices from "all the chapters combined."[34]

In summary, creative syncretists in NACA cultivated deliberative learning by organizing communication among cost accountants, business managers, and trade association executives. In doing so, they created a heterarchical organization that multiplied functions across its divisions and fostered projects that narrowed the sharp distinction between research, standard setting, and education. Among the most significant of these projects in the 1920s was a self-conscious effort to conceptualize developmental associations.

The U.S. Chamber of Commerce

Formed in 1918, the U.S. Chamber's Manufacturing Division took up where Hurley's FTC accounting project had left off three years earlier. It polled its members about cost accounting; assembled managers, cost accountants, and trade association officials to conceptualize developmental associations; and set down their ideas in a series of widely distributed pamphlets. By 1924, the Manufacturing Division had succeeded in turning a series of fragmented experiments into a coherent program.

During its first months in operation, the division's chair, E. W. McCollough, appointed a cost committee to work with trade associations and hired Robert Belt to chair it. The committee polled manufacturers on cost accounting. It found that although most manufacturers were familiar with the basic concepts, cost accountants rarely had the

[34] *NACA, Year Book, 1923*, 31–33. Compare federalism in the American Society of Certified Public Accountants with the AIA, where it served to ameliorate conflict between national and local accounting firms, instead of educational and deliberative ends. See Miranti, *Accountancy Comes of Age*, where it is a theme throughout the book.

authority to act within firms. Thus, despite general sympathy for cost accounting among manufacturers, it was underutilized.[35]

McCollough, Belt, and the cost committee reviewed their options and decided to organize several national meetings to conceptualize developmental associations. Like the FTC, they considered a demonstration project, but rejected it as too costly, impractical, and impolitic. Instead, they decided to encourage trade associations and cost accountants to work together to upgrade competition. Building on the success of the old cost committee's 1919 conference, McCollough organized two other national meetings in 1923 and one in 1924. Like the FTC, the department culled generalizations from which it conceptualized developmental associations and set them down in two pamphlets, one devoted to trade association cost accounting, the second to the acceptance and installation of uniform methods.

Thus, like NACA and the FTC, the Department of Manufacturing assembled practitioners to draw analogies from the "interchange of experiences," rather than enlisting autonomous professionals to devise scientific accounting standards. Although meeting participants heard technical papers by professionals, trade association functionaries delivered most of the presentations. Practitioners from associations in lumber, newsprint, plywood, milk, portland cement, tents and awnings, tanning, printing, and lithography explained how they mobilized interest, formed cost committees, managed deliberation and system design, and diffused uniform methods throughout their industries. Discussion rarely turned only on technical accounting questions. Instead, participants told stories about the relationship between the mobilization of members, conceptualization of accounting categories, diffusion of best practices, and trade association management.[36]

Approximately six hundred participants attended the U.S. Chamber's four national meetings. The vast majority represented trade associations in specialty and batch sectors: metalworking, construction and construction supplies, furniture, graphic arts, lumber and wood products, garments, shoes, toys, jewelry, dry cleaning and dyeing, candy, and surgical

[35] See statement by T. E. Howard (Charge of Cost Accounting, U.S. Chamber of Commerce), CofC, October, 1923, 88–89.

[36] Frank Wilbur Main, Main and Co., Pittsburgh, Advisory Committee, CofC, October, 1923, 86–94; E. W. McCollough, CofC, March, 1924, 1–7. See also E. W. McCollough's discussion at *National Association of Cost Accountants, 1921, Third Annual Conference Proceedings* (New York: National Association of Cost Accountants, 1922), 214–16.

equipment. But trade association executives from continuous process and mass-production industries, such as pulp and paper, chemicals, pharmaceuticals, and textiles, also participated. Observers from some of the nation's leading mass-producers also attended the U.S. Chamber's meetings: AT&T, Kodak, Bethlehem Steel, McCormick, John Deere, Stromberg Carlson, Johnson and Johnson, National Cash Register, General Tire, Corona Typewriter, Peerless Tube, and Standard Chemical. Among the other participants were attorneys, cost accountants, university professors, and representatives from local or state chambers of commerce, boards of trade, and manufacturing associations.

In short, the U.S. Chamber of Commerce took up the FTC's challenge to upgrade competition through trade associations. In 1918, it created a Manufacturing Division, which devoted its first decade to assembling cost accountants, trade association executives, business managers, and government officials to conceptualize and diffuse developmental associations.

American Trade Association Executives

The American Trade Association Executives (ATAE) was the third organization to advance developmental associations. Formed in 1919, the ATAE was a professional association dedicated to improving the efficiency, skills, and ethical standards of trade association executives.[37] The association served as an informal labor market for trade associations – interviewing prospective employees, maintaining a list of experienced executives, and making recommendations to prospective employers. It also exchanged names and information about open positions with the U.S. Chamber of Commerce.[38]

Like NACA, the organization of the ATAE in 1919 signaled the professionalization of management engineering and its relationship to the trade association movement. Leading ATAE members came not from law or financial accounting, but from manufacturing, engineering, and cost accounting. Men like NACA president Charles R. Stevenson, who began his career in the steel industry and then formed a cost accounting

37 American Trade Association Executives, *Proceedings and Addresses,* Second Annual Convention, October 26–28, 1921 (Cleveland: American Trade Association Executives, 1922), 31.

38 See Report of Secretary Treasurer, Mrs. Margaret Hayden Rorke, *Proceedings and Addresses of the Seventh Annual Convention of American Trade Association Executives, 1926* (Cleveland: American Trade Association Executives, 1926), 127.

partnership (Stevenson, Jordan, and Harrison), became prominent in the ATAE. Stevenson was joined at the ATAE by E. F. DuBrul from the machine tool industry, Roland Zinn from tanning, G. A. McClatchie from cotton finishing, W. H. Coye from furniture, William Miller from printing, S. E. Wulpi from plywood, George Bearce from newsprint, Claire Weikert from tents and awnings, and H. L. Ashworth from knitted outerwear. Together, these men led the movement to professionalize trade association work, and along the way they provided a third forum to conceptualize developmental associations.[39]

CONCEPTUALIZING DEVELOPMENTAL ASSOCIATIONS

By 1924, participants in NACA, ATAE, and U.S. Chamber deliberations had created a model of developmental association drawn from their experiences. I call it collaborative learning. Its goal was to perturb management habits and spark individual inquiry through interfirm comparison and discussion. There were four means to collaborative learning: a uniform cost accounting language, deliberation, benchmarking, and price stabilization. By conceptualizing developmental associations, creative architects hoped to make them available for criticism, imitation, and improvement. This section outlines developmental associations as an ideal type.

Before I do so, however, a theoretical caveat is in order. Developmental associations were not, as institutionalists who adopt game theoretic interpretations suppose, designed to monitor compliance, coordinate preferences, or solve prisoners' dilemmas. In that view, cost and price data allowed firms to monitor one another's preferences and behavior, and decide whether to cooperate with tacit pricing norms in the next round of play.[40] But such interpretations mistakenly assume information sharing was no more than an elaboration of earlier price fixing efforts and their preoccupation with mass production's overcapacity problems. In doing so, they miss crucial features of the design, operation, and performance

[39] For a brief biography of Stevenson's career, see *National Association of Cost Accountants, Year Book, 1927, Proceedings of the Eighth International Cost Conference* (New York: National Association of Cost Accountants, 1927), 20. For information on Zinn, see CofC March, 1924, 106; McClatchie, CofC, March, 1924, 151–54; Wulpi, CofC, October, 1924, 80–82; Ashworth, CofC, October, 1924, 76–78; Miller, CofC, October 1924, 89–89–93; Weikert, CofC, October, 1923, 12–17; Coye, CofC, October, 1923, iv; DuBrul, CofC, March, 1924, 182–85; and Bearce, CofC, March, 1924, 18.

[40] See note 4.

consequences of developmental associations. Although it is true that the architects of developmental associations hoped to foster price stability, their goals were both more and less ambitious than this perspective suggests. They were less ambitious because they neither expected compliance nor sought to eliminate competition. They were more ambitious because they aimed to foster dynamic efficiency and new forms of competition through reflexivity, deliberation, benchmarking, and collaborative learning. In the end, the architects of developmental associations were less concerned about a member's temptation to cheat than about showing where that member needed to improve and providing information unavailable from the market or the firm about how to improve. And although they sought price restraint, it was their careful coupling of stability with learning, improvement, and productivity enhancement that constituted the distinctive and qualitatively new logic of this associational form.

A Common Language

As Arthur Eddy learned, there was a seamless web between mobilizing members and the first feature of collaborative learning: the creation of a common language. Discussions of fair competition inevitably provoked productivity comparisons, which were impossible without a common "cost lexicon."[41] Many associationalists came to see their members' "natural curiosity" for comparison as the means to the end of uniform cost accounting. When associations initiated cost experiments in printing, milk distribution, drug manufacturing, silk, and metal casting, they reported "great consternation" among members. "Everyone knew that actual differences in production costs could only account for a small part of the range in estimates."[42] They were equally surprised at how few members spoke with "a uniform tongue."[43] Simple comparisons in metal casting "proved remarkably successful in convincing ... skeptical [manufacturers] of the need for and benefits from uniform cost accounting."[44]

[41] See statement of Plywood Manufacturers' Association Commissioner, M. Wulpi, CofC, October, 1924, 81.

[42] S. V. Dunkel, CofC, October, 1923, 14–17.

[43] R. E. Little, "The Results of Twelve Month's Intensive Work in the Milk Industry," CofC, October, 1923, 3–4.

[44] S. V. Dunkel, CofC, October, 1923, 14–17. See also Harry Green of the Cracker and Biscuit Association, who noted "the point, which impressed upon me more vividly than ever before, is the great need for all of us to speak the same language.... If we were all to get down to using a common language and to calling the same things by the same names, I believe about seventy-five per cent. [*sic*] of our troubles would be eliminated,"

The cost accountants captured the language problem more abstractly, but no less cogently. NACA's second vice president, Eric Camman, noted how his profession accorded the term "standard costs" with two meanings: ideals and yardsticks. The former were "objects of attainment," set centrally by management, associations, or the state. As such, they were used as targets against which to monitor and discipline performance. Managers set targets for labor costs and then used them to monitor, evaluate, and control workers. Government regulatory agencies (e.g., ICC) measured the costs of corporate capital in order to create an ideal rate base upon which to set rates. And cartels set uniform costs for all members so they could monitor compliance with pricing and output rules. Ideals necessitated widespread confidence in the objectivity of measurement, the authority of measurers, and the probity of accounts. Otherwise, the exercise of authority would appear capricious. In the second meaning – yardsticks – "standard costs" were no more than social conventions, whose effectiveness depended upon agreement among practitioners. Uniformity of costs provided practitioners with a common language to make comparisons of their own performance over time or to compare performance across diverse circumstances. Yardsticks, Camman wrote, were no more than "point[s] of departure, a place to start from." Once participants agreed on a metric (a yardstick), they could evaluate how well they were progressing or how well they were doing in comparison to one another. They could also revise yardsticks, when participants no longer thought they were effective or hoped to realize new collective ends through comparison and discussion. Developmental associations needed yardsticks, whereas cartels needed targets. The former provided information for deliberation and learning, the latter for monitoring compliance and control. In order to create yardsticks, it was necessary to design deliberative forums to build consensus on their meaning.[45]

Deliberation

Like the cost accountants, associationalists learned that they needed to build costs and revise systems from the bottom up, because professionally

in *National Association of Cost Accountants, Year Book, 1921* (New York: National Association of Cost Accountants, 1921), 163–64.

45 Eric A. Camman, *Basic Standard Costs: Control Accounting for Manufacturing Industries* (New York: American Institute Publishing, 1932), 34–35. For evidence of Camman's vice presidency, see NACA letter to Cost Accounting Unit of the Research and Planning Division of the National Recovery Administration, in RG 9, Entry 256, Box 1.

designed systems were too complex, cumbersome, and abstract for most practitioners. Foundry, photoengraving, cotton finishing, tent and awning, refractory, and portland cement associations devoted substantial resources to such systems only to see them languish on a shelf. In these and other sectors, associations learned how cost accounting systems had to be built from the bottom up through deliberation among practitioners. To be sure, many hired professional consultants and full-time association accountants. But, as Camman predicted, the bulk of their work involved arbitrating conflicts and forging agreements over common standards. Moreover, it was typical to devise a simple system and then send it out into the field for testing and refinement.[46] As NACA president and association secretary, Charles Stevenson, put it, the goal of deliberation was to create cost systems "as perfect as possible, working right and as nearly standard as we can, but the most important thing ... is the *use* made of that machine." It is better to install imperfect systems, "see the differences in the work ... being done in various plants," and revise accordingly.[47] Nor did deliberation end with system formation. Cost committees became permanent, and in recognition of the constant learning process associated with uniform cost accounting, many associations placed their systems in loose-leaf binders, so they could be readily reformed with new learning.[48]

Benchmarking

Once association members had learned to speak the same language, it became possible to submit data to the associations, which would calculate and disseminate useful industry benchmarks. These were usually detailed average costs (e.g., the labor, machinery, or overhead costs of a particular operation), but sometimes associations also provided detailed

[46] On portland cement, see CofC, October, 1923, 34; paper boxes, see CofC, October, 1924, 70; cotton finishing, see G. A. McClatchie, Chairman of the Cost Committee of the National Association of Cotton Finishers, CofC, March, 1924, 152–155; foundries, see W. B. Greenlee, Chairman Committee on Costs of the American Foundrymen's Association, "Section E-Cost Accounting Committees," CofC, October, 1923, 6; tents and awnings, see CofC, March, 1924, 175–177; and photoengraving, see CofC, October, 1924, 66–67.

[47] C. R. Stevenson, "The Future of Trade Association Cost Work," *National Association of Cost Accountants, Year Book 1923* (New York: National Association of Cost Accountants, 1923), 297; Ronald Zinn, CofC, March, 1924, 113–14; T. J. Bolitho, International Milk Dealers' Association, CofC, October, 1924, 16–20.

[48] On the use of loose-leaf binders, see George J. Warmbold Jr., Vice President of the Printing Ink Cost Bureau, CofC, October, 1924, 5–11; and Zinn, CofC, March, 1924, 117–18.

data on the lowest costs in their industry. The goal of benchmarking was to disconcert, to shake firms loose from habits born of narrow vision. No matter how good an internal cost system, there were limits to self-reflection. Comparison inevitably raised questions unthinkable from internal monitoring alone.

In their efforts to mobilize members, associations benchmarked modestly and early. The photoengravers, for example, began with a "batting average," which ranked concerns "in order of [operating] efficiency."[49] Others conducted simple comparisons of aggregate manufacturing and commercial expenses. Once in place, however, benchmarking became more frequent and complex. Monthly statistical reports might show "average cost per hour in different departments, average costs of the different kinds of products, and average costs of different kinds of operations."[50] The more detailed the benchmarks, noted G. A. Ware of the Newsprint Bureau, the more it "stirs up inquiry; ... stirs up curiosity."[51] And, added Charles Stevenson, when "you work against figures and facts that other people have developed, finding out what the best performance in the industry is and use that as your standard to compete against, it gives you something to shoot at and is bound to have a tremendous effect on your own operations."[52] Or as NACA's first president, J. Lee Nicholson, wrote:

> If a manufacturer can not make money in competition with other concerns when using the same methods of figuring costs, he can only conclude that his goods or his marketing, or both of them, are costing him too much. His next step, naturally, is to analyze closely the methods and conditions under which he is manufacturing and marketing his product, until he finds and corrects the inefficiencies which are handicapping him so seriously.[53]

Price Stabilization and Improvement

Although many associations had abandoned price fixing for collaborative learning by the 1920s, price stabilization continued to be an important

[49] W. B. Lawrence, Director, Cost Accounting & Statistical Dept, American Photo-Engravers' Assn., CofC, March, 1924, 23–25.

[50] W. B. Lawrence, Director, Cost Accounting & Statistical Dept, American Photo-Engravers' Assn., CofC, March, 1924, 23–25.

[51] G. A. Ware, Newsprint Service Bureau, CofC, March, 1924, 166–72.

[52] Stevenson, "The Future of Trade Association Cost Work," 299, and Stevenson's 1926 Address before ATAE on Standard Costs.

[53] Cited in U.S. Federal Trade Commission, *Report on Open Price Associations* (Washington, DC: Government Printing Office, 1929), 12.

goal. Many association secretaries agreed with FTC chair Edward Hurley when he said those who knew their costs were unlikely to price below them. If everyone were to track overhead, depreciation, and product costs, cutthroat pricing would fade away. Cost accounting taught others, such as the printers, that they poached one another's markets when they overvalued volume. As the following chapter will show, the printers succeeding in dampening cutthroat pricing, which accompanied volume, by tracking the costs of individual products more carefully and specializing on the ones where they had an advantage.

Still other associationalists believed more direct pricing rules remained necessary, despite the salutary effects of cost accounting. In 1927, Charles Stevenson called for affirmative rules against pricing below cost and for individual firms to price off of their own running averages, or "normal costs."[54] Four years later, with the economy in depression, Stevenson argued that progress in cost benchmarking made it possible for manufacturers to price off of industry average costs. Unlike price or information cartels, however, the stabilization of prices or market shares was not an end in itself; rather, developmental associations coupled price stability with systematic improvement. Although it might raise prices in the short run, Stevenson thought prices would come down over the long run, as firms responded to nonprice incentives to improve. As he put it:

> It is evident that if an average industry price were established, certain companies would make more than normal profit and certain companies would make less.... In a desire to make more than normal profit, constant efforts to increase the efficiency of the industry would be made. Individual initiative would be preserved, and fair industry price would be gradually reduced so that the public would be able to buy more of the products or secure them at a lower price.... Inefficient companies would be gradually forced out of business or compelled to modernize and improve their own efficiency, which, in turn would further reduce the industry price level.[55]

Thus, in Stevenson's view, benchmarking average costs not only provided firms with an incentive to improve, but also provided them with information unavailable from the market or from the firm about how to improve, effectively upgrading interfirm competition.

[54] Charles R. Stevenson, "The Economic Effect of Taking Business At or Below Normal Cost," *National Association of Cost Accountants, Year Book, 1927, Proceedings of the Eighth International Cost Conference of the National Association of Cost Accountants* (New York: National Association of Cost Accountants, 1927), 25.

[55] *NACA, Year Book, 1934*, 63–64.

THE DEMOGRAPHY OF DEVELOPMENTAL ASSOCIATIONS

How widespread were developmental associations? What impact did they have on economic performance? Did they really depart from price fixing and cartelization in practice? The next chapter explores these and other questions through a study of the commercial printing industry. The remainder of this chapter gains some traction on these questions by surveying the quantitative salience, distribution, and performance of developmental associations across U.S. industries.

To conduct these analyses, economic sociologist Marc Schneiberg and I created a cross-sectional data set of associations and their activities between 1920 and 1925 in 344 industries.[56] We created this data set in three steps. First, we used documents from the U.S. Chamber of Commerce conferences between 1920 and 1924 and a 1925 FTC investigation of open price associations to compile a list of all associations and firms that discussed, participated in, or operated cost accounting systems, information pooling, or benchmarking schemes.[57]

Second, we used the conference and investigation documents to code associations according to their level of involvement in accounting and benchmarking activities. We assigned a code of "any involvement" to all associations who participated in any conference or were identified by the FTC report as either having uniform systems or being engaged in cost accounting, deliberations over costs, or information sharing. This category is designed to capture all associations that were *at least* demonstrably interested in developmental associationalism. It is the broadest, most inclusive category. Although many associations in this group did more, all were sufficiently interested in developmental associationalism

[56] This section is from Gerald Berk and Marc Schneiberg, "Varieties *in* Capitalism, Varieties *of* Association: Collaborative Learning in American Industry, 1900–1925," *Politics and Society* 33, no. 1 (March 2005): 66–77.

[57] As noted in the first section of this chapter, the U.S. Chamber of Commerce formed its own uniform cost accounting group, and convened a series of conferences in April 1920, October 1923, and March and October 1924, bringing together hundreds of firms and associations to discuss cost accounting systems and their implementation. These conferences provide us with lists of participants, as well as proceedings and papers describing what particular associations had done to develop and operate classification schemes, costs manuals, and benchmarking systems. In addition, the Federal Trade Commission conducted an extensive investigation of open price associations in the 1920s, generating an inventory of associations that had "Uniform Systems" and a table documenting the activities of those organizations in some detail in its 1927 report. Taken together, these sources provide a wealth of detailed data on developmental associations and their activity across American industries in the period 1920–1925.

to pay attention to cost accounting and monitor its adoption elsewhere. We assigned a code of "substantial involvement" to associations actively engaged in institutionalizing uniform cost accounting systems within their industries. Associations were coded into this category if they convened meetings among their members to discuss cost, product standards, and categories; formed a dedicated committee or cost accounting department; developed or distributed cost manuals; helped members install accounting systems; or collected or pooled cost data. Finally, we assigned a code of "benchmarking" to those associations who used manuals, uniform cost plans, and accounting systems to generate and disseminate cost averages broken down by department, product, or specific operation. This category denotes full-fledged developmental associationalism and includes only those associations who provided firms with the capacity and information for systematic interfirm comparisons.[58]

Third, we coded associations (and their level of involvement) to industry classifications in the 1919 U.S. *Census of Manufacturing*. In so doing, we generated a data set of 344 *Census* industries in 14 *Census* industry groups. This data set let us map the distribution of developmental associations across manufacturing industries and link information on associations to the data provided by the *Census* on industry characteristics, organization, and performance.[59]

Overall Salience

Developmental associations diffused extensively in the U.S. economy. Figure 6.1 summarizes the distribution of associations and industries by levels of participation in collaborative learning or benchmarking systems. Between 1920 and 1925, 246 associations in 95 industries expressed

[58] In compiling this list, we focused on *associations* – they dominated the conference proceedings numerically and were the only organizations listed in the FTC study. Yet we also kept track of businesses, typically large corporations such as Kodak, Bethlehem Steel, and AT&T, who attended conferences, but as *individual firms* rather than as officers, representatives, or members of associations.

[59] Note that in constructing these data sets, we took a conservative approach in assigning higher levels of involvement to associations and industries. We coded them to the "substantial involvement" or "benchmarking" categories *only* when archival materials and reports provided detail on those associations *and* when that information supported such categorizations. In contrast, all associations for which such information was absent were restricted to the minimal, or "any involvement," category, even though it is quite possible that some in this group were more deeply involved. As a result, our data likely underestimate the number of associations and industries substantially or fully involved in benchmarking activities.

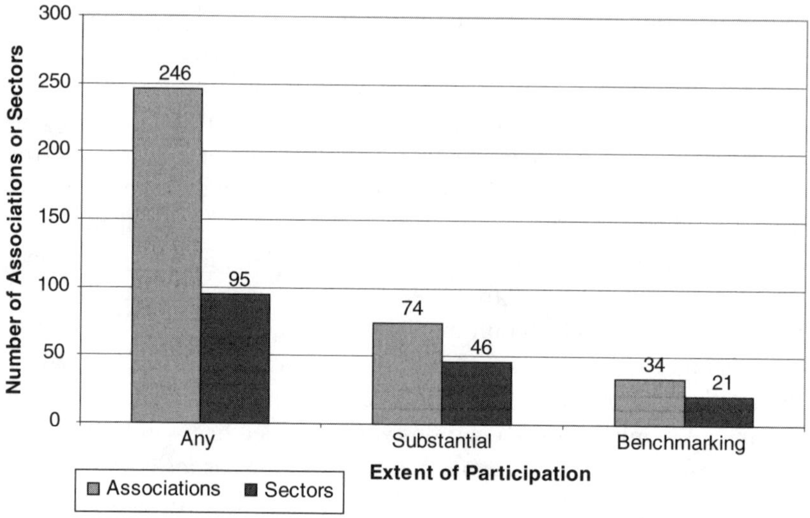

FIGURE 6.1. Participation in Collective Benchmarking by Associations and Sectors
Source: Taken from Gerald Berk and Marc Schneiberg, "Varieties *in* Capitalism, Varieties *of* Association: Collaborative Learning in American Industry, 1900–1925," *Politics and Society* 33, no. 1 (March 2005): 68.

clear interests in these systems ("any involvement"), and were joined in the U.S. Chamber conferences by 30 individual corporations from at least 8 additional industries.[60] In other words, roughly 30 percent of U.S. manufacturing industries and between 25 and 41 percent of the national and regional business associations in the United States devoted resources in this period to at least participate in discussions about developmental association and benchmarking and to monitor their development.[61]

[60] This group of firms included AT&T and Stromberg Carlson, Kodak, Johnson and Johnson, National Cash Register, Standard Chemical, and Harrisburg Shoe, as well as General Tire, Deere, Corona Typewriter, and a number of large steel producers including Bethlehem, Laclede, and Peerless Tube.

[61] The figures presented are calculated as percentages of (1) the total number of manufacturing industries listed in the *Census* in 1919, and (2) estimated number of national and regional business associations in existence in the United States in the 1920s. Reliable estimates of associations during this time period vary from 600 to 1,000. For perhaps the most comprehensive study, which results in the lower estimate, see Howard Aldrich and Udo Staber, "Organizing Business Interests: Patterns of Trade Association Founds, Transformations and Deaths," in Glen Carroll, ed., *Ecological Models of Organization* (Cambridge, MA: Ballinger 1988), 123; Howard Aldrich, Udo Staber, Catherine Zimmer, and John J. Beggs, "Minimalism and Organizational Mortality:

Smaller numbers of associations and industries went beyond deliberation and monitoring to implement these systems. But 74 associations in 46 industries took substantial steps toward instituting collaborative benchmarking, either by pooling information, creating cost manuals or departments, or collecting cost data ("substantial involvement"). That is, more than 13 percent of U.S. manufacturing industries and somewhere between 7.4 and 12.3 percent of all national and regional business associations in existence implemented collaborative learning or benchmarking systems in whole or in part. And 34 associations (or 3.4–5.7 percent of all associations) in 21 industries (over 6 percent of all manufacturing sectors) institutionalized fully developed versions of this organizational form ("full involvement").

To be sure, these figures hardly suggest a manufacturing economy that was organized primarily around developmental associations. Yet, when considered in context, these numbers indicate that a significant proportion of the U.S. economy participated in this project: nearly as many *industries* institutionalized developmental associations in whole or in part as experienced corporation consolidation during the great merger wave.[62] Moreover, at least one-fourth of all business *associations* in existence in the United States participated in some fashion in the construction of this collaborative alternative to mass-production corporation, with up to half that number institutionalizing some or all of its core features. Contrary to conventional accounts, associations were neither

Patterns of Disbanding among U.S. Trade Associations, 1900–1983," in Jitrendra Singh, ed., *Organizational Evolution* (Beverly Hills, CA: Sage 1990), 33. Studies from the 1920s to the 1940s vary between 500 and 1,500 (although the latter includes about 500 fraternal associations). After careful review, the National Industrial Conference Board concluded there were between 800 and 1,000 national or interstate business associations in 1925. See NICB, *Trade Associations: Their Economic Significance and Legal Status* (New York: NICB 1925): 319–26. Jay Judkins, *National Associations of the United States* (Washington, DC: U.S. Department of Commerce, 1949), viii; and *National Trade and Professional Associations of the United States* (New York: Columbia Books, 1990), 7, both report approximately 1,000 trade associations in 1920. We report the interval between 600 and 1,000.

[62] In *The Great Merger Movement in American Business, 1895–1904* (Cambridge: Cambridge University Press, 1985), 88 fn1, Naomi Lamoreaux finds that 52 of the 232 industries in her study, or 22 percent, experienced significant consolidation activity during the great merger wave, a figure broadly consistent with Neil Fligstein's reanalysis, which finds that 21 percent of 230 sectors, or 48 industries, underwent consolidation in *The Transformation of Corporate Control* (Cambridge, MA: Harvard University Press, 1990), 318–19. Curiously, there are no established metrics or benchmarks in the literature on economic organization for establishing when or where a particular form, institutional logic, or industrial order becomes significant or dominant within an economy.

eliminated as governance forms in the great merger wave, reduced to a handmaiden of mass production, nor confined to variations on cartels.

Distribution Across Industries

Looking across industries likewise reveals that developmental associations showed up in a wide variety of industries and that deeper involvement emerges in related clusters of industries. Figure 6.2 maps the distribution of developmental associations across the fourteen *Census of Manufacturing* industry groups, showing the number of *associations* within each industry group for each level of involvement. The broadest measure of involvement, "any," denoted by the light gray bars, reveals two results. First, developmental associations captured the attention of a broad cross section of U.S. industries. With the exception of tobacco manufacturers, associations and industries from every *Census* industry group participated in discussions about benchmarking and actively monitored its development. Second,

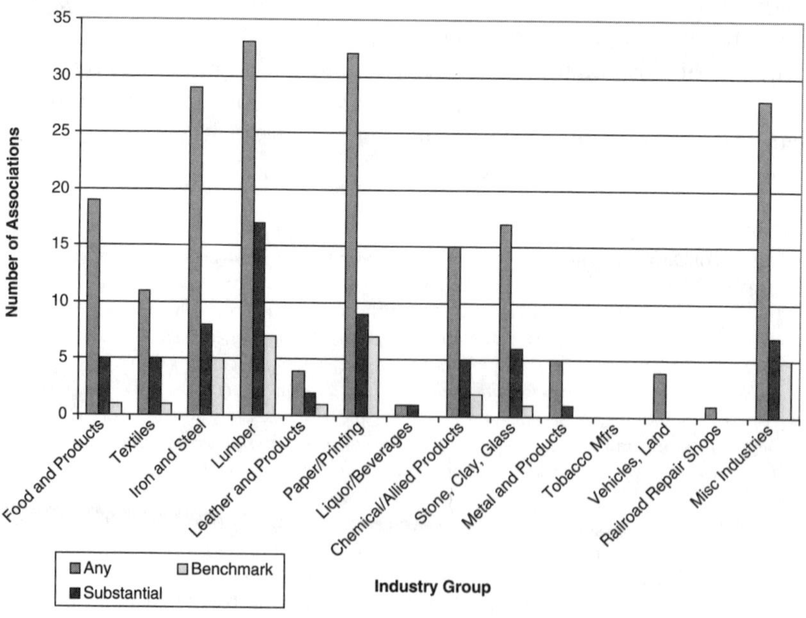

FIGURE 6.2. Extent of Participation in Collaborative Learning Systems, by Industry Group
Source: Taken from Gerald Berk and Marc Schneiberg, "Varieties *in* Capitalism, Varieties *of* Association: Collaborative Learning in American Industry, 1900–1925," *Politics and Society* 33, no. 1 (March 2005): 69.

industry groups varied significantly in the number of associations and industries involved. Three groups stand out: paper and printing, lumber, and iron and steel. More than twenty-five associations in nine to thirteen industries in each group participated in developing benchmarking. Four other groups occupied the middle range: food and food products; stone, clay, and glass; chemicals; and textiles. More than ten associations and eight to ten industries in each group participated in developing benchmarking. Finally, four groups had strikingly fewer numbers of interested associations and industries: land vehicles, leather, liquor, and railroad repairs.

At higher levels of involvement, participation becomes more focused (see the dark and light bars in Figure 6.2 and Appendix). Three points are noteworthy. First, four industry groups drop out at higher levels of involvement. Associations in land vehicles and railroad repair were only monitoring developmental associations; and although some associations in liquor and metal products took substantial steps toward benchmarking, none fully implemented it. Second, despite this winnowing, a wide array of groups surpassed simple monitoring to implement benchmarking systems in whole or in part: associations and industries in eleven of the fourteen *Census* industry groups displayed substantial involvement; those in nine of the fourteen groups implemented full-fledged benchmarking systems. Third, the three leading groups retained their vanguard status. Eight associations in iron and steel industries were substantially involved in collective benchmarking, with five instituting full-fledged benchmarking systems. Nine paper and printing associations and seventeen lumber associations were substantially involved, with seven in each group operating fully developed systems. In short, developmental associations show up in a wide variety of industries and those sectors most deeply committed to the form, such as printing, paper, ink, and wood products, appear to be vertically related.

Performance Correlates

Although a statistically confident account necessitates multivariate analysis, three cautious inferences emerge from a simple presentation of performance data according to levels of industry participation in developmental associations. First, although there is no clear relationship between depth of involvement in developmental associations and productivity, manufacturing sectors with developmental associations perform better than sectors without them; second, developmental associations are not in "sick" industries; and third, they do not exhibit performance effects associated with cartels. Table 6.2 presents standard measures of

TABLE 6.1. *Benchmarking Sectors and Associations by Industry Group*

Food and Kindred Products
Food preparation
National Cooperative Milk Producers Federation

Textiles and Their Products
Awnings, tents, and sails
National Tent and Awning Manufacturers Association
Dyeing and finishing textiles
National Association of Finishers of Cotton Fabric

Iron and Steel and Their Products
Foundry and machine shop products
American Malleable Casting
Steel Founders Society
Stoves and hot air furnaces
Stove and Furnace Manufacturers Association
Tin plate and terneplate
National Association of Sheet and Tin Plate Manufacturers
Typewriters and supplies
Carbon and Ribbon Exchange

Lumber and Its Remanufactures
Lumber and timber products
North Carolina Pine Association
Hardwood Manufacturers Institute
West Coast Lumbermen's Association
Western Pine Manufacturers Association
Lumber and planing mill products
Millwork Cost Information Bureau
Plywood Manufacturers Association
Maple Flooring Manufacturers Association

Leather and Its Finished Products
Leather, tanned, curried, and finished
Tanners Council/Leather Accts Assn

Paper and Printing
Boxes, paper and other, not elsewhere specified
National Container Association
Cardboard, not made in paper mills
Binders Board Manufacturing Association
Paper and wood pulp
News Print Service Bureau
Cost Accounting Assn, Paper Industry
Photoengraving
American Photo-Engravers Association
Printing and publishing, book and job
United Typothetae of America
NY Employing Printers Bureau

Chemicals and Allied Products
Druggists' preparation
Manufacturing Drug Industry Association
Paints
Paint Association

Stone, Clay, and Glass Products
Brick and tile, terra-cotta, and fired clay products
American Face Brick Association

Miscellaneous Industries
Roofing materials
Asphalt Shingle and Roof Association
Prepared Roofing Association
Rubber tires, tubes, and rubber goods
Rubber Association of America
Washing machine and clothes wringers
American Washing Machine Manufacturers Association

Source: Taken from Gerald Berk and Marc Schneiberg, "Varieties *in* Capitalism, Varieties *of* Association: Collaborative Learning in American Industry, 1900–1925," *Politics and Society* 33, no. 1 (March 2005): 70.

industry productivity, employment, and growth in 1919–1929, broken down by levels of involvement in developmental association.[63]

First, there is no positive monotonic relation between productivity improvement or growth and the level of participation in developmental associations. Value added per worker and employment rates do not grow at a progressively higher rate between 1919 and 1929 the more deeply that industries commit to these forms. At the same time, productivity among sectors where there is a substantial or high level of participation in developmental associations is higher than in sectors with no participation at all. So, overall, the evidence shows developmental associations have a salutary effect on productivity.

[63] These are industry-level data from the 1919 and 1929 *Census of Manufactures*. Productivity data consist of (1) the average of the value added per worker for all of the industries falling in each category for 1919, and (2) the average of the increase in the value added per worker from 1919 to 1929 for all industries in each category. Growth data consist of (1) the average of the number of workers employed per industry for all of the industries falling in each category for 1919, and (2) the average of the increase in employment from 1919 to 1929 for all industries in each category. The averages are not adjusted for the sizes or initial productivity. Note that the involvement categories listed here are mutually exclusive and exhaustive.

TABLE 6.2. *Productivity, Employment, and Growth by Level of Involvement in Developmental Association*

	No Involvement	Conferences, Monitoring Only	Substantial, but Not Full Involvement	Full Benchmarking
Productivity				
Average value added per worker in 1919	3,169	2,803	3,426	3,306
Average increase in value added per worker, 1919–1929	270	494	298	390
Growth				
Average number of workers employed in 1919	15,030	42,187	58,312	86,316
Average increase in employment, 1919–1929	2,002	34,88	24,720	12,876

Source: Taken from Gerald Berk and Marc Schneiberg, "Varieties *in* Capitalism, Varieties *of* Association: Collaborative Learning in American Industry, 1900–1925," *Politics and Society* 33, no. 1 (March 2005): 72.

Second, the data undermine a widely held conclusion about associations in the 1920s, namely that they were a new form of cartel designed to rationalize or manage long-term decline in "sick" industries. The data for 1919 show that developmental associations emerged in some of the most productive, high-performance sectors of U.S. manufacturing. The average value added per worker for substantially involved and full benchmarking sectors in 1919 was $3,426 and $3,306, respectively, exceeding the $3,169 and $2,803 average value added for industries with no or minimal involvement.

Third, there is no evidence that developmental associations produced the performance outcomes typically associated with cartelization: reduced productivity improvement and decreases in output or growth. On the contrary, industries with developmental associations performed as well as, if not better than, industries without them. They were certainly no worse off in terms of productivity improvement than sectors without developmental associations. And industries with substantially or fully developed benchmarking systems enjoyed a striking advantage in employment growth over those with no or minimal involvement.

THE PIECES REASSEMBLED

Regulated competition was institutional syncretism. Its architects and practitioners cobbled together a system of governance from ideas and institutions old and new: republicanism, scientific management, cartels, and administrative government, to name only a few of the parts. This was not a clean Madisonian process, in which policy implementation followed a line from delegation back to representation and politics. Instead, policy intellectuals and legislators drew on practice and practitioners conceptualized. Nevertheless, by 1925 regulated competition had a recognizable form. However uncomfortable, its parts fit together into a describable whole. Therefore, it is time to take stock, to reassemble the pieces of regulated competition into a historically linear ideal type.

We return to 1911 and Brandeis's theory of regulated competition. As he saw it, the victors of capitalist rivalry were always tempted to turn temporary advantages into unassailable privileges. When allowed or encouraged, the result undermined competition, concentrated power, and removed incentives to improve. The role of economic governance was to channel rivalry from predation to improvement in products and production processes. For Brandeis, however, there were many institutional forms to realize these ends. Some combination of private contracts (e.g., resale price maintenance), public regulation (e.g., rules against tying contracts), and organization in civil society (e.g., trade associations) was necessary. The exact mix depended on dispositions, resources, and politics.

In 1911, Brandeis thought the state's police power sufficient to check predatory competition. By 1913, he joined the majority in favor of a trade commission and turned his imagination to public administration. Drawing on his experience at the ICC, Brandeis sketched the design for a cultivational agency with powers to foster economic improvement. Deliberation, cost accounting, and benchmarking were his chosen means to these ends.

In 1914 the FTC took up Brandeis's agenda. Without a mandate to coerce uniform cost accounting or the resources to benchmark business performance, however, the FTC turned to civil society. It assembled trade associations to design codes of fair competition and uniform cost accounting systems and it turned to peak business and professional associations to conceptualize and diffuse the associational project. In order to distinguish the former from cartels, I have called them developmental associations. In order to distinguish the latter from corporatist organizations, I have called them deliberative polyarchy.

This chapter has shown how the FTC successfully cultivated deliberative polyarchy in the U.S. Chamber of Commerce and the NACA. Between 1918 and 1925, the NACA and the U.S. Chamber assembled cost accountants, government officials, trade association executives, managers, and corporate leaders to conceptualize developmental associations. Together, they formulated a model of economic governance I have called collaborative learning. When practiced by developmental associations, collaborative learning involved deliberation, uniform cost accounting, benchmarking, and price stabilization. Like the FTC, peak business and professional associations inscribed their deliberations in print. The U.S. Chamber published two pamphlets on developmental associations and NACA distributed its deliberations over trade association cost systems in professional journals, working papers, and annual reports. Although it is impossible to measure the precise effects of deliberative polyarchy on the growth of developmental associations, they spread from craft to batch to continuous processing sectors throughout the 1920s. By the end of the decade, developmental associations had shown up in nearly 15 percent of all manufacturing industries, where they improved productivity without falling prey to cartelization. Built from the shards of old price cartels and new cost accounting techniques, conceptualized and elaborated by the FTC, the U.S. Chamber of Commerce, and the National Association of Cost Accountants, developmental associations realized much in Brandeis's vision for regulated competition.

Chapter 7

From Collective Action to Collaborative Learning

Developmental Association in Commercial Printing

Was collaborative learning successful? Did it channel rivalry from cutthroat competition over volume into improvements in products and production processes? Did benchmarking perturb habits and spark inquiry? Did collaborative learning circumvent collective action problems? What exactly was the FTC's role in establishing and diffusing collaborative learning? This chapter addresses these and other questions through a case study of the commercial printing industry.

Commercial printers were pioneers in developmental association. In 1909, they launched the American Printers Cost Commission to develop a uniform cost accounting system. Two years later the United Typothetae of America (UTA) took up the commission's work. After a year of work, the UTA completed its first Standard Cost System; by 1913, it distributed its first benchmarking data to commercial printers. Cost work had positive effects on the UTA. Membership tripled, local chapters bloomed, and hundreds of printers adopted the cost system. But progress stalled in 1916 and UTA leadership turned to the state, where they found helpful encouragement from the Federal Trade Commission. Armed with a fresh sense of public purpose, the UTA launched a three-year organizing campaign in 1918. By the early 1920s, one-third of all commercial printers in the United States were using the standard cost system and many of those were actively benchmarking. The result was to end cutthroat price competition in many cities, increase product diversity, augment labor skills, advance technological innovation, treble productivity, and increase industrial fragmentation. Collaborative learning was successful in commercial printing.

I chose the printers for three reasons. First, printing was important to institution building because it was a nodal case, watched and copied by many key actors. The UTA developed the first and most comprehensive system of cost accounting, deliberation, and benchmarking. Therefore, the U.S. Chamber of Commerce, the ATAE, NACA, and the FTC monitored its progress,[1] and trade associations in other industries mimicked its success. In short, the UTA stood at a junction of a network of public and private actors concerned with regulated competition, whose members drew meaning from its experience and altered their behavior accordingly.

The second reason for studying printers is that, like Brandeis, they were temporal syncretists who decomposed nineteenth-century republicanism and recombined its parts with practices drawn from twentieth-century engineering. Printers were classic artisanal republicans, small proprietors who derived their sense of manhood and citizenship from their craft.[2] Their patron saint was Ben Franklin.[3] During the period 1910–1929, however, they recomposed their identity as well as their industry. United Typothetae of America organizers insisted it would be impossible to sustain widespread proprietorship, independence, and craftsmanship unless printers also learned to become modern managers. Developmental associationalism taught them how to do that.

[1] For evidence of ATAE and U.S. Chamber attention to the printers, see Edward T. Miller, "Uniform Cost Systems," American Trade Association Executives, Proceedings and Addresses, Second Annual Convention, 1921, 67; and E. T. Miller, *Uniform Cost Accounting Conference* held at Congress Hotel, Chicago, Illinois, October 28–29, 1924, 92; Hagley Museum and Library, Papers of the U.S. Chamber of Commerce, Acc. 1960.

[2] See Ava Baron, "An 'Other' Side of Gender Antagonism at Work: Men, Boys, and the Remasculinization of Printers' Work, 1830–1920," in Ava Baron, ed., *Work Engendered: Toward a New History of American Labor* (Ithaca, NY: Cornell University Press, 1991), 47–69; Ava Baron, "Acquiring Manly Competence: The Demise of Apprenticeship and the Remasculinization of Printers' Work," in Marc C. Carnes and Clyde Griffen, eds., *Meanings for Manhood: Constructions of Masculinity in Victorian America* (Chicago: University of Chicago Press, 1990), 152–63.

[3] On the printers' fascination with Ben Franklin, see John Clyde Oswald, "Printing Organization and Education: Ben Franklin as a Great Leader in the Printing Industry of the Eighteenth Century – Colonial Competition – His Interest in Education and His Founding of a University," *Typothetae Bulletin* 22, no. 15 (January 11, 1926): 459–60; Henry L. Bullen, "Colonial Printing Office Equipment: Franklin's Printing Plant and How He Used It – His Methods of Securing New Business – Printing Production in the Colonial Printing Plant – 'The Good Old Times,'" *Typothetae Bulletin* 22, no. 15 (January 11, 1926): 461–62; Harry L. Gage, "Benjamin Franklin as a Typographer," *Typothetae Bulletin* 22, no. 15 (January 11, 1926): 463; Harry T. Hemming, "Proposal for the Education of Youth: Franklin's Notable Plan for the Establishment of a Seat of Learning in 'Pennsylvania,'" *Typothetae Bulletin* 22, no. 15 (January 11, 1926): 469–70; Francis H. Bird, "Craftsman or Business Man – Which? An Imaginary Discourse between Ben Franklin and a Printer Friend on the Necessity of Common Sense in the Printing Business," *Typothetae Bulletin* 22, no. 16 (January 18, 1926).

The third reason for studying printers is that they are an excellent case to test my constructivist interpretation of trade associations, which shared information during the 1920s, against the dominant institutionalist interpretation. I argue these were developmental associations devoted to collaborative learning, whereas institutionalists see them as price fixing cartels by another means. In the conventional story, trade associations turned to information sharing after their efforts to fix prices were outlawed by antitrust. Often in "sick" industries, plagued by overcapacity, they "cunningly" distributed price and cost information so that individual firms could coordinate pricing without being detected by the Department of Justice.[4] Historian Colin Gordon and sociologist Scott Bowman have added precision to this interpretation by analyzing information pooling with the tools of game theory. They argue that trade associations learned to coordinate collective action by providing their members with information, which allowed them to decide whether they were better off by cooperating with tacit price norms and to monitor whether others were doing the same. When it worked, cooperation was "spontaneous," because it did not depend upon enforcement. In this view, benchmarking was an example of a "coordination game."[5]

By contrast, in my constructivist perspective, the goal of information pooling was to perturb habits, foster collective deliberation, and spark individual inquiry into improvement. In this approach, firms are conceptualized as creative syncretists. Although they often acted on the basis of habit, they also had the capacity – individually and collaboratively – to reflect on destructive habits, and to recompose association resources to experiment with, conceptualize, elaborate, and evaluate alternatives.

[4] Robert Himmelberg, *The Origins of the National Recovery Administration* (New York: Fordham University Press, 1976), 7–9; William G. Robbins, "Voluntary Cooperation vs. Regulatory Paternalism: The Lumber Trade in the 1920s," *Business History Review* 41, no. 3 (Autumn 1982): 358–77. For a similar interpretation of the information pooling provisions of the National Recovery Administration, see Ellis W. Hawley, *The New Deal and the Problem of Monopoly* (Princeton, NJ: Princeton University Press, 1966), 59–60, 63–64, 85–86, 99–100.

[5] John R. Bowman, "The Politics of the Market: Economic Competition and the Organization of Capitalists," *Political Power and Social Theory* 5 (1985), 35–88; John Bowman, *Capitalist Collective Action: Competition, Cooperation and Conflict in the Coal Industry* (New York: 1989); Colin Gordon, *New Deals: Business, Labor, and Politics in America, 1920–1935* (Cambridge: Cambridge University Press, 1994), 15–20.

	Agency	Relation To Competitors	Conditions For Success
Coordination Game	Individual Profit maximizing	Autarky or Collective	Information sharing Small numbers Standard products High entry barriers
Collaborative Learning	Social Habitual Reflexive	Customary or Deliberative	Common language Benchmarking Deliberation Price stabilization with improvement

FIGURE 7.1. Two Theories of Information Sharing by Trade Associations

The key to success in a coordination game, argues Bowman, is not only an effective system of information sharing, but also the proper structural conditions for success: small numbers, relatively homogeneous products, and high entry barriers. Price coordination is impossible when there are many firms, because the cost of monitoring outweighs the benefits of price fixing. Uniform costs, which serve as a pricing signal, are impossible to calculate when products are too diverse. And cooperation with pricing cues is likely to collapse if new players constantly enter the game.[6] The conditions for success in collaborative learning were outlined in the last chapter: a common accounting language, structured deliberation, performance benchmarking, and a mechanism to couple price stabilization with improvement. (See Figure 7.1.)

Printing is a good case to arbitrate the debate over how to characterize trade associations in the 1920s because it had a highly developed system of information sharing, but none of the features necessary for a successful coordination game. In 1915, there were 12,000 commercial printers in the United States. This was largely a custom and batch production industry. And there was a large market for used equipment. Laid off during recessions, journeymen printers needed little capital to set up "basement" shops. Therefore, if information sharing was successful in

[6] Bowman, "The Politics of the Market," 54.

the commercial printing industry, it is likely that something other than spontaneous cooperation was going on. In order to assess whether the UTA is an example of collaborative learning or a coordination game, this chapter traces the process of information formation, sharing, and use. Why did the printers assemble a cost commission in 1909? What did they do once they came together? What principles drove the design of the standard cost system and UTA benchmarking? What were the defining features of the standard cost system? How did individual firms use the standard cost system and benchmarking data? Did they use them to improve production, marketing, and pricing, or to coordinate pricing? What was the outcome of uniform cost accounting? Did production decrease and innovation decline, as game theory predicts? Or did printers learn to channel rivalry from cutthroat pricing to improvements in product quality, service, and nonvolume forms of productivity, as the theory of collaborative learning predicts? In short, is the UTA better understood as an information cartel or as a developmental association?

This chapter proceeds in five sections. The first section explains the origins of developmental association in commercial printing. The second section shows how printers renamed the cause of cutthroat price competition. Where they once assumed it was the result of technology and greed, they came to see it as the result of prizing volume over all other forms of production. This "volume illusion," they hypothesized, was an artifact of poor accounting conventions, not fixed economic constraints. Alter accounting conventions and printers would reconfigure production and competition. The third section outlines the defining features of the UTA cost system and shows how those features were intended to overcome the illusion by channeling production from volume to quality, service, and nonscale forms of productivity. The fourth section describes the diffusion of collaborative learning through a three-year organizing plan. The fifth section assesses the effects of developmental association on economic performance in the printing industry.

THE ORIGINS OF DEVELOPMENTAL ASSOCIATION

Nineteenth-century printers had a long history of solidaristic associations, which came under stress during the early twentieth century. In 1908, after a long and bitter struggle, the International Typographers Union (ITU) won the eight-hour day. This was a major defeat for printers' associations, who had staked their prestige on defending members from unions. The UTA watched its membership plunge by half. If this were not enough,

New York City printers looked on helplessly as the thriving market for mass-market magazines migrated from the district. Add to this a nationwide recession after the panic of 1907, and competition turned fierce, as printers battled for shrinking markets in the face of rising costs.[7]

Local associations remained tenacious during the crisis. In 1908, they regrouped to assess the damage and address an intractable profit squeeze. In the Midwest, master printers reorganized under the name they had long associated with craft solidarity and republican manhood: *Ben Franklin* Clubs. In the East, printers resurrected city boards of trade. In 1909, there was one thing on every local's mind: stabilizing price competition.

The printers had a checkered history of price cartels to draw upon. They first organized recession cartels in the deflation after the Civil War. A decade later, when mechanized typesetting saddled printers with debt, they organized price agreements to cope with cutthroat price competition. In the 1890s, they formed printers' trusts, with a variety of novel enforcement mechanisms. As institutionalists predict, cartels usually failed because it was so difficult to fix price schedules; detect cheating; or restrict entry in the highly fragmented, custom-products industry. The few successful cartels fell prey to state-level antitrust. Thus, by the time of the great merger wave, it appeared as though the printers had the same two options as every other U.S. industry: free markets or consolidation. Magazine printers began to consolidate. For the rest, cutthroat rivalry seemed the only possibility.[8]

The printers invented a third option: developmental association. In 1908, a Joint Conference Board of New York, Boston, and Baltimore printers met to set wage and price standards. Like Eddy's open price associations, the board found it impossible to arbitrate disputes for want of reliable cost information. When it administered an accounting questionnaire to 6,000 printers, the board found widespread ignorance and diversity in method. Officers cobbled together a rudimentary cost system, but it had little effect. Nonetheless, the Midwest's Ben Franklin Clubs looked on with great interest and they called a national meeting to consider accounting reform in July 1909. The result was the American Printers' Cost Commission. A developmental association was born.

[7] Leona M. Powell, *The History of the United Typothetae of America* (Chicago: University of Chicago Press, 1926), 71–72. The International Typographical Union boasted that it had "reduced the working hours of its members to a greater extent than any other labor organization in the world." See *The Typographical Journal* 36, no. 5 (May 1910): 612.

[8] Emily Brown, *Book and Job Printing in Chicago: A Study of Organizations of Employers and Their Relations with Labor* (Chicago: University of Chicago Press, 1931), 56–58; Powell, *History of UTA*, 76, 85–91.

NAMING THE "VOLUME BUG"

Once assembled to consider cost accounting, creative printers renarrated the cause of their distress. The trade was demoralized not because of greedy workers, the high cost of technology, or opportunism, but because faulty cost accounting – or none at all – led to the illusion that success was best measured in volume. As a result, competition took the form of zero-sum rivalry over market share and the printers fell into a destructive vortex. The more success was measured in volume, the more printers chased technology to increase speed and throughput; the more they perceived capital this way, the more they rushed off in pursuit of volume. Competition turned cutthroat and everyone suffered. The industry had fallen prey to a "volume illusion," complained the American Printers' Cost Commission, echoing Brandeis and FTC commissioner Nelson Gaskill. Change accounting customs, the commissioners suggested, and printers would find an alternative to cutthroat competition and unenforceable cartels.

The printers broached the discussion by reconceptualizing the relationship between technology and production. W. R. Ashe, the cost manager of the New York Employing Printers Association, took the habitual story and stood it on its head:

> Nearly all printers put the cart before the horse in trying to adjust volume to equipment, instead of equipment to volume.... The average printer is prone to hang a millstone around his neck. He puts in every machine his competitor happens to have, before sufficient profitable volume has been acquired for running machinery the necessary productive hours at which its maintenance cost is absorbed.[9]

Acting on habit, not managerial reason, "artisan" printers fell prey to the unscrupulous "supply man," who made inflated claims about productivity and cost, added cost commissioner A. M. Glossbrenner. Although circumstances varied dramatically, virtually all printers fell prey to manic investment.[10]

The millstone in place, there appeared but one alternative: increase volume in the hope of covering debt and realize scale economies. Trapped, thus, by the "*affliction of the volume bug*," Ashe complained, the printer believes he had no choice but to slash prices. And "*bang* goes the price" level, as he joins his rivals in their desperate "effort to get business."[11] Though he is occupied,

[9] W. R. Ashe, "The Value of the Standard Cost Finding System to Management," *Typothetae Bulletin* 32, no. 7 (November 17, 1930): 231–34, quote on 233.

[10] *Proceedings of the Second International Cost Congress of Employing Printers of America* (Chicago: American Printers' Cost Commission, 1910), 47–51.

[11] Ashe, "The Value of the Standard Cost Finding System to Management," 233, emphasis added.

complained cost commissioner Henry Porter, the printer's bank account is empty. Though satisfied to hear his machinery running at "top speed year round," the "musical printer" reaps nothing but "worn out machinery" and "red ink" at year's end, added a *Typothetae Bulletin* editorial.[12]

Virtually all production and marketing decisions were driven by the volume bug, complained the commission. In slack seasons, printers take on "fillers" (unprofitable jobs) to keep the presses running. Or, like the railroads, they slash prices on competitive jobs, hoping to make up revenues on jobs in which they held a monopoly. Some printers offered free products and services; others ignored sound estimating procedures in pursuit of volume.[13]

The result was perverse. Like a "dog chasing its tail," Ashe protested, "the tail is always ahead of the dog, because lower than cost rates are used in attracting sales, with no attempt to conform actual costs to these rates."[14] There is no more illusory yet taken for granted principle, Porter agreed, than "mere volume *is* profit."[15]

Printers had a choice: "Craftsman or Business Man – Which?" asked the director of UTA research.[16] A good cost system, the commissioners hypothesized, will lift the artisan from his prejudice and "remove the haze caused by filling [one's] plant with work at a loss."[17] It will "eliminate the profitless job" and, in all likelihood, "cause a loss of business." But printers will learn – many for the first time – that "the matter of losing business and losing money are two separate propositions." More often than not, less business will "result in increased profits."[18] A good cost system will

[12] H. P. Porter, "Press Room Output," *Proceedings of the 24th Annual Convention of the United Typothetae of America, 1910* (Washington, DC: United Typothetae of America, 1910), 98–101, quotation on 100. "Production," *Typothetae Bulletin* 21, no. 4 (April 27, 1925): 54.

[13] *Proceedings of the Thirty-first Annual Convention of the United Typothetae of America*, published as *Typothetae Bulletin* (December 1917): 51. See also Mabel Dwyer, "The Value and Use of Standard Costs in Profit Gains," *Typothetae Bulletin* 25 (September 19, 1927): 493–94, where she writes "many jobs are taken on a cut price because the management thinks their cost is high on account of low productive time. They think they can cut this price, get the job and it will increase by productive time and lower their hour cost. And the chances are they cut too low. If they had a cost based on a normal percentage [a budget] they would know that they could not cut it – in fact the excuse for cutting is taken away."

[14] Ashe, "The Value of the Standard Cost Finding System to Management," 233.

[15] Porter, "Press Room Output," 100, emphasis original.

[16] Bird, "Craftsman or Business Man – Which?"

[17] F. I. Ellick, "The Results a Cost System Should Bring," *Proceedings of the 26th Annual Convention of the UTA* (Chicago: United Typothetae of America, 1912), 68; *Proceedings of the 28th Annual Convention, United Typothetae and Franklin Clubs of America, New York* (Chicago: United Typothetae of America, 1914), 83.

[18] W. O. Foote, "Will the Use of the Cost System Cause a Loss of Business, and the Results?" *Proceedings of the Second International Cost Congress of Employing Printers*

heal the volume bug by enabling artisan printers to distinguish profitable from unprofitable work, to evaluate investment decisions more carefully, and to improve efficiency without increasing volume. It will, Ashe said (again echoing Brandeis and Hurley), replace "poor quality" competition ("volume at cut prices") with rivalry over "better service," "quality work," and "minimized cost" at "less volume."[19] In other words, better cost accounting promised to heal the volume bug by regulating competition.

By renarrating the cause of cutthroat competition, creative printers brought a background constraint under deliberate scrutiny. No longer an ineluctable feature of modern technology, high fixed costs were a sign of weak cost accounting and so subject to human reflection, recomposition, and evaluation. Cutthroat price competition was an artifact of management convention. Alter the language of accounting, the American Printers' Cost Commission hypothesized, and commercial printers would discover alternatives to the volume illusion.

CONCEPTUALIZING THE STANDARD COST SYSTEM

Drawing on technical innovations in cost accounting, creative printers conceptualized a standard cost system to regulate competition. The American Printers' Cost Commission completed its work in 1911. A year later, the UTA took over its cost work and in 1913 it published the *Typothetae Standard Cost System*. Four aspects of the UTA system were designed to overcome the volume bug: departmental costs, product costs, overhead distribution, and benchmarking. The first allowed printers to trace costs back to their source. The second allowed them to distinguish the cost of various classes of products. The third provided a technique to reduce fixed costs. And the fourth provided printers the means to individual improvement through collaborative learning.

Departmental Costs

The heart of the UTA *Standard Cost System* was a monthly worksheet called Form 9-H. (See Figure 7.2.) Like today's spreadsheet, the columns on Form 9-H broke printing into departments or "cost centers," including

of America (Chicago: American Printers' Cost Commission, 1910), 114–118.

19 Ashe, "The Value of the Standard Cost Finding System to Management," 231. Indeed, Ashe speculated, "under minimized expense ... volume does not have to exceed 50% of plant capacity to break even." See also Emily Brown, *Book and Job Printing in Chicago*, 267, who notes that, like the railroads, as long as printers prized volume first, "detailed cost information appeared useless."

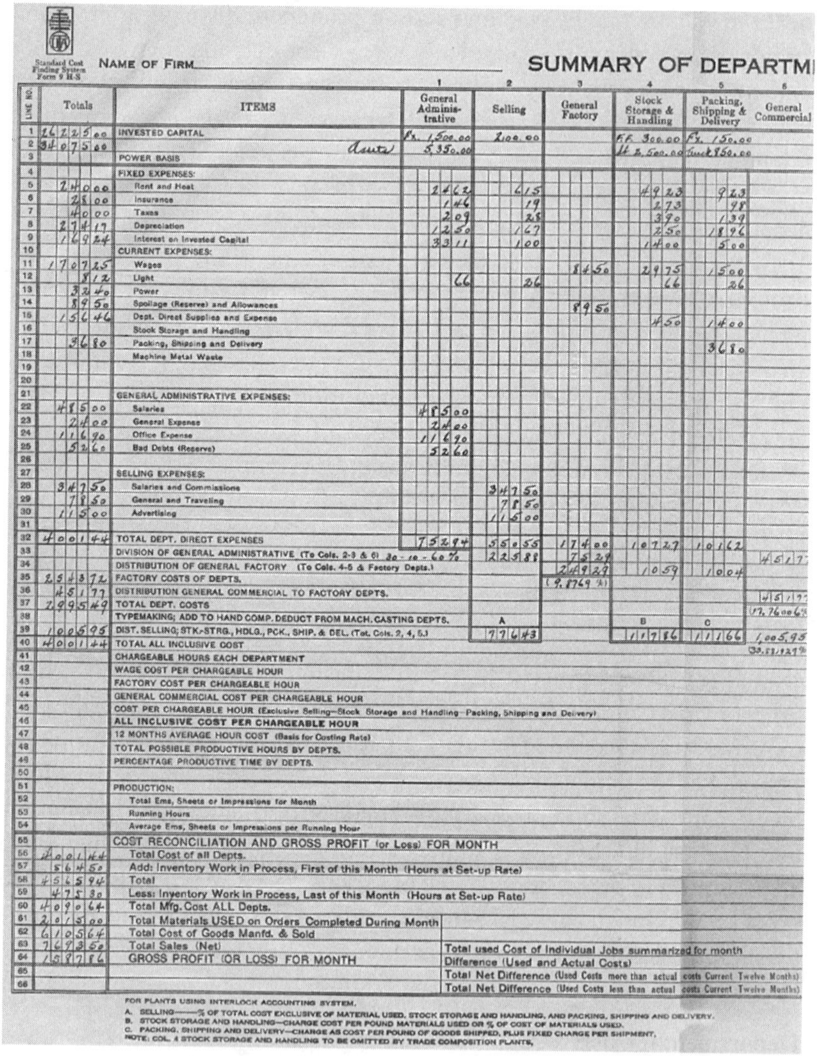

Line No.	Totals	Items
1	26225 00	INVESTED CAPITAL
2	34075 00	
3		POWER BASIS
4		FIXED EXPENSES:
5	240 00	Rent and Heat
6	28 00	Insurance
7	40 00	Taxes
8	274 17	Depreciation
9	169 24	Interest on Invested Capital
10		CURRENT EXPENSES:
11	1707 25	Wages
12	8 12	Light
13	32 40	Power
14	89 50	Spoilage (Reserve) and Allowances
15	156 46	Dept. Direct Supplies and Expense
16		Stock Storage and Handling
17	36 80	Packing, Shipping and Delivery
18		Machine Metal Waste
19		
20		
21		GENERAL ADMINISTRATIVE EXPENSES:
22	485 00	Salaries
23	24 00	General Expense
24	116 90	Office Expense
25	52 60	Bad Debts (Reserve)
26		
27		SELLING EXPENSES:
28	347 50	Salaries and Commissions
29	78 50	General and Traveling
30	115 00	Advertising
31		
32	4001 44	TOTAL DEPT. DIRECT EXPENSES
33		DIVISION OF GENERAL ADMINISTRATIVE (To Cols. 2-3 & 6)
34		DISTRIBUTION OF GENERAL FACTORY (To Cols. 4-5 & Factory Depts.)
35	2543 72	FACTORY COSTS OF DEPTS.
36	451 77	DISTRIBUTION GENERAL COMMERCIAL TO FACTORY DEPTS.
37	2995 49	TOTAL DEPT. COSTS
38		TYPEMAKING; ADD TO HAND COMP. DEDUCT FROM MACH. CASTING DEPTS.
39	1005 95	DIST. SELLING; STK.-STRG., HDLG., PCK., SHIP. & DEL. (Tot. Cols. 2, 4, 5.)
40	4001 44	TOTAL ALL INCLUSIVE COST
41		CHARGEABLE HOURS EACH DEPARTMENT
42		WAGE COST PER CHARGEABLE HOUR
43		FACTORY COST PER CHARGEABLE HOUR
44		GENERAL COMMERCIAL COST PER CHARGEABLE HOUR
45		COST PER CHARGEABLE HOUR (Exclusive Selling—Stock Storage and Handling—Packing, Shipping and Delivery)
46		ALL INCLUSIVE COST PER CHARGEABLE HOUR
47		12 MONTHS AVERAGE HOUR COST (Basis for Costing Rate)
48		TOTAL POSSIBLE PRODUCTIVE HOURS BY DEPTS.
49		PERCENTAGE PRODUCTIVE TIME BY DEPTS.
50		
51		PRODUCTION:
52		Total Ems, Sheets or Impressions for Month
53		Running Hours
54		Average Ems, Sheets or Impressions per Running Hour
55		COST RECONCILIATION AND GROSS PROFIT (or Loss) FOR MONTH
56	4001 44	Total Cost of all Depts.
57	564 50	Add: Inventory Work in Process, First of this Month (Hours at Set-up Rate)
58	4565 94	Total
59	475 30	Less: Inventory Work in Process, Last of this Month (Hours at Set-up Rate)
60	4090 64	Total Mfg. Cost ALL Depts.
61	2015 00	Total Materials USED on Orders Completed During Month
62	6105 64	Total Cost of Goods Manfd. & Sold
63	7693 50	Total Sales (Net) — Total used Cost of Individual Jobs summarized for month
64	1587 86	GROSS PROFIT (OR LOSS) FOR MONTH — Difference (Used and Actual Costs)
65		Total Net Difference (Used Costs more than actual costs Current Twelve Months)
66		Total Net Difference (Used Costs less than actual costs Current Twelve Months)

Column headings: 1 General Administrative; 2 Selling; 3 General Factory; 4 Stock Storage & Handling; 5 Packing, Shipping & Delivery; 6 General Commercial

FOR PLANTS USING INTERLOCK ACCOUNTING SYSTEM.
A. SELLING——% OF TOTAL COST EXCLUSIVE OF MATERIAL USED, STOCK STORAGE AND HANDLING, AND PACKING, SHIPPING AND DELIVERY.
B. STOCK STORAGE AND HANDLING—CHARGE COST PER POUND MATERIALS USED OR % OF COST OF MATERIALS USED.
C. PACKING, SHIPPING AND DELIVERY—CHARGE AS COST PER POUND OF GOODS SHIPPED, PLUS FIXED CHARGE PER SHIPMENT.
NOTE: COL. 4 STOCK STORAGE AND HANDLING TO BE OMITTED BY TRADE COMPOSITION PLANTS.

FIGURE 7.2. United Typothetae of America Form 9-H
Source: Taken from Elmer J. Koch, *The Standard Book on Cost Finding for Printers* (Chicago: United Typothetae of America, 1928).

composition, typesetting, presswork, binding, and proofreading. The rows provided space to enter expenses within each department, from rent and wages to overhead and administrative costs. In a small plant, specializing in a single process, one department might be sufficient.[20] The

[20] On Form 9-H, see Elmer J. Koch, *The Standard Book on Cost Finding for Printers* (Chicago: United Typothetae of America, 1928), 31–33; United Typothetae of

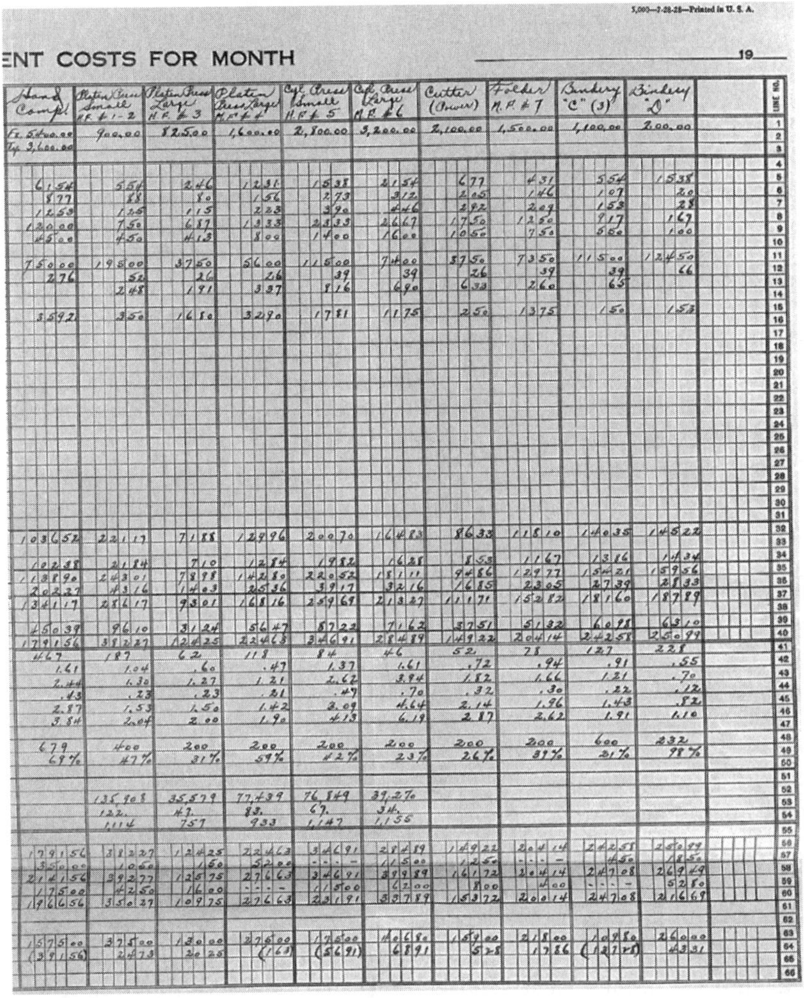

majority of printing establishments, however, had two or more departments (columns). A typical large plant might begin by identifying five production cost centers like those listed above. But departmentalization was meant to be flexible: a single machine, such as a small platen press,

America, *Standard Cost Finding System* (Chicago: United Typothetae of America, 1927), 6–19, 24–25; "Resolutions Submitted by the Cost Commission," *Proceedings of the Twenty-seventh Annual Convention of the United Typothetae and Franklin Clubs of America* (Chicago: United Typothetae of America, 1913), 107–8.

or labor category, such as binder, could also be defined as a cost center. It all depended upon what a printer wanted to learn.[21]

Departmentalization ensured that all expenses would be recorded. No longer would printers assume that volume reduced average costs. Now they would have the information to carefully track costs to their sources, where they might locate costly bottlenecks, inappropriate materials, unproductive machinery, or misplaced labor skills. In short, departmentalization was necessary to finding nonvolume means to cost reduction.

Product Costing

The second aspect of the UTA *Standard Cost System* intended to overcome the volume illusion was "product costing," or tracing job costs back to their origins within departments. As noted in the preceding section, the American Printers' Cost Commission believed that many printers chased volume because they were unable to distinguish profitable from unprofitable work. Instead, they often assumed it was cost effective to cross-subsidize jobs or take on fillers to amortize debt and keep workers busy. The *Standard Cost System* tutored printers to distinguish between costs "chargeable" directly to a job and "unchargeable" costs, incurred in debt service, administration, maintenance, or idle time. In this way they could begin to develop categories and information for distinguishing more carefully profitable from unprofitable work, and make more informed decisions about volume.[22]

The American Printers' Cost Commission hypothesized that printers, who learned to segregate the costs of their products – or "product cost" – should "eliminate unprofitable jobs of all kinds." In many cases, product costing should cause a loss of business, but an increase in profits.[23] It should teach printers to specialize in their most profitable lines of work. As a result, competition should shift from volume to quality, price, and service, and industry conditions should improve.

[21] On departmentalization, see F. I. Ellick (Omaha member of cost commission), "Exposition of the Standard Cost Finding System," *Proceedings of the Second International Cost Congress of Employing Printers of America* (Chicago: American Printers' Cost Commission, 1910), 76–84; F. I. Ellick, "Cost Accounting," *The Typographical Journal* 44, no. 1 (January 1914): 11.

[22] On product costing, or the "productive hour method," see Ellick, "The Results a Cost System Should Bring," 67–78.

[23] Foote, "Will the Use of the Cost System Cause a Loss of Business?" 114–18; Ellick, "The Results a Cost System Should Bring," 68.

Overhead Distribution

The third aspect of the *Standard Cost System* intended to overcome the volume illusion was overhead distribution. Many printers, the American Printers' Cost Commission noted, overestimated fixed costs because they did not know how to distribute overhead expenses to departments where they were incurred. Rent, heat, insurance, taxes, depreciation, and clerical and management salaries seemed the same, regardless of output. Where possible, the *Standard Cost System* urged printers to trace these and other overhead costs to the actual departments and activities in which they were incurred. Where it was impossible, it outlined a uniform method. Printers should calculate the percentage of total annual costs incurred by each department and then allocate untraceable overhead costs according to this proportion. Either way, the *Standard Cost System* provided techniques to monitor overhead costs and compare them over time and across departments. With that information, it was possible to reduce costs once thought fixed.[24]

Benchmarking

The fourth aspect of the UTA's cost system intended to overcome the volume bug was benchmarking. These were detailed industry cost averages, published and revised regularly in a volume called the *Typothetae Standard Guide*. By providing printers with nonprice incentives to improvement and information about how to improve, benchmarking promised to channel competition from market share to quality, specialization, and nonscale productivity.

Cost accounting, the American Printers' Cost Commission noted, inevitably provoked comparisons. As prominent Detroit printer William Chantery put it,

> You may have the finest set of ... production records in existence. You may be maintaining, day in and day out, the average of your plant, but are you sure that

[24] On overhead distribution, see Koch, *The Standard Book on Cost Finding*, 14; H. W. J. Meyer, "What Constitutes the Standard Cost Finding System and Distribution of the Overhead Burden?" *Proceedings of the Fourth International Cost Congress, Chicago, September 1912* (Chicago: United Typothetae of America, 1912), 227–37; "Report of the Committee of Twelve Appointed by the First International Cost Congress of Employing Printers of America," *Proceedings of the First International Cost Congress of Employing Printers of America, 1909* (Chicago: American Printers' Cost Commission, 1909), 117–18.

the average of your plant is equal to the average of your city or the average of the country as a whole? There is only one way for you to determine this, and that is by comparison of your averages with averages obtained from other sources.... By compiling average records you have the means by which the efficiency of your plant may be brought before your eyes.[25]

Or as Mabel Dwyer, secretary of the Typothetae Cost Accountants Association, put it, "there is considerable satisfaction in knowing just where your business stands in relationship to others in the same industry, and if your statement is below average this knowledge acts as an incentive for you to try to improve it."[26]

In 1915, the UTA published its first *Composite Statement*, a compilation of industry cost averages broken down by department and the average costs of a variety of standard products. Four years later, the association replaced the *Composite Statement* with the *Typothetae Standard Guide*. In addition to a more complete account of departmental average costs, the *Standard Guide* introduced physical data, that is, a detailed list of machine time averages for many specific operations.[27]

Industry benchmarks, Chantery said, were intended to disconcert, that is, to raise questions unthinkable from firm-level data alone. In Dewey's language, they were meant to perturb habits. As such, they were useful for evaluating volume; diagnosing bottlenecks; and identifying excess labor, make-ready, or administrative costs. Benchmarking, as Dwyer pointed out, also provided a nonprice incentive to improvement. Printers who knew where they fell short had reason to do better.

But UTA officials also thought benchmarks were useful for pricing. Commercial printing was a custom- and batch-product industry, where prices were typically set (or "estimated") prior to production. By the time of World War I, UTA accountants had begun to tutor members in estimating prices by benchmarking. Industry averages, they said, promised to improve pricing in three ways. First, estimating by benchmarking would reveal consequential errors. Because UTA benchmarks were so specific,

[25] F. A. Chantery, "Division of Records and Estimates as an Aid in Management," *Proceedings of the Fortieth Annual Convention, UTA, 1926, Typothetae Bulletin* 24, nos. 4–5 (October 25, 1926), 113–15, quotation on 115.

[26] Mabel H. Dwyer, "Departmental Cost Analysis," *Proceedings of the Forty-fourth Convention of the UTA* (Chicago: United Typothetae of America, 1930); *Typothetae Bulletin* 32, no. 3 (October 27, 1930): 100–103, quotation on 100.

[27] Powell, *History of the UTA*, 168–73; *Proceedings of the Thirtieth Annual Convention of the United Typothetae and Franklin Clubs of America* (Chicago: UTA, 1916), 45–46.

estimators could compare the costs of many distinct operations to industry averages. Large deviations would indicate the need for further inquiry and, perhaps, price adjustment. Second, estimating by benchmarking promised to raise questions about layout and production. For example, were high estimates the result of genuine productivity differences or inappropriate machinery, labor, or materials? In some cases, UTA cost accountant George Voorhees said, estimating by benchmarking revealed

> ... ways of increasing production by seemingly illogical means. For illustration, production work and production records in some plants have shown that greater production on hand-operated machines can be obtained by running the machines slower. It would be hard to believe this as a fact without the use of average production records.[28]

Finally, estimating by benchmarking provided another technique to test the volume illusion. Suppose, one printer said, you felt compelled to take on fillers during a slack time. By comparing your cut-rate estimate to the industry average, you might find it does not pay.[29]

In sum, estimating by benchmarking was another technique to foster collaborative learning, not to coordinate price fixing. By improving the estimating process, benchmarking was intended to channel competition from market share to product quality and diversity, service, and nonvolume cost reductions.

THE THREE-YEAR PLAN

Despite its initial success, developmental association in printing stalled in 1916. The UTA lost members for the first time since the first cost congress in 1909 and new subscriptions to the *Standard Cost System* slowed to a crawl.[30] By the mid-1920s, the UTA had reversed its fortunes.

[28] George N. Voorhees, "The Use of Production Records: How Interest in Records Work Has Spread – Necessity of Accurate Estimating – Typothetae Average Production Records Provide Accurate Efficiency Gauge," *Proceedings of the Thirty-ninth Annual Convention, UTA 1925*, 22 *Typothetae Bulletin* (October 26, 1925): 136.

[29] George N. Voorhees, "Better Pricing of the Product of the Printing Plant," Address before the Convention of the Seventh District Typothetae Federation of Springfield, Ohio (November 9, 1920), NARA, in RG 122, Box 218, File 2/459–62, 8–9.

[30] UTA membership grew rapidly during the first five years of cost work, from 950 in 1911 to 1,852 in 1915. In 1916 it fell to 1,630. For UTA annual membership from 1888 to 1926, see Powell, *History of the UTA*, 192–93. For figures on the growth of local and regional associations, and cost system distribution, see *Proceedings of the Twenty-*

Membership boomed, many new locals appeared, and a third of all printers in the United States had adopted its cost system. The reason for the turnaround was a successful organizing campaign.

The state lifted the UTA from the doldrums in 1916, when the FTC enlisted the printers to its cost accounting program. Edward Hurley saw the UTA as a model association and the UTA's officers seized their new-found public purpose to redouble their organizing efforts.

In February 1916, U.S. Chamber of Commerce officials brokered a meeting between Chairman Hurley and UTA secretary Joseph Borden, and they discovered a common purpose. Hurley thought the printers a model of regulated competition, worthy of monitoring, approbation, and publicity. Borden thought FTC approval would be a boon to UTA cost work by legitimating it in the eyes of printers, suppliers, and customers. Hurley invited the UTA to submit its *Standard Cost System* to the commission's cost division for review.[31] In August, he announced the commission's endorsement. The UTA cost system, he wrote, "is comprehensive in scope, in accord with the best methods, and well designed along simple lines." It deserved to be publicized, studied, and adapted to parallel circumstances.[32]

Federal Trade Commission endorsement reconfigured the UTA's sense of purpose. Officers of the UTA told members that this was not merely government approval of a private project. The association was engaged in the "nation's work," endorsed not only by the FTC, but also by the president himself.[33] Chief Commissioner Hurley, they reported, had been "pleading earnestly" with business to improve cost accounting methods and to "compare their costs." Thus, the commission's endorsement was rife with surplus meaning: it demonstrated state recognition of the printers' work as a model system in service to the "common welfare."[34]

sixth Annual Convention of the UTA, September 3–6, 1912, 33–37; *Proceedings of the Twenty-eighth Annual Convention of United Typothetae and Franklin Clubs of America, 1914*, 98; *Proceedings of Twenty-seventh Annual Convention of the United Typothetae and Franklin Clubs of America, 1913*, 21–22; *Proceedings of the First Printers' Cost Congress of the Southeastern States, April 20, 1911*, 8–10. For a list of new locals, see *Proceedings of Twenty-seventh Annual Convention of the United Typothetae and Franklin Clubs of America, 1913*, 27–29.

31 *Proceedings of the Thirtieth Annual Convention UTA, 1916*, 13.

32 *Proceedings of the Thirty-first Annual Convention of the United Typothetae of America, Typothetae Bulletin* (December 1917): 27.

33 Fred W. Gage, "The Trend of Modern Business toward Standardization," *Proceedings of the Thirtieth Annual Convention, United Typothetae and Franklin Clubs of America, 1916*, 45–46.

34 Gage, "The Trend of Modern Business," 44–46.

In practical terms, UTA officers thought that the FTC endorsement would be of "inestimable advantage" in converting new printers to the *Standard Cost System.* Borden announced his intention to lithograph, frame, and distribute Hurley's letter for display to every printer using the *Standard Cost System.* In this way, all customers, suppliers, and competitors would gain confidence in new forms of management.[35] Armed with a fresh sense of public purpose, the UTA executive committee met to consider a national organizing campaign. Speaking for the committee, Fred Gage told rank-and-file printers that the UTA was engaged in a civic enterprise. There was no industry better poised to realize the FTC's goal to upgrade competition through developmental association. Commissioner Hurley, he said, challenged American business to reduce the "class of dangerous competitors" to 10 percent of U.S. industry through management accounting. The hard work of designing a cost system behind it, the UTA was ready to diffuse it to 90 percent of U.S. printers. He moved that the association launch a "three year period of organization, education and standardization." It passed overwhelmingly.[36]

The three-year plan was the brainchild of Secretary Borden. Although the printers had made great strides since the first cost congress, Borden told the executive committee that the UTA reached fewer than 10 percent of the 13,000 commercial printers in the United States. The problem, as he saw it, was to enlist printers to practical experience with cost accounting. Propaganda and formal education alone were ineffective. Only by experimenting with the *Standard Cost System* would printers realize its effects. But organizing experimentation on such a huge scale was a daunting task, well beyond the UTA's resources. The executive committee settled on a three-part strategy: enlist support from allied trades, make education contractual, and divide the nation into organizational districts.

In order to raise enough money to finance the three-year plan, the executive committee enlisted support from machinery manufacturers, type founders, paper manufacturers and jobbers, printing furniture manufacturers, photoengravers, electrotypers, and supply houses. In return, they invited allied-industry representatives to join a UTA advisory

[35] *Proceedings of the Thirtieth Annual Convention UTA, 1916*, 18–19; T. L. Moore, "The Establishment of a 'New Freedom' Policy: The Federal Trade Commission, 1912–1918" (PhD diss., University of Alabama, 1980), 112–13. See also *Official Report of Proceedings before the FTC, In the matter of FTC vs. UTA*, July 5, 1922, 982–86, in RG 122, Box 217, File 459–2–1.

[36] Gage, "The Trend of Modern Business," 43–49.

committee. The committee proposed subscribers contribute 0.1 percent of the 1915 sales to the three-year plan. Within two years, the UTA had raised over $200,000 from more than 300 subscribers.[37]

The UTA executive committee outlined three goals for the three-year plan: to increase the number of printers using the *Standard Cost System* and submitting data for benchmarking, to improve estimating, and to educate printers in marketing. The committee charged the UTA Department of Education to develop three courses to achieve these ends: one in cost accounting, a second in estimating, and a third in salesmanship.

Participation in the three-year plan was not completely voluntary. The UTA demanded participants sign a binding contract that committed them to send at least one student to each of the associations' year-long courses (hence the name three-year plan). They were also obliged to pay monthly dues for three years, to display the UTA trademark on company literature, to adopt the *Standard Cost System*, and to submit data for benchmarking.[38] Note how creatively syncretists in the UTA reconfigured contract and coercion from their use in cartels to new purposes in developmental associations. Instead of binding participants to market behavior (e.g., price ceilings or output quotas enforced by fines), the UTA contract committed printers to education and experience of sufficient depth and duration to enable the reconfiguration of habit through deliberation. In return, the three-year plan's contract obliged the UTA to provide all services at no additional cost, including expert consultancy on cost system operation and estimating.[39]

In order to facilitate organizing, the UTA partitioned the nation into regional districts, where they stationed a corps of field organizers, cost

[37] "Three-Year Plan Experimental Work," *Typothetae Bulletin* (September 1918), 26–32; Powell, *History of the UTA*, 182–84; "Three-Year Plan," *Proceedings of the 31st Annual Convention of the UTA, 1917*, 20–22; Testimony of Secretary Joseph A. Borden in *Federal Trade Commission versus United Typothetae of America, Hearings*, National Archives, in RG 122, Box 217, File 459–2–1, 354–62, 370–72; Testimony of Edward T. Miller, in the *Official Report of the Proceedings before the Federal Trade Commission*, Docket 459, FTC v. UTA, July 5, 1922, in RG 122, Box 217, File 459–2–1, 975–80. For lists of subscribers, see *Typothetae Bulletin* 12, no. 1 (July 1917): 1–2; *Typothetae Bulletin* 12, no. 2 (August 1917); and *Typothetae Bulletin* 12, no. 3 (September 1917): 20–21.

[38] "Meeting of the Executive Council of the UTA and the Advisory Committee of the Allied Interests, August 23 and 24, 1918," 3, in RG 122, Box 216, File 2/459–2.

[39] "Meeting of the Executive Council of the UTA and the Advisory Committee of the Allied Interests, August 23 and 24, 1918," 3, in RG 122, Box 216, File 2/459–2. Charles L. Estey, "Address on the Three-Year-Plan of the United Typothetae of America and Interrelated Industries, before the National Paper Trade Ass'n, the Writing Paper Manufacturers Ass'n, the Cover Paper Manufacturers Ass'n" (June 1919), 2, in RG 122, Box 218, File 2/459–2.

accountants, direct mail advertising experts, and paid secretaries.[40] After a six-month pilot program, implementation began in earnest in the summer of 1918.[41] By 1921, 64 locals were actively participating, 5,540 students had attended UTA classes, 8,000 copies of the UTA guide to benchmarking costs were in circulation, and 21 locals were independently benchmarking member costs.[42] Membership in the UTA had grown from 1,600 to 5,150. Borden's successor, Edward Miller, estimated that there were no more than 25 seriously active locals in 1918. By 1921, the number had grown to 130.[43] Positive reports came in from local secretaries throughout the country and many reported high levels of participation: 95 percent in Portland, Oregon, 85 percent in Washington, D.C., and 100 percent in Buffalo, New York.[44] By 1924, Secretary Miller estimated that four out of five UTA members had adapted and installed a UTA cost system (i.e., nearly one-third of all printers in the United States).

[40] *Proceedings of the Thirty-first Annual Convention of the UTA, 1917*, 20–22. On the critical activities of field organizers in mobilizing new members, see Eugene J. Roesch, "U.T.A. Workers in the Field," *Typothetae Bulletin* 13, no. 6 (December 1919): 38–39. So important were the field organizers that many became permanent local secretaries at the close of the three-year plan.

[41] "Meeting of the Executive Council of the UTA and the Advisory Committee of the Allied Interests, August 23 and 24, 1918," 3–4, in RG 122, Box 216, File 2/459–2; "Report of Secretary Borden to the 1918 Convention," *Typothetae Bulletin* 12 (November 1918): 27–29.

[42] *Development of the Three Year Plan*, "Resume of Progress Made by the UTA as Reported to Representatives of the Allied Industries at a Meeting with the Executive Council of the UTA on January 23, 1920," in RG 122, Box 218, File 2/459–2; Edward T. Miller, "Uniform Cost Systems," American Trade Association Executives, *Proceedings and Addresses,* Second Annual Convention, 1921, 67; Edward T. Miller, Uniform Cost Accounting Conference, Chicago, October 28–29, 1924; U.S. Chamber Papers, Acc. 1960, 91–105 [hereafter CofC, October, 1924].

[43] Miller, CofC, October, 1924, 92; Testimony of Miller, in the *Official Report of the Proceedings before the Federal Trade Commission*, Docket 459, FTC vs. UTA, July 5, 1922, 982, 990–991, in RG 122, Box 217, File 459–2–1.

[44] The national headquarters received successful reports from Denver; Tacoma; Spokane; Cincinnati; Toledo; Portland, Oregon; Trenton, New Jersey; South Bend, Elkhart, Mishawka, and Albany, Indiana. Locals from Wisconsin, Arkansas, Texas, Delaware, South Carolina, Michigan, and Oklahoma also reported new members, enthusiastic students, and an increasingly professional local staff. See Roesch, "U.T.A. Workers in the Field," *Typothetae Bulletin* 7; *Development of the Three Year Plan*, "Resume of Progress Made by the UTA as Reported to Representatives of the Allied Industries at a Meeting with the Executive Council of the UTA on January 23, 1920," in RG 122, Box 218, File 2/459–2; *The Portland Printing Industry* 1, no. 12 (July 15, 1919): 1, in RG 122, Box 218, File 2/459–2; "Testimony of Raymond Fennell, Secretary of the Portland UTA," *Report of Proceedings before FTC*, Portland, OR, 434, in RG 122, Box 217, 459–2–1; "Benefits Derived from the Three-Year Plan," *Typothetae Bulletin* 13, no. 6 (December 1919): 23–24. For additional local testimony see Roesch, "U.T.A. Workers in the Field," 39.

As the three-year plan came to a close in 1921, the UTA Department of Research conducted a detailed investigation of cost accounting practices in 664 plants. Of those, they found 502 were run well, submitted data to the UTA on a regular basis, and actively consulted industry benchmarks.[45] By all accounts, the three-year plan successfully enlisted thousands of new printers to collaborative learning.

PERFORMANCE

Collaborative learning improved printing performance in the 1920s. It helped individual printers escape the volume bug, local markets upgrade competition, and the industry as a whole to make technological innovations that tripled the rate of productivity growth.

Improvements in the Firm

National headquarters for the UTA received many testimonials of cost accounting's benefits from individual printers. They described how they had shed unprofitable work and useless machinery, improved labor and capital deployment, and stiffened their backbones in pricing. For some, the UTA cost system reconfigured the volume illusion directly. It "immediately ... impel[s] the printer to ... throw out a lot of unprofitable work, or to advance his prices," one Atlanta printer told the second cost congress. Of course, there are still plenty of "fool printers," he complained, willing to work for nothing. But if the UTA accounting system taught him anything, it was that "the matter of losing business and losing money are two separate propositions. Frequently...[lost] business ... resulted in increased profits."[46] Firms stayed small and prospered.

As a Lake George, New York, printer testified,

> I have for the past three years been using your cost system.... It works.... I have raised all my prices and still the cost system keeps telling me that I am losing every now and then on a job. I have lost a third of my business to my competitors, none of whom keep adequate cost records, but I seem to have as much money at the end of the year as ever.[47]

[45] Edward T. Miller, "Uniform Cost Systems," *American Trade Association Executives, Proceedings and Addresses, Second Annual Convention* (1921), 67; and Miller, CofC, October, 1924, 92.

[46] Foote, "Will the Use of the Cost System Cause Loss of Business, and the Results?" 114–18.

[47] Quoted in Edward T. Miller, "Uniform Methods and Standardized Costs," *National Association of Cost Accountants, Year Book, 1921* (New York: NACA, 1921), 150.

Another printer explained how product costing revealed "a great deal of [work] was being done at a loss." For the next three years, he made it a policy to "reduce volume" in order to "increase profit." As a result, he concentrated on his most profitable jobs and increased his profit rate from 7.4 to 21 percent in five years, even though his gross annual revenues fell by 29.7 percent.[48]

Yet another printer found that once he began to distribute overhead costs effectively, he learned that half of his long-term contract jobs were sold at a loss. As a result, he shed unprofitable work, charged remunerative prices, and watched net profits increase by more than 112 percent.[49] An Albany, New York, printer explained how product costing allowed him to determine for the first time "which branch of our business paid ... the most money." By dividing his work into eight categories (from "law books" to "express printing"), he analyzed the monthly spread between costs and sales. Now, he added, he no longer cross-subsidizes products – "each class of printing ... stands for itself" and he specializes in the most profitable work.[50] In other words, where he (like the railroad managers) had once assumed joint costs, product costing demonstrated there was a better way.

Other printers explained how they used benchmarks from the *Typothetae Standard Guide* to make improvements in production, reduce the pressure for volume through better investment decisions, and overcome the volume bug through product cost comparisons. A leading Detroit printer succeeded in reducing labor, rental, and shipping costs by comparing his performance to average costs in the *Typothetae Standard Guide*. A comparison of the firm's "chargeable hours per hour of wages" to the national average, for example, revealed two sorts of excess – supervisory and skilled labor costs. In neither case were nominal wages or salaries the problem. Instead, a careful investigation revealed "too many executives for the volume of business" and "first class compositors" routinely deployed for work more appropriately handled by apprentices. Another benchmark indicated above-average rental charges. Further investigation

48 "Profits Increased through Use of the Standard Cost Finding System," *Typothetae Bulletin* 12, no. 7 (January 1918): 3, in RG 122, Box 218, File 2/459–2.

49 Isaac H. Blanchard, "Cost System in the Large Plant," *Proceedings of the 28th Annual Convention, United Typothetae and Franklin Clubs of America* (October 6–8, 1914): 82–83.

50 "A Few Things the Cost System Has Done for the JB Lyon Co.," *Proceedings of the Second International Cost Congress of Employing Printers of America* (Chicago: American Printers' Cost Commission, 1910), 33–35.

revealed how excess idle space, not a high nominal rate, was the cause. Finally, benchmarking shipping expenses led to an investigation, which revealed it was cheaper to outsource to a subcontractor.[51] Once again, smaller was more efficient. Another printer explained how UTA benchmarks led him to reevaluate binder operations, with positive effects on the efficiency of each machine and employee.[52]

Benchmarking also reduced the pressure for volume by improving investment decisions. Irving Partridge explained how he used UTA *Typothetae Average Production Records* to evaluate current machinery and new investments. He found, for example, that instead of the vendor's inflated promise to reduce costs, a new folding machine would have cost fourteen cents more per hour than his current equipment. Benchmarking performance on one machine raised questions about others and turned out to be "instrumental in getting rid of ... over-equipment [and] obsolete machinery."[53] Lower capital costs, Partridge concluded, reduced the pressure for volume production and made it possible to prosper at a smaller scale.

Other printers explained how estimating by benchmarking raised questions unthinkable from internal data alone. One prominent New York printer explained how a comparatively high estimate on a routine job led him to investigate. He realized he was using premium paper, whereas others used stock, and adjusted his price and marketing strategy accordingly.[54] Still others found that some "guesstimates" for routine jobs were accurate, whereas others exposed wild mistakes. Benchmarking, in short, revealed alternatives to the volume bug by improving individual investment, product market, and estimating decisions.

Three UTA studies corroborated individual testimony on the value of developmental association to the firm. The first, a 1921 study of profit rates in 327 cities, found that printers earned on average 3.4 percent (total sales minus total cost). By comparison, for firms using the standard cost system and actively benchmarking under the three-year plan, average profit rates were 10 percent.[55] A second cross-sectional study, conducted

[51] Mabel H. Dwyer, "Departmental Cost Analysis," *Proceedings of the Forty-fourth Convention of the UTA*, *Typothetae Bulletin* 32, no. 3 (October 27, 1930): 100–103.

[52] "The Importance of Production Efficiency," *Typothetae Bulletin* 12, no. 3 (September 1917): 3 in RG 122, Box 218, File 2/459–2.

[53] Reported in George N. Voorhees, "Management and the Accountant," *Typothetae Bulletin* 22 (October 26, 1925): 143–45.

[54] Voorhees, "Better Pricing," 3–4.

[55] Testimony of Edward T. Miller, in *Official Report of Proceedings before the FTC*, Docket No. 459, In the Matter of FTC vs. UTA, Chicago, July 5, 1922, 990, in RG 122, Box 217, File 459–2–1.

by a UTA field organizer, also showed better performance. Between 1918 and 1919, Don Gerking visited 590 plants, of which 130 were operating with UTA cost systems. He found the latter earned an aggregate profit of 12.2 percent above cost, whereas the former incurred a 2.3 percent loss.[56] A third indicator, printers' credit ratings, also indicated vast improvements in individual performance as a result of development association. A 1924 ranking of industrial credit ratings found the printers in fifteenth place, up from thirty-fourth in 1919 and eightieth in 1910.[57] In 1917, the UTA conducted its own credit study, which revealed a first grade rating among 84 percent of UTA members who had adopted the *Standard Cost System*.[58]

Local Market Improvements

Like individual performance, competitive conditions in local markets also improved. Chapter secretaries of the UTA throughout the country reported better prices and profits as a result of the three-year plan.[59] Chicago printers, for example, found that the three-year plan had dramatically changed pricing customs in the second-largest printing market in the nation. In the first place, the more that Chicago printers used UTA estimating procedures, the more customers came to trust prices, because estimates had become so detailed. As a result, price variations decreased significantly. Second, Chicago printers witnessed a rapid growth in "cost-plus contracts" after implementation of the three-year plan. Customers no longer expected estimates to be the final word on prices; and printers routinely wrote contracts with room for cost overruns, change-orders, and unexpected inflation in materials costs. One printer estimated that by 1921 nearly 90 percent of all printing in the city was done on a cost-plus basis.[60]

56 Don V. Gerking, Field Representative, UTA, "A Message to Visitors," *Typothetae Bulletin* 13, no. 6 (December, 1919): 40–42.

57 Miller, CofC, October, 1924, 95. See also Miller, *Official Report of Proceedings before the FTC*, 928; George H. Gardner, "Price Control," *Typothetae Bulletin* 12, no. 5 (November 1918): 147–48.

58 William H. Sleepeck, "Composite Statement of Cost of Production for 1916," *Proceedings of the 31st Annual Convention, United Typothetae of America, 1917*, 25.

59 Locals from Springfield, Massachusetts; Newark, New Jersey; Rochester and Buffalo, New York; Elkhart, South Bend, and Goshen, Indiana; Des Moines; Kansas City; Milwaukee; Chicago; Louisville; Minneapolis; Detroit; and Cleveland reported higher prices and better profits. *Proceedings of the Twenty-fourth Annual Convention of the United Typothetae of America, May 17–19, 1910* (Assn, 1910), 29–97; Miller, "Uniform Methods and Standardized Costs," 150–51.

60 Miller, "Uniform Methods and Standardized Costs," 150–51.

A study of Grand Rapids, Michigan, found that the total profit rate for all printers had leapt from a loss of 1 percent before the three-year plan to a 12 percent profit at the end. Although part of the improvement was due to wartime prosperity, the same study also showed a 4.34 percent decrease in aggregate departmental and overhead costs.[61] Another survey of local markets by the UTA's chief field organizer showed "increases in returns as high as twenty per cent" and dramatically improved credit conditions in cities actively involved in a three-year plan.[62] Finally, a 1921 report by Dun and Bradstreet's credit rating service showed that 90 percent of the failures in the printing business during the previous year were in cities or towns without a UTA local.[63]

Productivity and Technical Change

As the three-year plan came to a close in 1921, the printers embarked on an ambitious program of electrification and technological change, which successfully combined the republican ends of artisanship and independent proprietorship with engineering improvements in production. Coupled with the management improvements associated with the UTA's program in collaborative learning, technological change wrought substantial increases in productivity, labor skills, and the viability of small enterprise. Three aspects of these innovations are critical to our story. First, developmental association preceded technical change. Commercial printers were unable to exploit existing innovations or create new ones until they put their managerial house in order. Second, technical change mirrored the shift from volume to specialty production. Third,

[61] "Development of the Three Year Plan," 3.

[62] Don V. Gerking, "The Relation of Fieldmen to Members," *Typothetae Bulletin* 14, no. 2 (October 1920): 22.

[63] "The Proof of the Puddin'," *Typothetae Bulletin* 17, no. 25 (September 17, 1923): 389. As early as 1916, the UTA recognized the importance of the cost system to improving confidence between printers and their bankers, suppliers, and customers. As a result, they issued a Certificate of Cost Finding, signed by the chairperson of the American Printers Cost Commission and the secretary of the UTA, to all printers who had adopted the Standard Cost System. With Chairman Hurley's approval, a copy of the Federal Trade Commission's endorsement of the UTA system accompanied the certificate. Both were "printed on heavy ledger paper for the purpose of framing and display in the business office." The UTA noted that the certificate "stands in the same relation [to the printer] as a diploma to the professional man." See "The Work of the United Typothetae and Franklin Clubs of America," *Inland Printer* 59 (1917): 781–82; H. W. J. Meyer, "Report of the American Cost Commission," *Proceedings of the 31st Annual Convention, United Typothetae of America, 1917*, 90.

commercial printers rationalized craft or specialty production, whereas managerial enterprise rationalized mass production.

Two technical innovations improved productivity and product quality in commercial printing: electrification and press redesign. By making it possible to isolate power to individual machines, electrification improved plant layout, reduced space requirements, reduced power costs, increased control over individual machines, and made it possible to install better lighting. Although newspaper printers had pioneered electrification, commercial printers did not follow until the end of the three-year plan. Collaborative learning was a precondition for technological change, because it improved managerial capacity, reduced cutthroat competition, and made credit widely available to commercial printers. But, rooted as it was in republican dispositions, it also reshaped the goal of technical innovation from volume to specialization.

Newspaper printers were the first U.S. manufacturers to electrify, making the shift in the 1890s. By the time commercial printers launched the first cost congress, their cousins in the newspaper trade had completed two decades of technical innovation. Like the mass-producers who electrified in the 1920s, newspaper printers increased high volume throughput by applying electricity to enormous high-speed rotary presses.[64] When commercial printers began to electrify in 1919, they took a different path. Driven by their desire to combine independent artisanship with modern management, they adapted technology to augment skill and product quality and diversity. The more they reconstituted cost accounting to shift

[64] As a result of gains in energy efficiency, plant layout, and the scale economies associated with large rotary presses, productivity in newspaper printing grew at an average annual rate of 8.2 percent between the turn of the century and World War I, while productivity grew at an annual average rate of .7 percent in book and job printing during the same period. On newspaper printing and productivity, see Warren D. Devine Jr., "Technological Change and Electrification in the Printing Industry, 1880–1930," Institute for Energy Analysis, Oak Ridge Associated Universities, January 1985, Research Memorandum ORAU/IEA-84-8 (M), 21–35, Table 11 (p. 42). For an excellent summary of this report see Walter D. Devine Jr., "The Printing Industry as a Leader in Electrification, 1883–1930," *Printing History* 7, no. 2 (1985): 27–36. On the early recognition of efficiency advantages of individually driven electric motors over steam power and belt and shaft systems in printing and other sectors, see George A. Damon, "The Electrical Equipment of a Model Printing Establishment," *The Electrical World* 32, no. 20 (November 12, 1898): 499–504; "Electric Distribution of Power in Workshops," *Journal of the Franklin Institute* 151, no. 1 (January 1901): 1–28; W. H. Tapley, "The Practical Application of Electric Motors to Printing Press Machinery," *Journal of the Franklin Institute* 148 (October 1899): 259–79; and Frank C. Perkins, "The Modern Use of Electricity in Printing," *Scientific American* 86, June 14, 1902, 415.

the printer's attention from volume to quality, service, and flexibility, the more the printer demanded appropriate machinery. Instead of adapting electricity to increase speed, commercial printers used it to augment skill by increasing the pressman's control over machinery. The 1920s saw innovations in small-scale, flexible, automatic paper feed, high-speed electric presses, capable of multicolor and two-sided printing. They diffused rapidly after the three-year plan. Commercial printers bought an average of 3,916 presses per year between 1918 and 1929, an increase of 1,844 per year, or 50 percent, over the previous decade.[65] The UTA worked hard to ensure technical change was not limited to New York and Chicago. In the 1920s, the UTA launched two new education programs devoted to specialization and technical skills: one on electrification, a second on custom and specialty product marketing.[66] As a result, more than two-thirds of all commercial printing presses sold after the three-year plan were installed outside of the largest printing centers.

Coupled with improvements in managerial capacity, fostered by benchmarking and the *Standard Cost System*, these technical improvements yielded substantial productivity increases. Value added per worker in commercial printing leapt from an annual average increase of 0.7 percent before the three-year plan to 3.2 percent after, and doubled the already striking productivity advantage printers enjoyed over U.S. manufacturing industries overall.[67] (See Figure 7.3.)

To be sure, World War I witnessed growing electrification, yielding across-the-board productivity increases in manufacturing. But as business

[65] Elizabeth F. Baker, *Displacement of Men by Machines: Effects of Technological Change in Commercial Printing* (New York: Columbia University Press, 1933), 18–24, 201. Baker divides her figures on press sales at 1913. In order to adjust for the effects of uniform cost accounting, I reconfigured her calculations to break at 1916.

[66] On UTA electrification education, see Carl F. Scott, *Power for Operating Machinery in Printing Houses* (Chicago: United Typothetae of America, 1918), 2–3, 23–24. On UTA marketing education see A. L. Lewis, "The UTA Marketing Program," *Typothetae Bulletin* 22, no. 4 (October 26, 1925): 94–97. Commercial marketing in the 1920s became preoccupied with creating markets for novel custom products made possible by new printing techniques. See, for example, E. J. Clary, "Contact with the Customer's Plan Will Multiply Your Sales," *Inland Printer* 81 (September 1928): 60–62; Frederick Black, "Six Tips for the Printing Salesman," *Inland Printer* 81 (September 1928): 63–64; Herbert C. Hall, "Customers Will Buy Ideas Where They Won't Buy Printing!" *Inland Printer* 81 (September 1928): 57–59.

[67] Between 1900 and 1919, value added per worker in book and job printing increased from $26,372 to $31,118. These levels exceeded the average value added per worker for all American manufacturing industries by $3,825 to $7,864. Following the three-year plan, value added for printers increased from $31,118 in 1919 to $50,411 in 1929, levels that exceeded the American manufacturing average by $9,058 to $14,469.

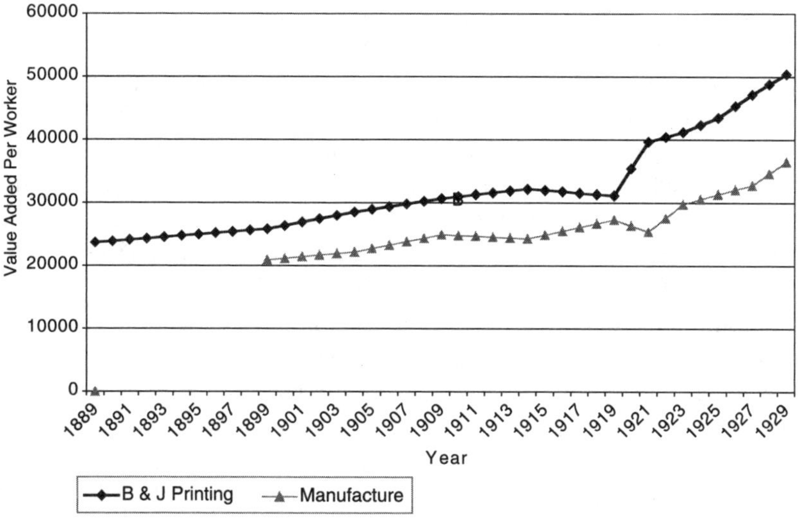

FIGURE 7.3. Value Added per Worker in Commercial Printing and Manufacturing, 1899–1929
Source: United States Department of Commerce, *Commerce Yearbook 1923* (Washington: Government Printing Office, 1924): 347–349; United States Department of Commerce, *Commerce Yearbook 1930* (Washington: Government Printing Office, 1931): 48–49; United States Department of Commerce, *Commerce Yearbook 1932* (Washington: Government Printing Office, 1933): 473–474.

historian Alfred Chandler shows, technological change never translates directly into productivity gains; it must be accompanied by organizational innovation. Indeed, the previous round of innovation in commercial printing – mechanized typesetting in the 1880s and 1890s – yielded labor strife, cutthroat competition, and only modest productivity growth. It was not until commercial printers began to track departmental and product costs, benchmark, and price with reference to cost that they began to catch up to newspaper printers in technology and productivity – and widened their advantage over U.S. manufacturers overall.

Furthermore, printers succeeded in realizing their republican experimentalist goals to improve productivity without incorporating, increasing the size or decreasing the number of firms, or deskilling their employees. In fact, developmental association, electrification, and automation increased the number of small, independent proprietorships and the proportion of skilled workers in the industry. For example, as printers automated paper feeding on presses in the 1920s, they shed thousands of unskilled feeders. But as productivity, specialization, and product quality increased, markets grew and printers hired more and more skilled pressmen. Thus, the ratio of skilled to unskilled workers increased. In addition, printing became less, not more, concentrated over time. Printing plants remained small. In 1889, the average number of employees per establishment in the book and job printing industry was 14.2. Forty years later, in 1929, that number had grown to 16.1. And when ranked with other industries by the percent of total industry sales made by the four largest sellers (the four firm concentration ratio), printing placed second to last in 1901, with a figure of 1.0, falling to last place in 1947, its four firm concentration ratio virtually at zero.[68]

In summary, developmental association improved individual firm performance and competitive conditions in local markets, and enabled technological innovations, which trebled productivity in commercial printing. In doing so, it realized the printers' republican experimentalist aspiration to combine independent proprietorship, craftsmanship, and democratic deliberation with the techniques of modern management. Developmental association in printing demonstrates the viability of creative syncretism.

A NOTE ON PRICE FIXING

In 1921 the FTC investigated the UTA for price fixing, which would appear to corroborate the institutional interpretation of information pooling, but did not. In addition to benchmarking costs, the commission charged the UTA with publishing a *Standard Price List* and advocating its members' price off of average costs.[69] Three pieces of evidence undermined the FTC's case. First, the UTA did not rely on price coordination to achieve its ends; second, the UTA abandoned its price list before the FTC investigation; and third, the FTC negotiated a consent agreement with the UTA, which undermined price fixing but left the techniques of collaborative learning intact.

Consider first the UTA price list. Investigation revealed that it was of little use for the vast majority of printer's products, because it covered

[68] Devine, *Technological Change and Electrification in the Printing Industry*, 58–59; Baker, *Displacement of Men by Machines*, 48–80. Nor was the continued decentralization of the industry a foregone conclusion. In the late teens and early twenties, *Census* data seemed to show the opposite and some knowledgeable commentators predicted continued concentration. See Lewis, "The UTA Marketing Program," 96.

[69] *United States of America before Federal Trade Commission, Complaint in the Case of Federal Trade Commission v. United Typothetae of America*, Docket 459, March 1, 1922, in RG 122, Box 215, File 459. See also "Federal Trade Commission Finally Reaches a Finding," *Typothetae Bulletin* 17, no 22 (August 27, 1923): 339–40, for an account of the initial complaint.

no more than 5 percent of total national output. Moreover, its categories were too crude to be useful for pricing the vast diversity of custom and batch products typical of the industry. Indeed, price lists, like average costs, were most useful for locating egregious mistakes in estimating.[70]

Second, UTA officers worried about the antitrust implications of the three-year plan, so they abandoned the *Standard Price List* two years before the FTC investigation. By the time the commission issued a cease-and-desist order against the price list in 1922, it was a moot point.

Third, the UTA and the commission agreed in 1922 that the UTA's publication of industry cost averages, the *Typothetae Standard Guide,* would no longer include aggregate production costs. (Apparently, the commission's legal staff believed these data were most likely to be used for price coordination.)[71] This agreement, however, had little effect on performance benchmarking, which relied, after all, on comparing detailed information gleaned from Form 9-H. Thus, although the data necessary for spontaneous cooperation were purged from UTA benchmarks, the data necessary for collaborative learning remained intact.

In summary, there is little evidence that printers used UTA data to coordinate prices or to monitor one another's preferences and behavior. They abandoned the list most useful for pricing in 1919 and under FTC scrutiny purged aggregate cost data from benchmarks in 1922. Despite this, productivity and profits improved steadily throughout the 1920s. It is far more likely that this outcome was due to collaborative learning than to spontaneous cooperation.

CONCLUSION

Creative syncretists at United Typothetae of America successfully combined traditional principles and practices of artisan republicanism with modern techniques of business management. In doing so, they reconfigured the UTA from a brotherhood to a cartel to a developmental association. Unable to rely on traditional craft solidarities or the modern techniques of enforcement, they turned instead to collaborative learning.

70 *Brief of United Typothetae of America, and Others,* Respondents before the FTC, Docket No. 459, FTC v. UTA, et al., 22–34, in RG 122, Box 215, File 459.

71 *Petition to Review Order of Federal Trade Commission,* United Typothetae of America (Petitioner) v. FTC (Respondent) in the U.S. Circuit Court of Appeals for the Seventh Circuit, October Term A.D. 1923, in RG 122, Box 215, File 459; *Brief of United Typothetae of America, and Others* (Respondents), before Federal Trade Commission, Docket No. 459, FTC v. UTA, et al., in RG 122, Box 215, File 459.

The UTA fostered collaborative learning in three ways. First, as printers came together to discuss costs, they began to renarrate the causes of their distress. They asked whether cutthroat competition was the inevitable result of technology, greed, and modern capitalism, or was an artifact of accounting habits that prized volume over all other forms of productivity. Alter the habits, they conjectured, and printers would channel rivalry from cutthroat pricing to quality, service, and nonvolume forms of productivity. Second, the UTA fostered collaborative learning through benchmarking. By providing information unavailable from the market or the firm, benchmarking disconcerted old habits and artisanal dispositions and raised questions unthinkable without comparison. Third, once the UTA had shown the way from the volume illusion to specialization, the printers embarked on an ambitious program of technical innovation, in which they adapted electricity and machinery to the ends of civic enterprise.

The state enabled the diffusion of collaborative learning in printing in three ways. By approving the UTA's cost plan, the FTC raised the association's social position, revised the identity of its leaders from private to public agents, and enhanced the legitimacy of cost accounting and benchmarking to rank-and-file printers. The result was a highly successful organizing drive, which trebled UTA membership and increased the number of printers operating its cost system to one-third of the industry.

The success of UTA cost accounting, in turn, enabled an ambitious program of product specialization, technical innovation, and productivity growth. Between 1918 and 1928, printers adapted electricity and press technology to enhance specialization, product quality, marketing capacity, and nonvolume forms of efficiency. Developmental association, in short, provided a distinctive path to improvement, overlooked by institutionalists. Instead of cartelization, spontaneous cooperation, or concentration, commercial printers did better by increasing product diversity, labor skills, and industrial fragmentation. This was no mean feat for an industry, which grew to 15,000 establishments by the 1920s.

It is difficult to make sense of the transition from cartel to developmental association or the success of the UTA without something like the theory of creative syncretism. For institutionalists, there was only one problem for trade associations who adopted information pooling: how to manage overcapacity. And the structural conditions in the printing industry made this impossible. From a constructivist point of view, creative associationalists scanned their institutional environment through the lens of republican experimentalism and found resources where institutionalists see only constraints. By retelling the causes of their distress and reconceptualizing the nature and purpose of cost accounting, they were able to mobilize those resources for a creative experiment in collaborative learning.

PART III

REGULATED COMPETITION CONTESTED

Chapter 8

The Politics of Accountability

Conflict over the meaning of antitrust reemerged in the 1920s, when the Department of Justice and private litigants challenged the legality of trade practice conferences and developmental associations in court. These cases pit two methods of assessing accountability against each other. On one side were the critics of regulated competition: the Department of Justice, the courts, and the economists. Like the progressive economists and laissez-faire constitutionalists we encountered in Chapter 2, they wanted to subject regulated competition to standards of classification. They asked whether trade practice conference rules and trade association instruments were instances of perfect competition or artificial monopoly, which served public or private interests. Adopting deductive categories from economics, they hoped to establish a bright line between private rights and public authority and then measure trade practice rules and trade association instruments against that classification. On the other side were the partisans of regulated competition: Brandeis (now an associate justice on the Supreme Court), the FTC, trade associations, and the cost accountants. They wanted to subject trade practice conferences and developmental associations to standards of process, power, and performance. Like Brandeis's social theory of restraints of trade (explained in Chapter 2) or Gaskill's theory of customary competition (explained in Chapter 4), they asked: What was the historical process that resulted in problems that trade practice rules or trade association instruments were intended to solve? Did they alter the distribution of power in a way that sustained possibilities for productive rivalry? What were the effects of trade practice rules or developmental associations on economic performance?

The partisans of regulated competition lost the struggle over accountability, but won noteworthy concessions. When they were defeated in the courts, they took their case to Congress, where they proved too disorganized to make their case. Classification became the dominant model of accountability and the practice of regulated competition was contained. Nevertheless, the critics of regulated competition accepted many of its most distinctive instruments, as long as they passed the test of classification. The FTC and developmental associations adjusted trade practice conferences and information pooling in response. Thus regulated competition survived the struggle over accountability, even if not in the forms initially envisioned by its architects.

This chapter recounts the politics of accountability in four sections. The first section tells the story of the struggle over trade practice conferences. I explain the clash between the courts and the commission and then show how the FTC accommodated trade practice rules to conform to judicial reasoning. The second section recounts the struggle over information pooling by trade associations during the Harding and Coolidge administrations (1920–1928). I explain the clash between Brandeis and the Supreme Court majority and then show how creative syncretists in the majority accommodated features of benchmarking by borrowing a new form of classification from economics. The third section describes how the partisans of regulated competition lobbied Congress to legislate their theory of accountability and explains why they failed. The conclusion shows how some practices of regulated competition survived, whereas others perished, as a result of the victory of a classification theory of accountability.

ACCOUNTABILITY FOR TRADE PRACTICE CONFERENCES

Court versus Commission

In 1921, the FTC tested the legal viability of its conferences when it hauled the Standard Oil companies into court for violating trade practice rules. This was a critical case because it tested the commission's authority to enforce regulated competition and prevent the regional companies, which had emerged from Standard Oil's dissolution in 1912, from reconsolidating power over their industry. It raised two other important questions. Could trade practice conferences channel rivalry from a contest over power to improvement in products and production processes? Could the commission offer a coherent method to hold trade practice rules accountable to statutory and constitutional ends?

On June 20, 1920, the FTC sponsored a trade practice conference on gasoline distribution in Chicago. Among the most controversial issues was a leasing system devised by Standard Oil of New York and copied by many of its largest competitors. Standard leased tank and pump units to retailers for $1 per year and restricted its retailers, who took the leases, from buying gasoline from other refiners. Conference participants were virtually unanimous in their opposition to restrictive leasing. They declared it an unfair method of competition, in which the refiners with the deepest pockets, rather than the best and cheapest product, prevailed. In December the FTC held a second conference in Denver, which reached the same conclusion.[1]

The conferences produced three rules against restrictive leasing. The first recommended that equipment should be sold at full cost. The second conceded that if equipment were to be leased, lessees should a pay minimum annual rate of 10 percent of the equipment's sales value, with due allowance for depreciation. The third rule condemned restrictive covenants, which forced retailers, who took cheap leases, to buy gasoline from a single source.[2]

The commissioners unanimously approved the gasoline distribution rules and proceeded to issue cease-and-desist orders against three Standard Oil companies and thirty-two other corporations. They asked defendants to stop leasing equipment at a price that did not yield a reasonable profit and to abandon restrictive covenants. The refiners refused to comply. They reasoned the FTC had exceeded its jurisdiction; the leases were private matters; and the trade practice rules served factional business interests, instead of the public's interest in freedom of contract and maximizing the number of distribution outlets.

Early in 1921, the commission filed suit to enforce.[3] Drafted under Commissioner Gaskill's guidance, the FTC's brief is a model of a process, power, and performance methodology to assess the accountability

[1] See U.S. Federal Trade Commission, *Trade Practice Conferences* (Washington, DC: Government Printing Office, 1929), 21–29; Federal Trade Commission, *Annual Report, 1919* (Washington, DC: Government Printing Office, 1920), 49–50; FTC v. Standard Oil of Indiana, 2 FTC 26 (1920). For a list of FTC hearings and stipulations against oil company distribution methods, see FTC v. Maloney Oil and Manufacturing Co., 2 FTC 346 at 357.

[2] The conferences also produced a model contract. Federal Trade Commission, *Trade Practice Conferences*, 25–28.

[3] See Thomas C. Blaisdell Jr., *The Federal Trade Commission: An Experiment in the Control of Business* (New York: Columbia University Press, 1932), 49; see also FTC v. Maloney Oil & Manufacturing Co., 2 FTC 346; Federal Trade Commission v. Lubric

of trade practice rules. The first part recounted the history of predatory competition in gasoline distribution; the second compared performance in firms and regions with unfair leasing to those without it.

Gasoline distribution was a young and rapidly changing industry, wrote the commission, in which practices that had worked well ten years earlier turned destructive under new circumstances. Following the tradition in kerosene, gasoline was initially distributed in barrels owned by the refiners. Custom held that refiners lent barrels to retailers for storage between deliveries at no extra cost. When in-ground tanks and pumps were introduced in the teens, Standard Oil extended its free leases to the new technology. Whereas uncompensated barrel loans increased competition over distribution, it suppressed it with pump and tank technology, charged the commission. Most refiners could not afford the subsidies. (The Standard Oil companies administered over 8,000 free leases in New York and New England alone.) Moreover, restrictive covenants made it impossible for competing refiners to market their products. Thus, customs once functional turned predatory under new circumstances.[4]

There was nothing inevitable about this development, added the commission, because comparison showed that refiners were perfectly capable of improving productivity and competing effectively without unfair methods of competition. The gasoline conferences revealed two counterfactuals: the Atlantic Oil Company and distribution in the western United States. Like the Standard Oil companies, Atlantic was a large, vertically integrated corporation that marketed under a trade name and managed a vast distribution system. However, Atlantic leased equipment to fewer than 20 percent of its customers and none of its leases included restrictive covenants. The company competed by providing customers with professional accounting and engineering services, data on regional sales, and generous loans. As a result, Atlantic had a sufficiently large market to cut production and distribution costs.[5]

The FTC also invoked performance in western oil distribution to make its point. The Denver conference showed that although leasing was rare in the West, there was no loss to economy, brand names were

Oil Co. 3 FTC 68; FTC v. Thomas K. Brushart, Doing Business under the Firm Name and Style of the Motor Fuel & Lubricating Co., 3 FTC 78.

[4] *Brief for Respondent*, Standard Oil Company of New York (Petitioner) v. Federal Trade Commission (Respondent), United States Circuit Court of Appeals for the Second Circuit October Term, 1920, 3–4, 7–9, 11–18, in RG 122, Box 76, File 134 [cited hereafter as *Brief for FTC*].

[5] *Brief for FTC*, 19–23, 40.

protected, and distribution facilities were adequate to service growing demand.[6]

Thus, evaluated according to process, power, and performance criteria, trade practice rules against free leases with restrictive covenants were a legitimate exercise of regulated competition, which warranted enforcement. By precluding predatory competition over deep pockets, the FTC reasoned, the refiners would have little choice but to compete over price, service, and product quality. This was precisely Congress's intent. Section 5 of the Federal Trade Commission Act granted the commission prophylactic powers to block unfair methods before they turned into unassailable power. In issuing cease-and-desist orders against free leases, the commission signaled its intent to prevent Standard Oil's children from reconsolidating control over the industry and to preserve rivalry over products and distribution processes.[7]

The courts disagreed with the FTC and in doing so articulated a very different theory of accountability, in which trade practice rules would be judged according to whether they could be classified as serving public or private interests.[8] In the courts' view, this case involved three different questions. First, how should one classify the leasing system? Was it an ordinary method of competition or a monopolistic practice? Second, how should one classify the trade practice rules? Did they redistribute private advantages or realize the public's interest in regulation? Third, how should one classify the FTC's cease-and-desist order? Was it regulatory capture or a legitimate exercise of coercion? The commission assessed trade practice rules according to process, power, and performance, whereas the courts classified them as public or private.

Measured against the facts, the courts classified the gasoline leases as ordinary tools of competition, the trade practice rules as private, and the FTC's cease-and-desist order as capture. They found in favor of the refiners.

Consider first the leases themselves. The history of technological change, a federal court of appeals argued, was irrelevant. After all, pump and tank technology is "nothing more than ... a barrel with a faucet in it." The problem was one of classifications, in which it was the court's obligation to assess whether the leases were an instance of ordinary

[6] *Brief for FTC*, 37–38.

[7] *Brief for FTC*, 103–11, 130–35.

[8] In 1922, the federal courts consolidated thirty-three cases into four. A year later, the Supreme Court heard an appeal.

competition or monopoly. They were the former. The particular terms of Standard Oil's leases were ordinary "weapons," "inherent" in the "strife" of competition, no different from advertising, pricing, or service, wrote the court. Competition is a "battle." When some firms lose, the public wins.[9] Free leases served the public interest by weeding out the weak and providing consumers with a more extensive distribution network. Moreover, restrictive covenants were a legitimate method to protect the lessor's property rights in its brand name from unscrupulous retailers, who would adulterate their product. Thus nominal leases with restrictive covenants were ordinary methods of competition, which belonged in the private sphere.[10]

If the leases were private, then rules against them redistributed market advantages instead of serving the public's interest in competition, reasoned the court. Echoing the Supreme Court's logic in *Lochner,* the federal court condemned the commission for trampling the public/private distinction. If upheld, the FTC's cease-and-desist order would open the door to panoptic government – a state with virtually unlimited "power" to "watch over" all market activity and to "compel" every rival who is "too fast paced" to "slow down."[11] Congress did not intend to "bestow any such power" on the FTC, declared the Supreme Court on appeal. If it had, it would be unconstitutional. The FTC's cease-and-desist order against Standard Oil of New York was declared void.[12]

Commissioner Gaskill condemned the courts for downgrading competition, damaging economic performance, and usurping administrative authority. They stood regulated competition on its head. "You have transformed competition from ... quality, ... price and ... service" to the "ability to buy preference" and "security." "In the long run, the largest bank account will rule" and distribution costs will rise, as competitors outbid one another in the "lavishness of ... equipment furnished for free." Instead of regulating competition, the judiciary succeeded in channeling rivalry from improvement in products and distribution into predation.[13]

[9] Sinclair Refining Co. v. Federal Trade Commission, 276 Fed. 686 at 688.

[10] Standard Oil Co. of New York v. Federal Trade Commission, Texas Co. v. Same, 273 Fed. 478 at 480–81.

[11] Sinclair Refining Co. v. Federal Trade Commission, 276 Fed. 686 at 688.

[12] FTC v. Sinclair Refining Co. Same v. Standard Oil Co. (New Jersey). Same v. Gulf Refining Co. Same v. Maloney Oil & Mfg. Co., 261 U.S. 463 at 474–76.

[13] "Federal Trade Board View of Demonstrators," *American Perfumer and Essential Oil Review* (May 1924): 127–31. This was a general problem, Gaskill said. The article cited

Gaskill criticized the judiciary's method of classification as incoherent and obnoxious to the FTC's prophylactic warrant. Under the Court's logic, the FTC must prove monopoly *before* it occurred. But this was precisely Congress's intent, that is, to check "unfair competition" before it hardened into monopoly power. The Sherman Act had long been capable of reaching monopoly once it was in place. The Court asked the wrong question. Instead of classifying trade practice rules, judges should ask how well the FTC's conference procedure intervened in the historical process of custom formation to improve economic performance. As we saw in Chapter 5, Gaskill asked the judiciary to consider instead whether conference procedures identified "visionary" practices and held them out as a model. Did they provide cautious manufacturers, who compulsively followed routine, with information and incentives to copy visionaries? Did they police the "pirates," who exploited dysfunctional customs to perpetrate fraud, theft, and opportunism? This method of assessing accountability would better serve the public's interest in regulated competition.[14]

Accommodation

Gaskill's critique fell on deaf ears and the commission learned to accommodate the Court's demand for classification.[15] In 1927, the Trade Practice

here attacked the practice by perfume companies of placing "hidden demonstrators" (solicitors not identified as such on the manufacturer's payroll) in department stores.

14 Nelson Gaskill, "Public Interest versus Private Interest in the Federal Trade Commission Act," *Proceedings of the Academy of Political Science* 11, no. 4 (January 1926): 121–31, especially 127–28.

15 In addition to the courts, Gaskill failed to gain the ear of the president, Congress, or the press. Preoccupied with criticisms of lax antitrust enforcement, Harding had little capital to reform trade regulation. And even though many conservative Republicans supported trade practice conferences, they were more critical of the FTC's public investigations of the electricity, construction, and oil industries. When President Coolidge responded to that criticism by appointing William Humphrey to replace Gaskill in 1926, Democrats and progressive Republicans began to criticize the FTC. Robert LaFollette (R-WI), in his final years in the Senate, complained that the FTC had been captured by its "worst enemies." And the liberal press joined the chorus. On Humphrey and his critics, see G. Cullom Davis, "The Transformation of the Federal Trade Commission, 1914–1929," *Mississippi Valley Historical Review* 49 (December 1962): 437–55; E. Pendleton Herring, *Public Administration and the Public Interest* (New York: McGraw-Hill, 1936), 125–27; Address of W. E. Humphrey, Federal Trade Commissioner, before the Thirteenth Annual Meeting of the Chamber of Commerce of the United States, May 20, 1925, FTC Library; W. E. Humphrey, "The Economics of Cooperation as Exemplified by the Work of the Federal Trade Commission," Address before the Institute of Statesmanship, January 6, 1930, Winter Park, Florida, FTC Library.

Conference Division initiated a classification scheme. But this was not enough to satisfy the commission's critics, who had internalized judicial logic. So, in a second accommodation, the FTC's Legal Division rewrote all enforceable trade practice rules in a standardized judicial language.

In the spring of 1927, the Trade Practice Conference Division reviewed rules for the West Coast dairy industry for their legality and classified them into two categories. In doing so, they adjusted conference outcomes to judicial authority. Group I included all rules found consistent with current antitrust and administrative law. As such, they were enforceable under Section 5 of the Federal Trade Commission Act.[16] Group II included all rules considered "sound" business practice by the majority of the industry, but had no status in existing antitrust and administrative law. Thus, it was impossible to depend on judiciary authority for guidance. The division classified Group II rules as "advisory and optional provisions," unenforceable at law. During the next six months, the Trade Practice Conference Division refined its categories and reviewed all prior rules for classification.[17]

The effects of classification became evident when the oil industry returned for a second conference in 1929. Once again participants condemned free leases with restrictive covenants. This time, however, the FTC restricted its authority. The Trade Practice Conference Division

[16] U.S. Congress, Senate Committee Print, 76th Cong., 3d sess., Temporary National Economic Committee, *Control of Unfair Competitive Practices through Trade Practice Conference Procedure of the Federal Trade Commission*, Monograph no. 34 (Washington, DC: Government Printing Office, 1941), 4–6 [hereafter cited as TNEC, *Control*]. For an earlier statement, see summary of Commissioner McCollough before the Hickory-Handle Branch, Wood-turning Industry, July 18, 1928, in FTC, *Trade Practice Conferences*, 1929, 136, where he says that the FTC, in passing on resolutions adopted at trade practice conferences, determines "whether the things which the industry condemns are really unlawful, and if they are found to be so such rules will be approved and will be enforced by the commission against every concern who may violate them." On the other hand, the commission recognizes that trade practice conferences concern themselves with practices that are not "strictly unlawful," but that participants determine to be "good business rules and sound methods of doing business." The commission does not approve or disapprove of the latter, but accepts "such rules as expressions of the trade."

[17] Blaisdell, *The Federal Trade Commission*, 97–98; Federal Trade Commission, *Annual Report 1928* (Washington, DC: Government Printing Office), 8–10, 13; TNEC, *Control*, 4–5. See also Sumner S. Kittelle and Elmer Mostow, "A Review of the Trade Practice Conferences of the Federal Trade Commission," *George Washington Law Review* 8, no. 3 (January–February 1940): 434–37; James Hunker, "Trade Practice Conferences" (master's thesis, Ohio State University, 1949), 39–40, 77–80.

classified the rule against nominal leases in Group II, an expression, that is, of good practice unenforceable at law. Only restrictive covenants proved consistent with judicial precedent and warranted classification in Group I, where violations fell under the FTC's coercive powers.[18]

Accommodation failed to solve the FTC's legitimacy crisis before the courts and it spread to Congress and the press. Critics charged that the commission had been captured by business interests and called for new restrictions on trade practice conferences. The oil code, especially, came under fire for sanctioning price fixing. Representative Wright Patman (D-TX) charged that the commission had been captured by the American Petroleum Institute. The progressive press joined in. Trade practice conferences, wrote the *Nation* and the *New Republic,* had become the instruments of "business desire."[19]

Never one to shrink from a fight, Commissioner Humphrey bristled at the charges: neither the courts nor the Department of Justice had found a "single" trade practice rule illegal since the commission began to classify them in 1927.[20] But Humphrey's riposte only escalated the controversy, and business joined progressives in demanding his resignation.[21] Humphrey held his ground. Deeply worried about the commission's legitimacy before Congress and the public, his fellow commissioners responded with a second accommodation. They asked the Legal Division to review all trade practice rules for antitrust violations and rewrite them in a standardized judicial language.[22]

[18] See FTC, *Trade Practice Conferences,* 205–9.

[19] Robert F. Himmelberg, *The Origins of the National Recovery Administration: Business, Government, and the Trade Association Issue, 1921–1933* (New York: Fordham University Press, 1976), 95–99; Davis, "The Transformation of the FTC," 452–53. For Patman's attack, see Statement of Chairman Humphrey of the Federal Trade Commission to Honorable Clifton A. Woodrum, Chairman, House Sub-Committee on Appropriations for Independent Offices, House of Representatives, February 19, 1932, 1–4, FTC Library.

[20] Statement of Humphrey to Woodrum, 5.

[21] If congressional attack on FTC authority were not enough, the Supreme Court handed down a decision against the FTC's efforts to enforce trade practice rules for drug advertising, which declared that the "final determination" of an unfair method of competition lay with the "courts, and not ... the commission." See FTC v. Raladam, 283 U.S. 643 (1930) at 643.

[22] Blaisdell, *The Federal Trade Commission,* 94–98; Herring, *Public Administration,* 131–33; William E. Koviac, "The Federal Trade Commission and Congressional Oversight of Antitrust Enforcement: A Historical Perspective," in Robert J. Mackay, James C. Miller III, and Bruce Yandle, eds., *Public Choice and Regulation: A View*

Fighting over the status of trade practice rules did not end with the second accommodation. Trade associations protested the FTC's retreat from conferences and formed an ad hoc association, the Congress of Industries (COI), to defend prior rules and current procedure. The fate of their movement, they beseeched the commission, depended on the integrity of the commission's deliberative process.[23] Humphrey joined in. "Carried to the extreme," he said, the "standardization" of rules in judicial language undermined the creative process of deliberation, discovery, and experimentation. "Conferences would consist in mailing to the members of the industry a copy of the antitrust laws"; and a "two-cent stamp" would replace the "guidance and the help and the intelligence of the commission."[24]

But the Congress of Industries and Humphrey's protests had little effect and trade practice rules went to review. All Group I rules were standardized into judicial language. Group II rules, however, remained open to deliberation. Responding to the COI's plea, the commissioners directed the Trade Practice Conference Division to open its review of Group II rules to trade association and industry representatives. As a result, most rules in this category emerged intact.[25]

By 1930, it appeared as though the courts had won the contest over accountability. Despite the most creative efforts of Brandeis, Gaskill, and Humphrey to articulate an alternative, the FTC accommodated judicial method. Instead of assessing trade practice rules according to the principles of process, power, and performance, the FTC turned increasingly to classification. The partisans of regulated competition, however, did not give in so easily. As the third section of this chapter will show, cost accountants and trade associations put up a fight. Before I recount that battle, however, I turn to the contest over developmental associations.

ACCOUNTABILITY FOR DEVELOPMENTAL ASSOCIATIONS

Although the fight over the accountability of developmental associations involved different institutional practices, it pitted the same theories and

from Inside the Federal Trade Commission (Stanford, CA: Hoover Institution Press, 1987), 72; Herring, *Public Administration,* 131.

[23] Himmelberg, *Origins of the National Recovery Administration,* 99; Herring, *Public Administration,* 131–32; Blaisdell, *The Federal Trade Commission,* 95–98.

[24] Statement of Commissioner Humphrey Regarding *The Standardization of Trade Practice Conference Rules,* Speeches of Commissioners, 2, FTC Library.

[25] Blaisdell, *The Federal Trade Commission,* 98.

many of the same actors against one another. The Department of Justice, the courts, and the economists classified. Did trade association activities facilitate competition or monopoly? Only the former were legitimate under antitrust and constitutional law. Initially, the Department of Justice and the courts classified information pooling, or benchmarking, by trade associations as monopoly pure and simple. Like institutionalists looking back, they argued it had no other purpose but to coordinate price fixing. Now an associate justice on the Supreme Court, Brandeis tendered a process, power, and performance theory of accountability. In a series of dissenting opinions, he posed a different set of questions from the laissez-faire constitutionalist majority. Did trade associations intervene effectively in the process of forming and reforming trade customs to channel rivalry from predation into improvement? Did their efforts equalize power? What were the consequences of trade association practices for economic performance? Information pooling, Brandeis dissented, upgraded competition, equalized power, and improved performance.

In 1926, the Supreme Court relaxed its objections to information pooling by trade associations, but rejected Brandeis's logic. Instead, creative syncretists in the majority drew on new distinctions from economics to develop a more complex typology of information exchange. Instead of classifying all information pooling as monopoly, the Court asked whether it was used to improve individual decision making or to facilitate collective action. The former was legal, because it facilitated the economists' theory of perfect competition. The latter was illegal, because it facilitated price fixing. Thus, the Court accommodated some features of developmental associations, even though it rejected a process, power, and performance theory of accountability. Classification triumphed, but many aspects of developmental associations survived.

Ambivalence

Fighting over trade associations began at the end of World War I. Americans were ambivalent about them. On the one hand, trade association participation in the war effort ensured their prestige. When the Republicans returned to power in 1920, they brought associations into the heart of their economic policy. President Harding appointed wartime food administrator and association enthusiast, Herbert Hoover, secretary of commerce. For Hoover, trade associations were syncretic wonders that reconciled American values of individualism with the technical necessities of modern industry. They could coordinate complex economic activity and yet preserve the identity of individual entrepreneurs. At the Commerce Department, he mobilized trade associations to standardize products, negotiate trade disputes, improve management techniques, and promote international trade.[26]

On the other hand, peace triggered price inflation and charges of cartelization among the trade associations. In New York and Illinois, state legislatures opened investigations into price fixing in construction in the nation's two largest cities. Information pooling and benchmarking came in for particular criticism. Investigators charged "Open Price" or "Eddy associations" with organizing price coordination through collective cost, price, and production data. Democrat Samuel Untermeyer, who led the New York investigation, charged the Harding administration with lax antitrust enforcement.[27] And the FTC, still controlled by Democrats, opened investigations into price fixing in meatpacking, coal, steel, and house furnishings. Thus, even though trade associations gained prestige in the 1920s, they remained vulnerable to charges of corruption, as did their defenders in the Harding and Coolidge administrations.[28]

Although Harding did not enter office a trustbuster, bad publicity prodded him to ask Attorney General Harry Daugherty to investigate trade associations, which pooled data, for violations of the Sherman Act. Between 1921 and 1924, the Department of Justice initiated actions against the Gypsum Industries Association, the Hardwood Manufacturers Association, the Linseed Crushers Council, the Tile Manufacturers Credit Association, the Cement Manufacturers Protective Association, and

[26] Himmelberg, *Origins*, 5–7; Ellis Hawley, "Herbert Hoover, the Commerce Secretariat, and the Vision of an 'Associative State,' 1921–1928," *Journal of American History* 61 (1974): 116–40; Ellis Hawley, "Three Facets of Hooverian Associationalism: Lumber, Aviation, and Movies, 1921–1930," in Thomas K. McCraw, ed., *Regulation in Perspective* (Cambridge, MA: Harvard Business School Press, 1982), 95–123; Marc Allen Eisner, *From Warfare State to Welfare State: World War I, Compensatory State Building and the Limits of the Modern Order* (University Park: Pennsylvania State University Press, 2000), 106–21.

[27] Samuel Untermeyer was a New York reformer and attorney who served as general counsel to the Pujo House Committee investigation of the "money trust." See Martin J. Sklar, *The Corporate Reconstruction of American Capitalism, 1890–1916* (Cambridge: Cambridge University Press, 1988), 287.

[28] Himmelberg, *Origins*, 7–11; Davis, "Transformation of the FTC," 441; Eisner, *From Warfare State to Welfare State*, 126–27; Federal Trade Commission, *Annual Report 1921* (Washington, DC: Government Printing Office, 1921), 38–57; Federal Trade Commission, *Annual Report 1922* (Washington, DC: Government Printing Office, 1922), 40–55.

the Southern Pine Association.[29] Armed with the Supreme Court's classification scheme, the government argued that information pooling was monopoly, pure and simple. Until 1926, the courts agreed.

Classification: "Real Competitors Don't Disclose Their Secrets"

Attorney General Daugherty instructed lawyers in the Antitrust Division to pursue three goals in their trade association work. First, they should fortify the state's commitment to the method of classification to assess the accountability of association activities to the law; second, they should persuade the legal profession there were only two relevant categories to evaluate associations – competition and monopoly; finally, they should demonstrate that information exchange constituted monopoly. Daugherty began his campaign with the American Hardwood Manufacturers Association, because it was prominent, well organized, and had an elaborate information pooling system. Influenced by Arthur Eddy's pioneering work in steel construction, the Hardwood Manufacturers Association launched an "open competition plan" in 1918, which exchanged data on prices, sales, production, inventories, costs, and market projections. The association mobilized four hundred participants, who accounted for more than one-third of domestic production.[30]

The Antitrust Division took particular aim at Eddy and Brandeis in its brief against the Hardwood Manufacturers Association: there was no third way between competition and monopoly, it wrote. "Regulated" or "cooperative" competition is an oxymoron: the "plain meaning of the words are opposed to each other." In genuinely competitive markets, information is always a private good. The most successful manufacturers "conceal every detail of their business from their competitors." There is no reason to pool price, cost, or production data than to foster collective action. The Hardwood Manufacturers Association's "open competition plan" is nothing more than antitrust subterfuge: an "old form of combination in restraint of trade" under a new name. This is no such thing as a "new form of competition," charged the Department of Justice.[31]

29 Himmelberg, *Origins,* 16–21; Eisner, *From Warfare State to Welfare State,* 121–25; Federal Trade Commission, *Open-Price Trade Associations,* U.S. Senate, 70th Cong., 2d sess., Document no. 226 (Washington, DC: Government Printing Office, 1929), 10–16.

30 American Column & Lumber Company et al. v. U.S., 257 U.S. 377 (1921); Himmelberg, *Origins,* 16–18; Eisner, *From Warfare State to Welfare State,* 122–23.

31 American Column & Lumber Company et al. v. U.S., 257 U.S. 377 at 386 (1921). See also United States v. American Linseed Oil Company et al., 262 U.S. 373–74.

From the government's perspective, the facts of the *Hardwood* case unambiguously proved monopoly. Although the agreement to fix prices was "tacit," the "fundamental purpose" of information exchange was "concerted" action. Like the "gentlemen's agreement" of days past, the Hardwood plan relied on "business honor" and "social penalties," instead of financial sanctions. But these were equally effective, when accompanied by "elaborate reports" that members used to monitor one another's behavior.[32]

The Supreme Court agreed: there is no doubt the Hardwood plan was a monopoly, whatever euphemism its architects invented to name it. The Court is not "blinded by words," when the plain "reality" is an "old evil in a new dress and with a new name." "*Genuine competitors*" hide their advantages from "their rivals." Information exchange has only one purpose: to "evade [a] law," which proscribes "combinations" and "conspiracies" in "restraint of interstate commerce." The Hardwood plan violated the Sherman Act, the Court concluded.[33]

The Supreme Court ratified Daugherty's three goals in the *Hardwood* opinion. It endorsed classification, convinced the legal profession that only two categories – monopoly and competition – were relevant to assess trade association activities, and found information exchange a form of monopoly. Although the Justice Department continued to win cases, the logic of classification did not go unchallenged. Brandeis dissented. In doing so, he outlined a process, power, and performance theory of accountability, which paralleled the FTC's method for evaluating trade practice rules.

Process, Power, and Performance

Drawing on his theory of regulated competition, Brandeis conceptualized information pooling differently than did the Department of Justice or the majority of his colleagues on the Supreme Court. Recall that, in his view, it was impossible to classify contracts as completely free or restraints on trade and economic behavior as purely competitive or monopolistic. All contracts restrained trade because they bound individuals together in social collaboration. The effects of competition were ambiguous. Sometimes it reduced prices and improved products and production processes; at other times, it undermined itself and locked in

[32] American Column & Lumber Company et al. v. U.S., 257 U.S. 377 at 399 (1921).
[33] American Column & Lumber Company et al. v. U.S., 257 U.S. 377 at 410 (1921).

stifling power. Thus, it was impossible to evaluate contracts according to the distinction between freedom and restraint or economic behavior according to the distinction between competition and monopoly. It was necessary to distinguish between productive and unproductive restraints of trade or productive and predatory forms of competition. In Brandeis's view, this could only be done by paying careful attention to the context in which contracts were devised or competition was exercised. Did they lock in power? Or did they facilitate rivalry over product quality, service, and productivity? Brandeis posed the same questions of information pooling by trade associations. What was the particular history of the problem it was intended to solve? Did it lock in power over competitors, dealers, and consumers? What were its consequences for economic performance?

In a world in which competition had a history and was always governed by custom, Brandeis wanted to know what the conditions were "before and after" information exchange was adopted. What was the "evil believed to exist" that this "particular remedy" was meant to solve? It was important to know intent, as well as history, not because it determined legality, but because he thought it would "help the court to interpret facts and predict consequences."[34]

In addition to process, Brandeis wanted to know about the distribution of power in the industry under scrutiny. Did association activities improve the quality of competition by equalizing power? Or did they oppress competitors, consumers, and retailers? The legality of an association's activities, he wrote, is determined not by its effects on prices or output, but by "the coercion" affected. The "essence" of unlawful restraint is "power." Thus, the distribution of power before and after information pooling was effected determined the context in which it must be interpreted.[35]

Finally, Brandeis asked about performance. What were the "actual or probable" "consequences" of information pooling? Was it likely to "limit freedom" so as to "narrow" a market? Or did it promote "intelligent competition," invention, and economic improvement?[36]

Reevaluating the facts of the *Hardwood* case through a process, power, and performance theory of accountability, Brandeis said, led him to a completely different interpretation from the one proffered by

34 In his *Hardwood* dissent, Brandeis drew amply upon his opinion in a case three years earlier. See Board of Trade of the City of Chicago et al. v. U.S., 246 U.S. 238–39.

35 American Column & Lumber Company et al. v. U.S., 257 U.S. 414.

36 Board of Trade of the City of Chicago et al. v. U.S., 246 U.S. 238–39.

the Supreme Court's majority. The purpose of information pooling was plainly to equalize asymmetries in power between small rural mills and powerful urban dealers, not to coordinate price fixing. Ignorant of the state of trade, their competitors' costs, and price trends, isolated mills fell prey to exploitation by powerful wholesalers. Only the largest mills, which had their own statistical bureaus, were able to compete effectively. By pooling data on prices, costs, and production, the Hardwood Manufacturers Association equalized power and made it possible for all manufacturers to compete more effectively on price and quality. Brandeis's point was constructivist. His colleagues on the Court had blinded themselves to the history and purpose of information exchange in the hardwood industry, because they classified it as monopoly before they looked at the facts. Only an inductive theory of competition, he said, which paid careful attention to context, could make sense of the association's activities.

Statistical exchange, Brandeis added, did not oppress association members, dealers, or consumers. The members of the Hardwood Manufacturers Association were responsible for only one-third of domestic production and accounted for a far smaller proportion of the total number of mills. There were no divisions of territory, price agreements, or restrictions on the distribution of information or who could attend district meetings. Industry prices had not become uniform. Members were perfectly free to set prices and production levels. The facts, Brandeis concluded, revealed no signs of coercion. Thus, the Hardwood Manufacturers Association's system of information exchange passed the test of equality.[37]

It also passed the test of performance. Competition, Brandeis wrote, had become "more intelligent" as a result of information exchange. Small manufacturers learned to better calibrate production to consumption, track their costs, and prophesize market trends. "Market letters" and "free discussion" provided firms with information about the best and worst practices in their industry. Information pooling equalized "opportunity" and regulated competition. Without it, Brandeis wrote, the hardwood industry would follow the inevitable path to concentration, and yet another trust would dominate competitors, distributors, employees, and the community. Economic innovation would decline, power would become unassailable, and the efforts of antitrust to reconcile the

[37] American Column & Lumber Company et al. v. U.S., 257 U.S. 417–18.

republican aspiration to equality with the modern aspiration to economic prosperity would be dashed.[38]

In sum, where the Department of Justice and the Supreme Court classified information pooling as price fixing by another means, Brandeis asked, what were the problems it was intended to solve, did it effect coercion, and what was its effect on performance? Classification prevailed in the *Hardwood* case. But Brandeis's dissent challenged the Court to rethink its categories.

Judicial Accommodation

The *Hardwood* decision left the Harding administration in confusion. On the one side, Attorney General Daugherty saw it as an unequivocal ruling. The Court would not tolerate information exchange in any form. In 1923, he initiated nineteen suits against associations that pooled price, cost, and volume data. On the other side, Commerce Department secretary Hoover saw the *Hardwood* ruling as conditional. Information exchange was lawful only if historical prices were published, the source of data was anonymous, and associations did not interpret data or encourage action. Hoover worked with FTC commissioner Gaskill to provide trade associations with advance advice on the legality of their information pooling plans. But their efforts amounted to little, because fundamental questions about how to conceptualize accountability remained unresolved. The National Association of Manufacturers and the American Trade Association Executives pressed President Harding for clarification and more favorable policy toward trade associations. But it was not until Coolidge took office in 1926 that they saw any movement.[39]

President Coolidge replaced Daugherty with an attorney general far more sympathetic to trade associations: Harlan Fisk Stone. Coolidge and Stone promised to clarify the status of information pooling by choosing cases that isolated it from well-accepted violations of antitrust law. They succeeded. By the end of the year, the Supreme Court had redrawn its earlier distinction. Instead of classifying all information exchange as monopoly, creative syncretists on the Court drew upon innovative work in economics to craft a distinction between individual and collective use of data. In doing so, the Court accepted some features of developmental associations without embracing the logic of republican experimentalism

[38] American Column & Lumber Company et al. v. U.S., 257 U.S. 418–19.
[39] Himmelberg, *Origins*, 26–40.

or regulated competition. Instead, the majority deepened its commitment to the laissez-faire constitutionalist method of classification in order to police the bright line between public and private.[40]

No sooner was Attorney General Stone sworn into office, than he directed his antitrust chief, William Donovan, to initiate a suitable case to test the limits of antitrust doctrine on information pooling. Donovan found the Maple Flooring Manufacturers' Association – an organization of 22 manufacturers, who accounted for 70 percent of domestic output. This association was appealing. It had an elaborate information-pooling program. There was no evidence of a price agreement, encouragement to alter behavior, or discussions of the data. Nonetheless, it was clear to Donovan that data on average costs, prices, and quantities were cues for pricing and output decisions. Information pooling was plainly a vehicle for collective action.[41]

Attorney General Stone never had a chance to supervise the government's case, because President Coolidge elevated him to the Supreme Court, where he wrote the Court's opinion in favor of the Maple Flooring Association.[42] Although Stone's opinion signaled a shift in the Court's attitude toward information pooling, it reinforced the laissez-faire constitutionalist majority's method of classification. Instead of classifying all information exchange as monopoly, drawing on innovations in economics, he reclassified it according to use. The *Maple Flooring* opinion turned on whether the association's information was used for individual or collective purposes. The former was perfectly consistent with the public's interest in better-functioning markets (perfect competition), while the latter served only the private interests of an association's members in higher prices (monopoly).

Stone drew from economists, not cost accountants or associationalists, to develop a new typology of information pooling. He began by explaining how individual use served the public interest. Citing recent works by J. A. Hobson and Frank Fisher, he showed how better information better aligned supply and demand by improving individual decision making.[43]

[40] Himmelberg, *Origins*, 38–47; National Industrial Conference Board, *Trade Associations, Their Economic Significance and Legal Status* (New York: National Industrial Conference Board, 1925), 350–53; *The Federal Antitrust Laws with Summary of Cases Instituted by the United States, 1890–1951* (Commerce Clearing House, 1952), 125, 128, 133.

[41] Maple Flooring Mfrs' Ass'n v. U.S., 268 U.S. 563–77 (1925).

[42] Himmelberg, *Origins*, 45–47.

[43] Maple Flooring Mfrs, Assn v. U.S., 268 U.S. 575, 583–84.

Fisher put it this way: all economic decisions involve uncertainty about the future effects of current actions. It was possible to ameliorate risk with better information. As a result, market economies invented mechanisms to improve the quality and distribution of data: government statistics, stock and commodity exchanges, and information pooling by trade associations.[44] Or as Hobson put it, secrecy might have served competition during an era of simple manufacture. But rivalry under modern conditions necessitated "perfect transparency of industrial operations" to ensure the balance of supply and demand. Otherwise, mass-producers were likely to overproduce. The economists, Justice Stone wrote, agreed that the better the quality of information, the better the decisions individual firms were likely to make and the closer a market economy came to realizing the marginalist ideal of perfect competition.[45] In other words, when used to enhance individual "intelligence" so that businesspeople were better able to "conform" to "economic laws," information pooling realized the public's interest in the efficient allocation of resources to their highest value. Congress, Stone concluded, meant to facilitate, not to "repeal economic law."

But Stone also thought information pooling was obnoxious to the public interest, and against the law, when it was used for collective action. The Sherman Act, he wrote, ignores the question of information exchange. It does, however, distinguish between "individual" and "concerted" action in markets and declares the latter unlawful when it unreasonably restrains trade. Here again, economics was useful. The economists had long shown that collective action to fix prices or limit output distorted the allocation of society's resources. Thus, when information was used collectively to raise prices above the level that would prevail if individuals made independent decisions, it was unlawful.[46]

The facts in the *Maple Flooring* case, Stone went on, set it apart from the *Hardwood* case, and ensured that the Court was following precedent by creating a more refined classification of information pooling. Where the Hardwood producers used data to monitor one another's pricing and output behavior, the Maple Flooring manufacturers used it only to

[44] See Irving Fisher, "Avoidance of Risk," reproduced in Leon C. Marshall, *Readings in Industrial Society* (Chicago: University of Chicago Press, 1918), 498–99; and Irving Fisher, *Elementary Principles of Economics* (New York: MacMillan, 1912), 427–32, both cited in Maple Flooring Mfrs Assn v. U.S., 268 U.S. 583.

[45] J. A. Hobson, *The Evolution of Modern Capitalism* (London: George Allen & Unwin, 1916), 403–5, cited in Maple Flooring Mfrs Assn v. U.S., 268 U.S. 583.

[46] Maple Flooring Mfrs Assn v. U.S., 268 U.S. 584.

improve individual decisions. The former served the public interest by approximating perfect competition; the latter served only private interests by creating monopoly power over prices.

Although Brandeis voted with the majority in the *Maple Flooring* case, the Court conceptualized information pooling very differently than he had in his dissent in the *Hardwood* case. Where Brandeis judged it by the standard of regulated competition (i.e., did it channel rivalry from predation to improvement?), Stone judged information exchange by the standard of perfect competition (i.e., did it balance supply and demand?). Where Brandeis thought all information was social, because it reflected custom and facilitated human deliberation, Stone distinguished individual and collective use of information. Where Brandeis asked how the facts of the *Maple Flooring* and *Hardwood* cases revealed a particular history, distribution of power, and consequence of information pooling, Stone perceived only those facts that corresponded to one of two abstract categories: the individual or collective use of information.[47] In 1926, Justice Stone's method of classification prevailed.

THE FAILURE OF STATUTORY REFORM

Once they failed in the courts, the partisans of regulated competition took their case to Congress, where they hoped to revise antitrust law to reflect a process, power, and performance theory of accountability. But peak business associations, like the U.S. Chamber of Commerce, and professional associations, like the National Association of Cost Accountants and the American Trade Association Executives, were designed for deliberation and collaborative learning, not political mobilization and influence. As a result, their efforts failed.

There were two initiatives to revise the principles of accountability. The first came from the National Association of Cost Accountants in 1927, but never went beyond a conference resolution. The second came from an ad hoc organization of trade associations, the Congress of Industries (COI), in 1931. Unlike NACA, the COI succeeded in finding a congressional sponsor, Senator Gerald Nye (R-ND). Although Nye introduced three bills and held hearings, his proposals never left the Judiciary Committee. This section describes these proposals and explains why they failed.

[47] For a different view of the *Maple Flooring* case, which sees it as a victory for Brandeisian logic, see Rudolph J. R. Peritz, *Competition Policy in America* (Oxford: Oxford University Press, 1996), 87–89, 91–94.

Led by NACA's sixth president, Charles Stevenson, the cost accountants called for statutory antitrust reform in 1927. Recall Stevenson's biography. A founding partner of a prominent management–engineering firm, Stevenson, Jordan, and Harrison, he had been active in NACA governance since its origins. Stevenson's clients included both individual firms and trade associations. He served as secretary to associations in the specialty paper and box industries.

As president of NACA, Stevenson asked the members to consider two resolutions. The first declared pricing below cost an unfair method of competition. The second asked Congress to reform antitrust law to reflect that principle and to accommodate trade association cost accounting.

Two changes had made it possible to implement a rule against pricing below cost by 1927, Stevenson told NACA members. First, a sufficiently large number of manufacturers had learned to measure their costs to implement a rule against pricing below cost. Second, and more important, the widespread use of benchmarking by trade associations made it possible for the FTC to hold developmental associations accountable to improved performance. By providing the state with detailed data on average costs, Stevenson argued, associations would allow the FTC to track whether industries, which had implemented rules against pricing below costs, did better because they took monopoly profits or improved productivity. To put Stevenson's proposal in Brandeis's language of regulated competition, Congress could check predatory rivalry by outlawing pricing below cost and ensure that industry did not abuse the right to police such practices by measuring its effects on economic performance.[48]

Although NACA members thought there was a variety of reasons to relax a strict rule against pricing below cost, well over 70 percent of the membership supported it. An even larger percentage supported a resolution to ask Congress to reconsider competition policy in light of the progress in cost accounting and trade association benchmarking.[49] Nevertheless, the political resolution lay fallow. There is no record of NACA publicizing its resolutions, mobilizing members, or lobbying Congress. Why?

[48] C. R. Stevenson, "The Economic Effect of Taking Business At or Below Cost," *NACA Year Book, 1927, Proceedings of the Eighth International Cost Conference of the National Association of Cost Accountants* (New York: National Association of Cost Accountants, 1927), 25, 49, 71, 78–84.

[49] *NACA Year Book, 1927,* 87–88.

The most plausible answer is that NACA was not well designed for politics. Compare NACA with its counterparts in financial accounting: the American Association of Public Accountants (AAPA) and its successor, the American Institute of Accountants (AIA). Recall that NACA was a heterarchical organization, designed to facilitate collaborative learning through discussion, consultation, and information exchange. The AIA was a hierarchical organization, designed to facilitate professional autonomy through state licensing, educational curriculum, ethical standards, monitoring, and discipline. NACA's project was decidedly apolitical, whereas the AIA's relied on state power for legitimacy and enforcement. The AAPA formed its first Committee on Legislation in 1892 to lobby state legislatures for professional certification laws. Over the next three decades, the AIA succeeded in pressing the states for laws governing licensure, standards for accrediting educational institutions, and professional ethics.[50] At the end of Stevenson's presidency in 1928, NACA still did not have a committee devoted to legislation or governmental affairs.[51] Neither did its leadership develop expertise in political mobilization, lobbying, or elections. To be sure, NACA members were not ignorant of the state. As was discussed previously, they worked closely with the FTC and the War Industries Board. Nonetheless, until Stevenson's initiative, NACA made no effort to mobilize the coercive power of government to advance its ends. Thus, it is not surprising that the cost accountants' appeal to Congress sat on a shelf.

A second initiative to legislate a process, power, and performance theory of accountability went much further than NACA's efforts, but stalled in Congress. In 1931, trade association executives formed an ad hoc organization to lobby the FTC on trade practice rules and Congress on antitrust reform: the Congress of Industries. The COI leaders took their case to the Senate, where they enlisted Gerald Nye (R-ND) to introduce three bills in the spirit of regulated competition. But the COI proved too weak to lobby effectively for their cause and Nye failed to gain President Hoover's support. Consequently, Nye's bills never left the Judiciary Committee.[52]

[50] Paul J. Miranti Jr., *Accountancy Comes of Age* (Chapel Hill: University of North Carolina Press, 1990), 13, 27–28, 47–56, 120–25, 183; Norman E. Webster, *The American Association of Public Accountants: Its First Twenty Years, 1886–1906* (New York: Arno Press, 1978), 207–70.

[51] The *NACA Year Book 1928* lists committees for chapters, constitution, education, lectures, membership, publications, publicity, research, and standardization, p. viii.

[52] Himmelberg, *Origins*, 161–64.

Nye was a progressive Republican who came to office in 1926 devoted to government control of banks, grain elevators, and mills. In the Senate, he joined fellow progressive, George Norris (R-NE), on the Judiciary Committee. After extensive consultation with the COI, Nye initiated three antitrust bills and convinced Norris to hold hearings on them.[53] The first legalized trade practice rules and provided immunity for firms operating under them, brought conferences under statutory procedure, and provided standards to adjudicate the legality of trade practice rules. The second created a specialized trade practice court with jurisdiction over cases arising under the Sherman, Clayton, and Federal Trade Commission Acts. The third empowered the FTC to enforce trade practice rules and outlawed pricing below cost and discriminatory pricing.[54] Nye's bills would have gone some distance toward integrating developmental associations into FTC regulatory practice; legitimating a process, power, and performance theory of accountability; increasing awareness of the volume illusion; and authorizing the FTC to enforce trade practice rules. The bills never left committee. Why?

First, the COI was an ad hoc organization, lacking the prestige, skill, or resources to influence Congress, the president, or the electorate. It was less than a year old when the Judiciary Committee held hearings on Nye's bills in 1932. Although it had been successful in protecting the FTC's Group II rules from standardization, the COI's legislative efforts evaporated in Congress. It is telling, moreover, that an ad hoc organization took up the cause of representing trade associations after 1930. The second reason Nye's initiative failed was the virtual absence of the U.S. Chamber of Commerce in the legislative process. The U.S. Chamber was the logical organization to lobby for regulated competition. After all, it had sponsored the most ambitious effort to conceptualize developmental associations and it had many of the capacities necessary for congressional lobbying: cordial relations with the executive branch, a federated structure, expertise, financial resources, and a large membership. But the U.S. Chamber had been conspicuously quiet on antitrust reform in

[53] On Nye, see Robert James Leonard, "From Country Politics to the Senate: The Learning Years for Senator Nye," *North Dakota History* 39 (Summer 1972): 15–23; Daniel Rylance, "A Controversial Career: Gerald P. Nye, 1925–1946," *North Dakota Quarterly* 36 (Winter 1968): 5–19.

[54] Himmelberg, *Origins*, 161–63; U.S. Senate, Committee on the Judiciary, *Hearings on Amendment of Federal Trade Commission Act and Establishment of a Federal Trade Court*, 72d Cong., 1st sess. (Washington, DC: Government Printing Office, 1932), 1–4; *Congressional Record*, 72d Cong., 1st sess., vol. 75, pt. 2, 1287–89.

the 1920s.[55] As we have seen, the U.S. Chamber was extremely diverse. Members were all over the map on antitrust. Instead of hammering out consensus or imposing authority, U.S. Chamber leaders accommodated diversity. In 1918, they created ten departments to service members from its many industries. This structure proved effective in organizing deliberation. The Manufacturing Division did an excellent job of organizing trade association executives and cost accountants to conceptualize development associations. But when it came to codifying those principles in statutory law, the Manufacturing Division was silent. Nearly a decade after the division had completed its work, U.S. Chamber leaders began to speak out in favor of antitrust revision, and then only after the COI had taken the lead. But there is no record of active lobbying in favor of Nye's bills. Unlike the more militant leaders of the National Association of Manufacturers, who pressed to legalize cartels, U.S. Chamber leaders made no attempt to mobilize members, influence President Hoover, or form a congressional majority in favor of regulated competition.[56] Like NACA, the U.S. Chamber was good at organizing collaborative learning, but poor at politics.

The third reason Nye's legislation failed is it lacked presidential support. As institutionalists Stephen Skowronek and Scott James have shown, every successful regulatory initiative since 1900 garnered presidential support.[57] Given Hoover's long-standing support for an "associative state," we might predict that he would have supported efforts to enforce trade practice rules or authorize a process, power, and performance theory of accountability for trade associations. But Hoover took the landscape of political possibility as he found it during his presidency. Like his Republican predecessors, Hoover tacked back and forth between the poles of the antitrust debate, instead of attempting to transform it. Compare Hoover to Wilson in this regard. Wilson was a minority party president who owed his office to a division in the majority party. As such, he attempted to forge a sustainable coalition between Democrats and progressive Republicans by developing a third way to reform antitrust. Instead of regulated monopoly or enforced competition, Wilson enlisted Brandeis to articulate the principles of regulated competition

55 Himmelberg, *Origins*, 80–81, 83, 161.

56 On the National Association of Manufacturers, see Himmelberg, *Origins*, 79–80, 125–26.

57 Stephen Skowronek, *Building a New American State* (Cambridge: Cambridge University Press, 1977); Scott James, *Presidents, Parties and the State* (Cambridge: Cambridge University Press, 2000).

to Congress and the public. The Republican presidents after Wilson, by contrast, hoped to maintain a coalition of business conservatives, many of whom wanted self-regulation, and progressives, who hoped to augment state power. But the more they moved in one direction, the more they garnered criticism from the other side. Harding turned the Department of Commerce into a haven for trade associations and then used the Department of Justice to attack them. Coolidge appointed Humphrey, but then oversaw FTC accommodation to its critics. And Hoover supported antitrust immunity for production agreements in troubled natural resource industries, such as coal and lumber, but refused to support any additional reform.[58]

In summary, although the partisans and practitioners of regulated competition proposed statutory reform to shift the principles of accountability from classification to process and performance, they had neither the organizational capacity nor the political support to mobilize Congress. Both NACA and the U.S. Chamber of Commerce proved good at deliberative polyarchy but bad at lobbying; and President Hoover hedged his bets on antitrust reform. In 1932, the courts, Department of Justice, and the economists retained authority over trade practice conferences and developmental associations and judged their instruments according to how well they fit into deductive categories.

CONCLUSION

The antitrust reforms of 1914 licensed regulated competition, but did not settle the debate over industrial order. It reemerged in the fight over accountability in the 1920s. On one side were the partisans of regulated competition, who attempted to hold trade practice rules and trade associations to standards of process, power, and performance. On the other side were the Department of Justice, the courts, and the economists, who evaluated trade practice rules and associational instruments according to whether they were competitive or monopolistic. The practitioners of classification won the struggle over accountability, but not the bigger war over industrial and regulatory practice. Although classification became

[58] On Hoover's ambivalence over antitrust reform, see Himmelberg, *Origins*, 31–33, 69–70, 90, 113–14, 159–60; Ellis W. Hawley, "Herbert Hoover and American Corporatism, 1929–1933," in M. L. Fausold and G. T. Mazuzan, eds., *The Hoover Presidency: A Reappraisal* (Albany: State University of New York Press, 1974), 101–19.

orthodoxy, it left ample space for those who would assess their activities according to different standards. In this world of multiple standards, the authority of the courts, economists, and the Department of Justice would always be partial. Some aspects of regulated competition would survive classification. Others would not.

For example, although the FTC accommodated the Court's demand for classification, it continued to cultivate regulated competition through trade practice conferences. Under Group I rules, the commission provided industries with opportunity to redirect unlawful customs *before* they necessitated litigation. Under Group II rules, the commission continued to sanction voluntary practices, such as uniform cost accounting and benchmarking. As we saw in the case of the printers, FTC sanction was critical to the success of the UTA's three-year plan. With a brief hiatus during the National Recovery Administration (1933–1935), the FTC's Trade Practice Conference Division has continued into the present. And although trade practice rules still have no independent legal status, the division has continued to foster reflection on industry customs.

Or consider benchmarking by trade associations. Seen from the perspective of classification, it was legal if used to improve individual management capacity. As long as trade associations did not organize collective discussion, interpret the facts, or encourage members to adopt uniform costs, benchmarking was likely to survive scrutiny. Seen from the perspective of developmental associations, benchmarking was neither individual nor collective action. It was an instrument of collaborative learning, in which actors deliberated over the nature and meaning of the data. Thus, mutual misrecognition ensured that some aspects of benchmarking would survive government evaluation, whereas others would not.

Compare the experience of the printers to the bolt, nut, and rivet industry. Heeling closely to judicial method, the FTC's Legal Division investigated the printers' benchmarking system in the early 1920s. As long as the UTA agreed to abandon all price lists and discussions of pricing, FTC lawyers classified benchmarking as a legitimate tool to improve individual management.[59] By contrast, the Justice Department

[59] United States of America before Federal Trade Commission, Complaint in the Case of Federal Trade Commission v. United Typothetae of America, Docket 459, March 1, 1922, in RG 122, Box 215, File 459. See also "Federal Trade Commission Finally Reaches a Finding," *Typothetae Bulletin* 17, no. 22 (August 27, 1923): 339–40; George K. Horn, President UTA, "Miles of Effort for Typothetae," *Typothetae Bulletin* 20, no. 3

successfully prosecuted the Bolt, Nut, and Rivet Association in 1928, because it put its cost system in service to a plan meant to preserve a wholesale distribution network. A U.S. District Court in New York concluded that information pooling was used to restrict free competition among hardware manufacturers, wholesalers, and retailers, instead of improving individual capacity.[60]

In short, although the adherents to regulated competition and perfect competition disagreed over principle, they agreed that some instruments of developmental associations and some trade practice rules were good for different reasons. Thus, even though the classifiers won the battle over accountability, they did not win the war over trade associations or FTC practice. Some aspects of regulated competition continued to thrive under their supervision. The practitioners of cultivational administration at the FTC and benchmarking in trade associations continued to find space for their work, and U.S. institutions in the twentieth century remained diverse, loosely coupled, and multivocal.

(October 20, 1924): 45; Edward T. Miller, "Coordinating the Year's Activities: Part I – Secretary's Report," *Typothetae Bulletin* 20, no. 3 (October 20, 1924): 52.

60 Gerald Berk, "Communities of Competitors: Open Price Associations and the American State, 1911–1929," *Social Science History* 3 (1996): 375–400.

PART IV

CONCLUSION

Chapter 9

Civic Enterprise

The builders of regulated competition created a new path to economic and political development, which successfully combined America's traditional aspiration to equality with modern management. Brandeis enhanced the cultural debate over industrial society during the election of 1912 by combining republican commitments to equality with progressive aspirations to mastery in the ideology of republican experimentalism. He devised a theory of regulated competition, which showed how business, trade associations, and government could work together to channel business rivalry from predation to improvement. And he drew on his experience in railroad and utility regulation to outline a blueprint for a cultivational commission devoted to regulating competition. In 1914, creative legislators combined the features of progressive, populist, and Brandeisian proposals for a federal trade commission and they forged a legislative majority by interpreting their work through multiple frames. The Federal Trade Commission Act of 1914 became law with multiple meanings that licensed numerous projects, including regulated competition. Creative administrators at the FTC cultivated experimental and deliberative capacities in peak, professional, and trade associations through two programs: cost accounting and trade practice conferences. Their efforts bore fruit. The U.S. Chamber of Commerce conducted a forum to conceptualize developmental trade associations. The National Association of Cost Accountants built an association devoted to information exchange and collaborative learning. And with the help of the FTC, the U.S. Chamber, and the cost accountants, 15 percent of trade associations in 25 percent of U.S. manufacturers transformed themselves from cartels into developmental associations. The economic effects of regulated competition were positive. Printers trebled productivity, revolutionized technology, improved product quality and service, and raised labor skills. Developmental associations in tanning, metalworking, paper, envelopes, lithography, and other industries upgraded competition, improved productivity, and increased employment.

Although the partisans of regulated competition lost a legal struggle over accountability to laissez-faire constitutionalists and economists, the law continued to make space for trade practice rules and developmental associations. Their preferred method of evaluating trade practice conferences and developmental associations – process, power, and performance – took a back seat to the method of classification. But the laissez-faire constitutionalists' aspirations to objectivity and universality through classification were vulnerable to ambiguity and misperception. Judges and economists divided the world into clear-cut dualities – freedom and coercion, competition and monopoly, and public and private – which failed to capture a third set of practices: deliberation, regulated competition, and public/private collaboration. As a result, the effects of judicial decisions upon regulated competition were indefinite. Some aspects of trade practice conferences and developmental associations were condemned, whereas others survived.

In the Court's view, the line between legal and illegal trade practice rules was clear. If they confirmed preexisting judicial opposition to a monopolistic practice, they were in the public interest and admissible. Otherwise, the Court presumed trade practice rules were unconstitutional because they used public power to redistribute private market advantages. Only the former warranted FTC coercion. The latter might be legitimate expressions of good economic practice, but, in the Court's view, compliance had to be voluntary.

The effect of the Court's classification on trade practice conferences was mixed. On the one hand, it undermined the FTC's prophylactic powers: it could not police industries' "pirates" before they locked in monopoly power. On the other hand, it left open the possibility that a majority of businesses, who had become habituated to destructive competition, might amalgamate with the visionaries instead of the pirates. Thus, although judicial logic did not capture the possibility of reforming trade custom through deliberation, it remained legitimate under the category of voluntary compliance. Judicial misclassification curtailed the FTC's coercive authority, but left its cultivational powers intact.

Likewise, some forms of information pooling by trade associations survived misclassification. By 1925, judges and economists classified benchmarking according to individual or collective use. The former perfected competition, whereas the latter suppressed it. But developmental associations used benchmarking for a third purpose: deliberation and collaborative learning. Therefore, judicial misclassification ensured that some forms of benchmarking would survive scrutiny, whereas others would not. As long as data were historical and unaccompanied by official commentary, benchmarking was likely to be classified as a service to individuals. Discussion would always be suspect, but might be acceptable if it avoided prices and output. Thus, even though judges misperceived the ends of benchmarking, in many cases it would survive official scrutiny.

In sum, misperception ensured that the dominance of the courts over the commission and economics over cost accounting would always be partial, and therefore it could not displace other modes of perception and practice. Although regulated competition lost the war over legal hegemony, the fact that the courts, the economists, and the Department of Justice would continue to misclassify many trade practice rules and features of developmental associations ensured that many of its important aspects of regulated competition survived.

CREATIVE SYNCRETISM

It is hard to make sense of regulated competition with institutionalist assumptions about technology, institutions, and agency. According to institutionalists, the high fixed costs of modern industry, patronage parties, an overbearing judiciary, and late state building constrained the options in the United States. Like other early efforts to build national administrative capacities, the FTC failed. Moreover, antitrust left industry far too autarkic to submit to corporatist intermediation or business–government cooperation. As a result, the twin economic problems of the age, overcapacity and distributive conflict, went unresolved.

But institutionalists are incorrect to conceptualize technology (costs) and institutions as constraints upon human agency. Costs were not unambiguous measures of technology. They were social constructions, freighted with extra-economic meaning. Accounting became the site of struggle over narrative identity and institutional form. Institutions were not combinations of complementary and tightly linked features. They were syncretic bundles of decomposable instruments. Human action was not rule bound, rational, or cognitively structured. It was reflexive, creative, and deliberative. The actors discussed in this book built institutions to regulate competition by retelling the stories of their difficulties in ways that made it possible to recombine institutional resources. Creative action continued after the founding of regulated competition. It was critical to the way in which the institutions of regulated competition functioned. Cultivational administration at the FTC, deliberative polyarchy in the National Association of Cost Accountants and the U.S. Chamber of Commerce, and developmental associations exploited the human capacities for reflection, deliberation, and experimentation.

Brandeis was a creative syncretist, one who drew liberally from nineteenth-century political economy and twentieth-century engineering to reconfigure law, institutions, and culture. In 1912 he recast the predicament of antitrust by retelling the history of economic prosperity and power. The trouble with the populists was that they reified self-regulating markets and in doing so, they refused to see their own complicity in the concentration of power in the American economy. By advocating enforced competition, they helped destroy many of the productive restraints that business devised to regulate competition, such as resale price maintenance and trade associations. The results were perverse: they hastened the coming of corporate capitalism. The trouble with the progressives was that they naturalized economic power when Americans had other choices. But neither the populist faith in the market nor the progressive faith in public administration was sufficient to place the United States back on the path to reconciling democracy and economic progress. Continuous monitoring, discussion, and experimentation were necessary to distinguish predatory from productive competition and to channel business activity from the former to the latter. Regulated competition was a superior option.

Brandeis understood that the antitrust debate raised fundamental questions about America's cultural aspirations to equality, individual development, and self-government; it would not be won on its technical merits alone. The election of 1912 divided populists and progressives over the problem of monopoly, but it also provided a unique opportunity to forge a coalition by reworking rival dispositions into a coherent perspective. From the populists, Brandeis drew on ancient republican aspirations of equality, individual development, and deliberative government. From progressives, he drew on aspirations to mastery through applied science, administration, and professionalism. Republican experimentalism challenged populists and progressives to reconcile science and democracy through collaboration, measurement, economic innovation, and disciplined comparison.

Institutionalists have blinded themselves to republican experimentalism and regulated competition because they periodize history into sharply defined eras and see human action as largely determined by institutional constraints. The Progressive Era was an age of adjustment to economic change in which the agents of adaptation, innovation, and stasis were marked by their positions in an institutional division of labor. According to this theory, Brandeis must have represented his petit bourgeois clients or prophesied regulation. He did both and neither. Once we recast institutions and culture as syncretic and action as creative, it becomes possible to see how Brandeis reached across the rifts of time to combine nineteenth- and twentieth-century ideas, institutional instruments, and economic practices in republican experimentalism and regulated competition.

Creative legislators were also master syncretists. They forged a coalition for the Federal Trade Commission Act by creating a discursive common carrier. They combined progressive, populist, and Brandeisian proposals in a legislative compromise. But mere combination was insufficient to circumvent cultural impasse. Creative senators explained their work with multiple frames. Francis Newlands told progressives that the statute achieved mastery by accepting monopoly and regulating it, whereas Albert Cummins told populists it protected the republic from monopoly by preventing it. Herbert Croly claimed victory for the progressives, whereas Brandeis claimed victory for the populists. The cultural ambiguity of the Federal Trade Commission Act has eluded institutionalists, who tag it a historical conjuncture that had clear winners and losers or successfully reconciled rival interests. But this book has shown how the statute licensed multiple projects and durable debate over its meaning.[1]

Creative trade commissioners built a cultivational FTC. They mobilized the U.S. Chamber of Commerce, the National Association of Cost Accountants, and trade associations to cost accounting and trade practice conferences. In search of Weberian bureaucracy, institutionalists have overlooked cultivational administration at the FTC. Instead, they explain the FTC's failure to realize hierarchy and autonomy by

[1] For a striking expression of the institutionalist tendency to reify law making as a historical conjuncture, regardless of the context, see Robert Lieberman's critique of social constructionism, where he writes, "In literary criticism, meaning can be constructed and reconstructed each time we read a text. But in politics, meanings are made concrete when we pass a law or adopt a policy." Robert Lieberman, "Social Construction (Continued)," *American Political Science Review* 99, no. 2 (June 1995): 440.

exogenous constraints: meager finances, political appointments, and links to industry. But the distinction between resources and constraints was in the eye of the beholder. To administrators committed to civic improvement, economic growth, and scientific learning, these conditions were resources. Commissioners Hurley, Gaskill, and Humphrey exploited internal debate, financial constraints, and the FTC's relationships to industry, associations, and embedded professionals to upgrade competition through cost accounting and trade practice conferences. Moreover, instead of building a bureaucratic organization, they multiplied functions within divisions, encouraged lateral communication, and flattened the FTC's hierarchy. The FTC succeeded in the 1920s not because it established legitimate authority over industry, but because it mobilized its staff and civil society to inductive learning.

Creative associationalists reconfigured cartels into developmental associations. By retelling the story of their distress, they combined old solidarities of republican manhood with modern accounting techniques to channel competition from destructive rivalry over volume into improvements in products and production processes. In search of corporatist organizations, with capacities to organize collective action, discipline defectors, and represent sectoral interests, institutionalists have overlooked developmental associations. In their account, trade associations failed to solve overcapacity crises in the 1920s, because antitrust left business too culturally individualistic and institutionally autarkic to submit to corporatist authority. But this book has shown how reflexive associationalists joined with the FTC to invent a new organizational form by renarrating the causes of their distress. Instead of exogenous constraints (e.g., high fixed costs, antitrust, or intractable collective action dilemmas), they speculated that accounting conventions that overvalued volume caused destructive competition. Alter those conventions and manufacturers would find new ways to prosper and compete. Uniform cost accounting, benchmarking, and deliberation became the means to that end.

It is also hard to make sense of why developmental associations succeeded without something like a Deweyan theory of creative or reflexive action. The United Typothetae of America (UTA) pooled information in order to perturb habits, spark inquiry, and foster discussion over improvement, that is, to promote creativity. They succeeded because printers responded by upgrading production processes, labor skills, technology, and products – not, as game theorists hypothesize, because information pooling coordinated collective action.

In sum, by retelling the history of antitrust and associations as a tale of creative syncretism, this book makes three contributions. First, it explains the origins and accomplishments of regulated competition. Second, it shows how institutional diversity and constitutional discord survived a putative conjuncture: the Federal Trade Commission Act of 1914. Third, it adds to a body of scholarship that shows how mass production and corporate capitalism were politically contingent, not economically necessary. By naming the volume illusion, Brandeis, Hurley, Gaskill, Stephenson, and the printers not only revealed the socially constructed and contingent nature of mass production. They also made it possible to build an alternative that, by many measures, better reconciled American aspirations to prosperity, individual development, and self-government.

EPILOGUE

When all is said and done, regulated competition might look like an intriguing eddy in the mainstream of U.S. history. However equivocal was the law, diverse were the institutions, or successful was regulated competition, skeptical readers will conclude that the struggle over accountability was conjunctural. Corporations dominated the twentieth-century economy, the FTC became a bit player in the modern state, marginalist economics became the queen of the social sciences, financial accounting eclipsed cost accounting, and modern liberalism became the reigning ideology of twentieth-century politics.

It is impossible to fully assess these claims without going beyond the evidence presented in this book. But two points can be made. First, how many conjunctures does it take to set institutional development on a narrow track? The antitrust decisions of the 1890s and the great merger wave should have made developmental associations impossible. The antitrust reforms of 1914 should have resolved the struggle over twentieth-century industrial order. If not in 1914, then the trade association and FTC cases of the 1920s should have put the cultural debate over monopoly to rest. They did not.

Second, a brief epilogue of antitrust, cost accounting, and mass production indicates that regulated competition endured, if not always in its original form. In antitrust, competition remained what William Connelly calls an "essentially contested concept" throughout the twentieth century.[2] The discursive struggle between cost accountants, financial accountants, and economists over how to measure economic performance continued in the New Deal's National Recovery Administration. Indeed, debates over the

[2] William E. Connelly, *The Terms of Political Discourse* (Lexington, MA: D. C. Heath, 1974), chapter 1.

purpose of industry codes and how to assess their performance continued to divide cost accountants, financial accountants, and economists.[3] When Congress passed the Robinson-Patman Act in 1937, which outlawed price discrimination, it raised thorny questions over cost accounting all over again. As the accountants pointed out, it was impossible to decide whether firms had engaged in illegal price discrimination without carefully measuring product and departmental costs. Finally, as historian Ellis Hawley and legal historian Rudolph Peritz have shown, the debate over antitrust did not end in the New Deal. The debates over developmental associations reemerged in the National Recovery Administration during the New Deal. The debates over whether discriminatory pricing allowed business to unfairly amass economic power reemerged in the debates over the Robinson-Patman Act in the late 1930s. And the debate over corporate power reemerged in Congress all over again in the 1950s. Americans have continued to disagree over the meaning of competition and monopoly throughout the twentieth century.[4]

Moreover, the victory of marginalist economics and financial accounting over cost accounting did not eliminate the cost accounting profession. As Christopher McKenna shows, the cost accountants of the 1920s created the "world's newest profession": business consulting. Many of the lessons cost accountants learned in the 1920s became the guiding principles of the consulting profession. Despite their promises to confidentiality, consultants became successful precisely because they developed a language to compare the diverse experiences of their clients. Thus, unlike the deductive disciplines of financial accounting and marginalist economics, business consulting remained a largely inductive field. The techniques pioneered in developmental associations and NACA in the 1920s – collaborative learning, disciplined comparison, and close coordination with clients to develop measurement techniques – became the

[3] Herbert F. Taggart, "Minimum Prices under the NRA," *Michigan Business Studies* 7, no. 3 (1936): 171–477; Herbert F. Taggart, "The Cost Principle in Minimum Price Regulation," *Michigan Business Studies* 8, no. 3 (1938): 150–332.

[4] Earl W. Kintner, *A Robinson-Patman Primer* (New York: MacMillan, 1970); Frederick M. Rowe, *Price Discrimination under the Robinson-Patman Act* (Boston: Little, Brown, 1962); Ellis W. Hawley, *The New Deal and the Problem of Monopoly* (Princeton, NJ: Princeton University Press, 1966); Ellis Hawley, "Democracy Railroaded: Review of *Alternative Tracks: The Constitution of American Industrial Order,* by Gerald Berk," *The Review of Politics* 57, no. 3 (Summer 1995): 549–51; Rudolph J. R. Peritz, *Competition Policy in America: History, Rhetoric, Law* (New York: Oxford University Press, 1996).

intellectual foundations of business consulting in the second half of the century.[5]

Finally, regulated competition continued to be a viable response to crises in mass production in the Great Depression, after World War II, and in the 1980s. Most studies of the National Recovery Administration (NRA) show how it failed to lift the United States out of the Great Depression. Instead, the NRA's industry codes suppressed competition and engendered intractable conflict among participants. But some industries learned from the successes of developmental associations in the 1920s. The leading cost accounting firm, Stephenson, Jordan, and Harrison, designed successful codes for the folding box, corrugated and solid fiber shipping container, envelope, and glass industries. Like many other codes, the "Stephenson Plan" set quotas on volume. But it also provided member firms with information and accounting tools to improve product quality, service, and nonvolume forms of productivity. Thus, despite its quotas, the box and container codes increased production, employment, profits, and innovation.[6]

A second example illustrates the enduring relevance of cost accounting and developmental association to crises of mass production. As World War II came to a close in 1945, the steel industry found itself saddled with overcapacity. Like the printers in 1908, the American Iron and Steel Institute (AISI) proposed that manufacturers diversify their product lines and find nonvolume methods to improve productivity. But when the AISI Statistics Department conducted a study to assess the industry's capacity to realize these ends, it found that management lacked the accounting tools to distinguish product and departmental costs. Like Brandeis's encounter with the railroads, the statisticians concluded that steelmakers had so overemphasized volume that it never occurred to them to trace

5 Christopher D. McKenna, "The Origins of Management Consulting," *Business and Economic History* 24, no. 1 (Fall 1995): 51–58; Christopher D. McKenna, *The World's Newest Profession: Management Consulting in the Twentieth Century* (Cambridge: Cambridge University Press, 2006).

6 "History of the Code of Fair Competition for the Envelope Industry," NARA, in RG 69, E. 25, Box 2160, File 13; Stephenson, Jordan and Harrison, "Rules for Accounting and Costing for the Folding Paper Box Industry," NARA, in RG 9, Entry 256, Box 5; R. A. Lawrence, "History of the Code of Fair Competition for the Corrugated and Solid Fiber Shipping Container Industry," NARA, NRA Microfilm, Reel 34, Part 34; Stephenson, Jordan and Harrison, "Brief in Explanation of the So-Called Stephenson Plan of Invoice Analysis," NARA, in RG 69, E. 25, Box 1689, File 22; Code of Fair Competition for the Corrugated and Solid Fiber Shipping Container Industry, Code History, NARA, in RG 69, E. 25, Box 1686, File 13; *Container News Digest* 1, no. 2 (April 1935): 1–4; *Container News Digest* 1, no. 3 (May 1935): 2.

the costs of different product lines back to their sources. The Statistics Department recommended that the AISI form a committee to draft a standard cost system for steel producers. The board agreed and requested that the AISI legal department conduct a detailed survey of developmental associations during the 1920s. Although the fate of the standard cost system is unclear from the AISI record, it is clear that the techniques pioneered by developmental associations in the 1920s remained valuable to associations coping with crises of mass production later in the twentieth century.[7]

The story of the Great Depression and postwar steel replayed itself once again when mass production fell into crisis in the 1970s and 1980s. Creative business consultants and consulting academics returned once again to cost accounting, benchmarking, and the volume illusion. In 1980, William Abernathy and Robert Hayes charged U.S. corporate management with a myopia born of prizing finance and law over production and marketing. Late-twentieth-century executives were more likely to respond to competition with financial restructuring than to take risks in technological innovation, product development, or process improvement.[8] Several years later, Robert Kaplan and H. Thomas Johnson recovered the relevance of early-twentieth-century cost accounting to contemporary management. They showed how U.S. corporations had progressively subordinated cost accounting to the ends of financial reporting. Although corporate cost accounting served shareholders, it failed to provide management with timely information to improve products, marketing, or production processes. In yet another example of historical syncretism that belies the lessons of path dependency, Johnson and Kaplan hurdled seventy years of business history to rediscover early NACA activists A. Hamilton Church, Clinton Scovill, and Charles Stevenson. They explained long-abandoned product costing, departmental costs, and production-based overhead distribution techniques to modern readers. In 1990, the National Association of Accountants officially

[7] See Memorandum for Mr. H. A. Moore, AISI, *Antitrust Considerations Applicable to Proposal to Publish So-Called 'Cost Accounting Manual'* (May 14, 1947), AISI papers, Series III, Box 7, Hagley Museum and Library; Walter S. Tower, President of AISI to Hoyt A. Moore, AISA papers, 6/6/47, Acc. 1631, General Correspondence, Series III, Box 7. See also "A Look at Costs through the Eyes of the Management Engineer," *Business Week*, September 24, 1949, 1–8, in AISI papers, Acc. 1631, Box 42.

[8] Robert H. Hayes and William J. Abernathy, "Managing Our Way to Economic Decline," *Harvard Business Review* 58 (1980): 67–77. See also Robert Reich, *The Next American Frontier* (New York: Time Books, 1983).

recognized their discovery when it published an anthology of articles from the first decade of NACA *Yearbooks* and *Bulletins*, titled *Relevance Rediscovered*.[9]

The 1990s also saw an explosion of business benchmarking, which grew out of contemporary efforts to reconfigure the volume illusion. Unlike developmental associations in the 1920s, individual corporations pioneered benchmarking in the 1980s. In 1979, motivated by its rapidly declining market share, Xerox Corporation tried to figure out why its competitors could sell products more cheaply than it could make them. This meant, first, tracking departmental and product costs in far more detail than they had done previously. But Xerox also implemented a private benchmarking system in which it detailed performance data from peer firms for comparison. Consultants, trade associations, and government took note of Xerox's accomplishments and began to experiment with benchmarking. By the late 1980s, the Saratoga Institute, the Strategic Planning Institute, and the Benchmarking Exchange provided private subscribers with benchmarking services. In 1987, Congress passed the Malcolm Baldridge Quality Act, which established the U.S. National Quality Award to be administered by the Department of Commerce's National Institute of Standards and Technology in cooperation with the American Society of Quality Control. The National Institute of Standards and Technology sets "best practice" standards through benchmarking and includes company benchmarking among its criteria for excellence.

Other benchmarking services followed in the 1990s. The American Productivity and Quality Center organized a consortium of more than ninety companies in the International Benchmarking Clearing House. Internationally, the International Organization for Standardization's ISO 9000 program and the Deming Prize (awarded by the Union of Japanese Scientists and Engineers) also offered manufacturers benchmarking services. A 1993 survey of 203 U.S. companies by the National Industrial Conference Board found that 67 percent had experimented with benchmarking. Among those, 59 percent replied that they had reduced costs, 53 percent that they had improved customer service, and 50 percent that

[9] H. Thomas Johnson and Robert S. Kaplan, *Relevance Lost: The Rise and Fall of Management Accounting* (Cambridge, MA: Harvard Business School Press, 1987); H. Thomas Johnson, *Relevance Regained: From Top-Down Control to Bottom-Up Empowerment* (New York: The Free Press, 1992); Richard Vangermeersch, ed., *Relevance Rediscovered: An Anthology of 25 Significant Articles from the NACA Bulletins and Yearbooks, 1919–1929*, vol. 1 (Montvale, NJ: National Association of Accountants, 1990).

they had improved product quality. In another survey, 96 percent of the companies polled predicted that benchmarking would continue to grow.[10]

Benchmarking also became an important tool for public administration reform in the 1990s. Government "reinventors" advocated benchmarking as a method to compare the performance of administrative units within an increasingly decentralized state. Like Brandeis's critique of early-twentieth-century railroad regulation, they noticed the contradiction between centralized standard setting and improvement. Although the former was necessary to ensure accountability, it tended to freeze privileges, foster opportunism, and undermine incentives for improvement. Still, regulation without standards, as political scientist Theodore Lowi charged at midcentury, cannot achieve moral or technical ends. It ratifies, rather than redistributes, the distribution of power in society and saps the modern state of legitimacy. Faced with analogous dilemmas of state power in public utility and railroad regulation, Brandeis turned to sliding scales and benchmarking. He thought these techniques would foster learning, create incentives for improvement, and provide revisable standards for acceptable performance.

Likewise, recent efforts to decentralize environmental planning to habitat conservation councils and education policy to local school councils have spawned experiments in public benchmarking. Like the FTC in the 1920s, the Environmental Protection Agency and urban school boards have used performance benchmarking to provide decentralized actors with incentives to improve and information, unavailable locally, about how to do it. Although the fate of public benchmarking remains

[10] On Xerox, see Tony Bendell, Louis Boulter, and Paul Goodstadt, *Benchmarking for Competitive Advantage*, 2nd ed. (London: Pitman Publishing, 1998), 8–9; and Robert C. Camp, *Business Process Benchmarking: Finding and Implementing Best Practices* (Milwaukee: ASQC Quality Press, 1995), 87, 315–45, 425. On coordinating agencies, see Bendell, *Benchmarking for Competitive Advantage*, 9–10; Camp, *Business Process Benchmarking*, 112–15; and "Multiple Choice: What's the Best Quality System," *Quality Progress* (July 2003): 45. On certifications and awards, see Mark Graham Brown, *Baldridge Award Winning Quality* (Milwaukee: ASCQ Quality Press, 1994); Donald C. Fisher, *Measuring Up to the Baldridge: A Quick & Easy Self-Assessment Guide for Organizations of All Sizes* (New York: American Management Association, 1994), 1–9; Bendell, *Benchmarking for Competitive Advantage*, 9, 171–82. On surveys regarding benchmarking, see Bendell, *Benchmarking for Competitive Advantage*, 5–7; Jerome P. Finnigan, *The Manager's Guide to Benchmarking: Essential Skills for the New Competitive Cooperative Economy* (San Francisco: Jossey-Bass, 1996), 23–24.

uncertain, it appears to be designed to resolve the same sorts of dilemmas of public administration Brandeis named nearly a century ago.[11]

Whether contemporary experiments in cost accounting, benchmarking, and cultivational administration will reopen Brandeis's deeper aspirations to republican experimentalism to broader public debate remains uncertain.[12] If the experience of regulated competition in the first third of the twentieth century is a reasonable guide, however, we can be sure that contemporary efforts to reconstruct business and government will be syncretic, diverse, and durably contested. There is little doubt, moreover, that Brandeis, Eddy, Gaskill, Stevenson, the cost accountants, and the printers will remain worthy interlocutors wherever reformers face squarely the challenges of reconciling economic prosperity, individual development, and egalitarian democracy.

[11] David Osborne and Ted Gabler, *Reinventing Government: How the Entrepreneurial Spirit Is Transforming the Public Sector* (Reading, MA: Addison-Wesley, 1992); David Osborne and Peter Plastaik, *The Reinventor's Fieldbook* (San Francisco: Jossey-Bass, 2000); U.S. National Partnership for Reinventing Government, Vice President Al Gore, *Balancing Measures: Best Practices in Performance Management* (Washington, DC: The Partnership, 1999). On environmental benchmarking, see Bradley C. Karkkainen, Archon Fung, and Charles F. Sabel, "After Backyard Environmentalism: Toward a Performance-Based Regime of Environmental Regulation," *American Behavioral Scientist* 44 (2000): 692; Bradley C. Karkkainen, "Collaborative Ecosystem Governance: Scale, Complexity and Dynamism," *Virginia Environmental Law Journal* 21 (2002): 189. On decentralization and benchmarking in education, see Archon Fung, *Empowered Participation: Reinventing Urban Democracy* (Princeton, NJ: Princeton University Press, 2004); James Lieberman and Charles F. Sabel, "The Federal No Child Left Behind Act and the Post Desegregation Civil Rights Agenda," *North Carolina Law Review* 81 (2003): 101–237.

[12] For recent efforts to elaborate the democratic potential of current efforts to reform business and public administration, which resonate with Brandeis's project, see M. C. Dorf and C. F. Sabel, "A Constitution of Democratic Experimentalism," *Columbia Law Review* 98 (1998): 267; Archon Fung and Erik Olin Wright, eds., *Deepening Democracy: Institutional Innovations in Empowered Participatory Governance* (New York: Verso, 2003); Jonathan Zeitlin and David Trubek, eds., *Governing Work and Welfare in a New Economy: European and American Experiments* (Oxford: Oxford University Press, 2003); Charles Sabel and Jonathan Zeitlin, "Learning from Difference: The New Architecture of Experimentalist Governance in the European Union," *European Law Journal* 14, no. 3 (May 2008): 271–327.

Appendix

Industries and Number of Associations with at Least Substantial Involvement in Developmental Association, by Industry Group

Food and Kindred Products (5 associations total)
- Bread and other bakery products (1)
- Confectionery and ice cream (1)
- Flour-mill and gristmill products (2)
- Food preparations, not elsewhere specified (1)

Textiles and Their Products (5)
- Awnings, tents, and sails (1)
- Clothing, men's (1)
- Clothing, women's (1 as above)
- Dyeing and finishing textiles, exclusive of that done in textile mills (1)
- Jute goods (1)
- Knit goods (1)

Iron and Steel and Their Products (8)
- Foundry and machine-shop products (3)
- Iron and steel, forgings, not made in steel works or rolling mills (1)
- Stoves and hot air furnaces (1)
- Tin plate and terneplate (1)
- Typewriters and supplies (1)
- Wirework, including wire rope and cable, not elsewhere specified (1)

Lumber and Its Remanufactures (17)
- Boxes, wooden packing, except cigar boxes (2)
- Coffins, burial cases, and undertaker's goods (1)
- Furniture (4)

Lumber and Timber Products (6)
- Lumber, planing-mill products, but not planing mills connected with sawmills (4)

Wood, turned and carved (1)
Wooden goods, not elsewhere specified (1)
Leather and Its Finished Products (2)
Belting, leather (1)
Leather, tanned, curried, and finished (1)
Paper and Printing (9)
Boxes, paper and other, not elsewhere specified (2)
Cardboards, not made in paper mills (1)
Paper and wood pulp (2)
Paper goods, not elsewhere specified (1)
Photoengraving (1)
Printing and publishing, book and job (2)
Liquors and Beverages (1)
Liquors, distilled (1)
Chemicals and Allied Products (5)
Druggists' preparation (1)
Ink, printing (2)
Paints (1)
Varnishes (1)
Stone, Clay, and Glass Products (6)
Brick and tile, terra-cotta, and fired clay products (3)
Cement (1)
Glass (1)
Marble and stone work (1)
Metals and Metal Products, Other Than Iron and Steel (1)
Smelting and refining, copper (1)
Tobacco Manufacturers (0)
Vehicles of Land Transportation (0)
Railroad Repair Shops (0)
Miscellaneous Industries (7)
Electrical machinery, apparatus, and supplies (2)
Roofing materials (2)
Rubber tires, tubes, and rubber goods, not elsewhere specified (1)
Stationery goods (1)
Washing machines and clothes wringers (1)
Other Associations, Not Categorized into Industry (8)

Index